Effective Business Administration and Communication

Desmond W Evans

A Student Handbook For BTEC First Diploma In Business & Finance
And NVQ Business Administration Courses At Level 1/2

PITMAN PUBLISHING
128 Long Acre, London WC2 9AN

A Division of Longman Group UK Limited

British Library Cataloguing in Publication Data
A catalogue record for this book is available from the British
Library.

ISBN 0 273 03778 1

Typeset by Avocet Typesetters, Bicester, Oxon
Printed and bound in Great Britain

Contents

Using this book

This book has been especially researched and written to help you in your NVQ-assessed course of study.

As the demands of studying for a National Vocational Qualification have become better understood, the importance of acquiring an up-to-date and practical body of business/public service knowledge to support newly acquired skills has come to be regarded as essential.

A current and accurate body of knowledge – of, say, what legal conditions a contract of employment has to fulfil, what range of British Telecom or Mercury telephone services are available, or how an imprest petty cash system is operated – gives a meaning to the myriad of day-to-day tasks which we all undertake in our daily work. Who can carry out effectively tasks whose purpose or reason is not fully understood?

So, when developing NVQ skills and competences during your course, make time to ask and to find out:

▶ What specialised knowledge do I need to underpin this particular skill and make it meaningful for me?

▶ Why is this specific task undertaken – what does it contribute to the goals and objectives of the organisation?

▶ What aspects of the particular skills I have just acquired can I use in other areas of my work?

▶ How do the competences I have just developed link in with others I have already acquired?

In this way, the NVQ competences you obtain will be rounded out by an understanding of the reasons for carrying out particular jobs and duties, and backed up by a body of up-to-date knowledge.

This book has been produced to help you obtain your NVQ award while encouraging you to look upon your own personal development and education as a life-long process. If you work hard to cement together the building blocks of knowledge, skill and experience, you can't go wrong!

Good luck and all success!

Desmond Evans
April 1992

Acknowledgements

The author gratefully acknowledges the help and support – including permission to reproduce copyright material – supplied by the people and organisations listed below. Without their generous interest and assistance, this text could not have been written:

Aldus Europe Limited (Pagemaker)
British Telecom
Business Equipment Digest
Canon (UK) Limited
The Coca Cola Company, Atlanta, Georgia
Epson (UK) Limited
Fellowes Manufacturing (UK) Limited
Graphic Books International Limited
Headway Computer Products Limited
Hewlett Packard (UK) Limited
Hogg Robinson (Travel) Limited
Hoover Limited
IBM United Kingdon Limited
Microsoft Limited
Minolta (UK) Limited
Pitman Publishing
The Plessey Company plc

Mr C H Longley (Rinnai UK)
Select Office Services, Chichester
Torus Systems Limited
Viking Direct Limited
Waterlow Business Supplies
West Sussex County Council
Wordstar International Incorporated

The production of a textbook – from initial idea to distributed printed copy – is dependent upon a publishing team comprising editors, designers, printers, distribution and administrative staff. The author also gratefully acknowledges their support and advice during the production of this text.

Throughout the book I have referred to an office assistant or manager with the generic 'he'. This has been simply for economy and fluency and is in no way intended to overlook the significant contribution made by women at all levels of business and public life. By the same token, I have used the term 'chairman' instead of 'chair' or 'Chairperson' to stand for a post-holder of either sex.

Part 1

Working in organisations: the work role

OVERVIEW

Before embarking upon a period of extended study about effective business administration, it is important to gain a clear insight into how organisations are structured, what different types of organisation exist in commerce and the public service, how they organise the work they do and what, as a new employee, you need to know in order to carry out your daily work.

Your work role requires that you know both your employee rights and responsibilities, that you understand the requirements of health and safety at work, that you are clear about the need for goals, targets and deadlines, realise the need to cope with continual changes and developments and are aware of the importance of your contribution to your organisation's image and to keeping your customers' goodwill. Part 1 examines all these important aspects in detail and thus acts as a sound foundation to the Parts that follow.

STARTING OUT

Starting out as a new employee in a large private or public sector organisation can prove very bewildering – until you think about what organisations are for, how they are structured and

NVQ references

This Part covers Competences 1–6 of the *Work Role* for the BTEC First Diploma In Business And FInance:

1 Act in accordance with rights and responsibilities of job role.
2 Use resources with economy and efficiency.
3 Contribute to achieving organisational goals and objectives.
4 Contribute to change and development of the organisation.
5 Present a positive image of the organisation.
6 Provide information and advice to customers/clients.

Part 1 also provides a detailed survey of the structure of organisations, how people are deployed within them and how work is shared by specialist departments.

how various people in different posts fit into them. Firstly, organisations start small and grow big – usually as a result of success in meeting their basic aims, whether to make a profit in the private sector, or to serve the public well and cost-effectively in the public sector. As you will see in this section, growing larger usually results in specialised departments being set up and in employees occupying tiers or 'hierarchic' layers in the organisation, according to their job responsibilities and levels of authority. Also, as markets and demands change, so do organisations, with the result that they are in constant process of development – they are dynamic rather than static.

DEFINING FEATURES OF A BUSINESS ORGANISATION

1 The profit motive

All business organisations are created and

developed in order to attain specific goals such as making and selling goods at a profit, selling a professional service, such as legal advice at a profit; or carrying out equipment maintenance under contract at a profit. Indeed, it is the ability of commerce and industry to make profits that keeps the country's economy going. The organisations make gross profits, from which taxes and other deductions are taken, to leave the net profits.

2 Clearly defined roles and responsibilities for employees

In order to achieve such goals or objectives, people in organisations are given clearly defined roles and responsibilities for particular activities which go to make up the overall purpose of the organisation. In manufacturing, the machine operator on the factory floor will concentrate upon only a small part of the process of making a motor-car. In the design office, the senior designer will be pondering over the shape and structure of a new model. At the top level of the organisation, the finance director will be concerned to ensure that *all* models produced are at the right price to cover costs and give a profit.

3 The hierarchy effect: the higher up, the more authority

In larger organisations, jobs vary in their scope and significance. As the jobs of certain people become more important to the organisation, so the people doing them are given more authority to see them properly carried out. This authority typically extends to having responsibility for the work of others, using the organisation's finances to buy and sell, and helping to decide upon the future direction the organisation should take.

4 The organisational pyramid

Most organisations work according to a cascade effect of delegation: most power and authority is located at the top of the pyramid and delegated outwards and downwards from directors via department heads and supervisors to office and factory personnel working at junior levels of the organisation.

As a result of this practice of granting more authority to fewer people, many organisations are said to be pyramidic in shape.

The layer-sandwich structure of the pyramid is termed an organisational hierarchy. In this, people work at different levels and receive instructions and action requests from senior staff, either to carry out themselves or to manage through staff reporting to them.

Fig. 1.1 The organisational pyramid

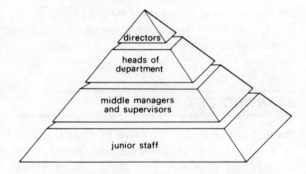

5 The stepped hierarchy or ladder in organisations

This stepped or hierarchical structure is a very common feature of both business and public sector organisations as you can see from the diagrams below of the structure of a typical company and of local government.

Fig. 1.2 The stepped hierarchy

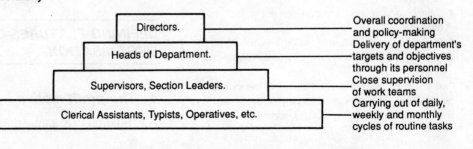

6 Division of activity into departments, sections and units

A further feature of organisations is the division of activity into specialised units or departments. As the activities of business became more complex, it made sense for groups or units of people within the organisation to concentrate upon an area which had a common theme – the actual making or production, the financial aspects of the business, the sales side and so on. Each department, section or unit forms part of the structure of the whole organisation.

The organisational chart

Many companies and public service institutions find it helpful to construct organisation charts and diagrams like the one shown in Fig 1.4 in order to illustrate clearly how the various parts of the organisation are related and interconnect to form the whole.

Fig. 1.3 Hierarchies in county councils: members and employees

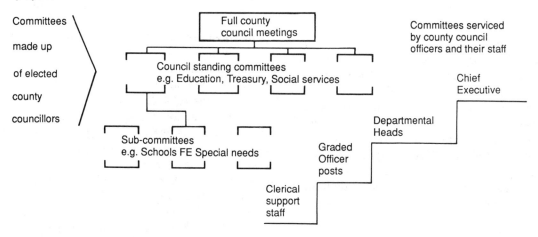

Fig. 1.4 The organisational chart

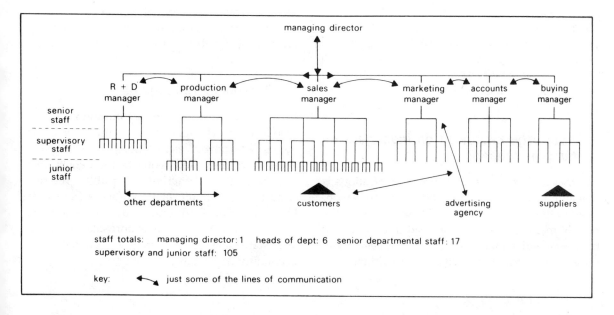

Factors which influence the structure of organisations:

▶ What they do
▶ How large they are
▶ Where they are sited
▶ Who their customers are
▶ What kinds of task employees do daily
▶ The impact of information technology applications

The impact of information technology has affected all aspects of the organisation – operation, size, siting and customer contact. With rapid telecommunications through electronic mail networks, facsimile transmission (fax) and interconnected databases on computer, it matters much less where a person works from. An employee can be linked by computer to the organisation's network while working alone at home and customers can order goods without visiting the shops.

7 Authority: bestowed on managers by general consent

Another defining feature of most organisations is that authority lies in the post and not in the person. In effect this means that staff will associate with the post of managing director or head of department the power and authority which goes with either job, rather than with the particular individual who

happens to hold it. Thus an organisation's personnel can move on or retire and successors can take on the vacant posts confident that they will be accorded due respect at the outset. Of course, the newcomers will have to continue to earn it by dint of personal example and leadership! In this way, organisations work as hierarchies because the people within them agree to abide by the custom of accepting reasonable orders or instructions from those whose posts give them the right to issue them.

8 Job descriptions: written schedules which communicate responsibilities

In small organisations, the various activities of, say, the shopkeeper and his assistants are pretty straightforward and understood most of the time by all concerned on the basis of the spoken word. Since everyone rubs shoulders all the time, there is very little need for messages to be written down and circulated. However, in large organisations word-of-mouth messages sometimes become garbled as the 'What did he say? Pass it on.' effect comes into play. Moreover, neither managers nor secretaries work very well without some clear notion – understood and communicated to all concerned – of the range and limit of their responsibilities. Thus the written job description serves to clarify the duties and responsibilities of all organisational personnel, and in open, sensible organisations, it is made available to those staff affected by the duties it defines and describes.

9 Organisational change

In order to survive, an organisation must be responsive to changes in, say, consumer buying habits or taxpayers' expectations. For example, as a result of increased requests for details about county councils' activities, public relations departments and information officials were added to county council structures. By the same token, new departments, such as export sales or training and staff development may be grafted on to expanding companies.

■ **DISCUSSION TOPIC**

Companies employing thousands of people – sometimes international companies spanning the globe – have grown considerably in the past fifty years. What problems do you think this poses for their managerial and support staff?

NEW TERMS AND PHRASES

Entire dictionaries of business terms and definitions have been compiled to aid students, and this initial checklist will get you started on drawing up your own personal list of terms and phrases. Make a habit of jotting down each new specialist word or phrase you encounter in your studies, since you will recall much better those entries you researched and set down yourself. Indeed, you and your fellow students may well wish to set up a computer database of such terms for constant access through the year.

Types of organisation

Franchise

Large companies marketing well-known products or processes sometimes license small entrepreneurs to use their name and (for a fee) help them to run successful outlets; franchising, for example, is popular in the fast-food market.

Limited company

Many small businesses are created as limited companies since in law their directors are not personally liable for the debts incurred by the business beyond their shareholdings in it; limited companies may be private, public or limited by guarantee. The Royal Society Of Arts Examinations Board is limited by guarantee and this type of company structure is favoured by charities.

Multinational

A term used to describe a private sector company or group of companies with divisions or wholly owned subsidiary companies in various countries.

Multiple

Retailing firms with numerous High Street stores or branches in a national network are often called multiples.

Nationalised industry

A state-owned industry like the British Coal Corporation and British Rail; *note*: many former nationalised industries have recently been privatised – turned into public limited companies (see below).

Partnership

A partnership is formed when between two and twenty people draw up a deed of partnership which formally sets down who does what and how profits and liabilities are shared out. Accountants, solicitors and doctors often form partnerships, sharing risks, workload and profits.

Public corporation

A term used to describe large state-owned organisations like the energy industries, now being privatised.

Public limited company (PLC)

These are usually large national or multinational (international) companies with an issued share value of at least £50,000; shares in such companies are offered for sale each day in stock exchanges and may be purchased by the general public; private limited company shares may not be sold in this way.

Quango

A 'quasi autonomous non-governmental organisation' to undertake specific tasks; the Equal Opportunities Commission is a good example of a quango.

Sole trader

The formal title given to the 'one-man-band' single owner business (which is how many multinationals started); note also the term 'proprietor' is used for the owner of a small business.

Key people in organisations

Private sector organisations

The shareholder

- private and public limited companies are financed by money (capital) from people buying shares in the company;
- shareholders may be individual members of the public, organisations like trade unions or other companies with cash to invest;
- public company shares may be purchased by anyone through a stock exchange, whereas private company shares can only be bought from the shareholder, and are usually held by the company's directors;
- shareholders attend annual general meetings and extraordinary general meetings of the company;
- they have legal rights of access to information;
- they vote to elect the directors;
- they may acquire sufficient shares to control or take over the company.

The chairman

- at the top of the organisational pyramid;
- elected by the board of directors;
- chairs meetings of the board of directors;
- may have executive status or may leave day-to-day running of the company to the managing director.

The directors

- decide on important matters at board meetings;
- have legal obligations and responsibilities under the Companies Act 1985;
- may exert influence on company activities by having extensive shareholdings in the company;
- the board of directors presents its annual report to the shareholders for approval at the end of each trading year.

The managing director

- the executive head of most organisations, with authority over all the staff;
- is a member of the board of directors.

The company secretary

- responsible to the managing director and board to ensure all the company's affairs are conducted according to legal requirements;
- services and attends meetings of the board of directors;
- attends to all correspondence involving shareholders and the calling of shareholders' meetings;
- usually responsible for fire, health and safety regulations, company contracts, trade mark registrations, etc;
- acts as legal advisor to the company.

The departmental manager

- responsible to the managing director for the work of one department in the organisation;
- directs the work carried out by the members of staff in the department;
- ensures targets are met, e.g. projected (budgetted) annual sales turnover is achieved at the desired level of gross profit (profit before tax);
- is provided by the company with the human, equipment and financial resources to reach the preset targets.

The section supervisor

- responsible to the head of department for the work of a section or unit in the department (e.g. a large accounts department may have sections for the sales ledger, purchase ledger, nominal ledger, payroll, credit control, etc.);
- reviews work in progress with the head of department to ensure targets are met;
- responsible for section staff.

The shop steward

- responsible for trade union matters within the section/organisation;
- represents the trade union members in negotiations with management;
- responsible to area branch secretary and trade unions' officers.

Public sector organisations

County councillor/District councillor

- elected by those registered to vote in each local area;
- usually a member of a political party;

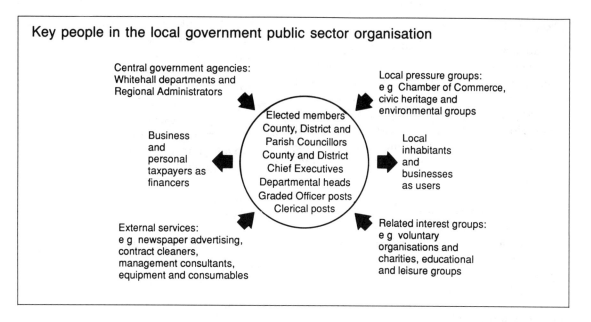

Key people in the local government public sector organisation

Central government agencies:
Whitehall departments and
Regional Administrators

Local pressure groups:
e g Chamber of Commerce,
civic heritage and
environmental groups

Business
and
personal
taxpayers as
financers

Elected members
County, District and
Parish Councillors
County and District
Chief Executives
Departmental heads
Graded Officer posts
Clerical posts

Local
inhabitants
and
businesses
as users

External services:
e g newspaper advertising,
contract cleaners,
management consultants,
equipment and consumables

Related interest groups:
e g voluntary
organisations and
charities, educational
and leisure groups

Fig. 1.5

▶ makes decisions in full council meetings or in committees;
▶ responsible for setting budgets and carrying out legally imposed duties.

Local government officer

▶ full-time official who carries out the policies of the elected members under the direction of a chief executive;
▶ officials are divided into departments and sections covering specific areas of the work.

The chairman of a public corporation

▶ responsible to a central government department for the administration of a public corporation; the central government department will be headed by a Permanent Secretary responsible to a Minister – a senior Government Member of Parliament;
▶ duties resemble those of a company chairman.

■ **DISCUSSION TOPIC**
'Organisations are not bricks and mortar or plant and equipment, or even neat little diagrams on paper. They are people!' Is this an over-simplified view of organisations?

The work of departments in business organisations

Although as an office assistant you will naturally be preoccupied with the work of your own department, it is important right from the start to appreciate that the success of any business enterprise depends entirely on the cooperation between departments which are interdependent. Furthermore, as an office assistant you will undoubtedly be in daily contact with many colleagues in other departments and so it is important for you to gain a thorough knowledge of what they do and what preoccupies them.

Research and development department

▶ designs and tests new products;
▶ improves and updates existing products;
▶ researches into new areas of interest;
▶ analyses and tests competing products;
▶ works with the production department to develop prototypes (initial models) and construct the equipment to manufacture new products;
▶ helps to ensure that new products comply with legal requirements, British Standards and safety laws.

Production department

▶ manufactures the company's range of products;
▶ monitors factors like wastage and costs of bought-in parts so as to maintain profit margins;
▶ designs tools to help make products and buys in the necessary plant and equipment;
▶ writes or buys in computer programs which control much of the set routines of production-line manufacturing – *Note*: 'Computer-Aided Manufacture And Design' (CADCAM) and the term 'robotics';
▶ controls and coordinates the rate and quantity of manufacture so as to meet given orders within pre-set deadlines – plans its activities in advance;
▶ monitors trends in production techniques internationally so as to remain competitive.

Accounts department

▶ is responsible for overall financial aspects of the organisation's activities;

▶ records and monitors all areas of financial activity: sales, purchases, running costs (heat, light, payroll, etc), manufacturing costs, dividends issued, etc and checks these against annual budgets;
▶ supplies timely information aimed at ensuring that the organisation works at a profit, i.e. that sales revenue is not exceeded by cost of sales; provides financial reports for senior management on a regular basis;
▶ produces information for shareholders at regular intervals – in the form of financial reports including balance sheets and profit and loss accounts;
▶ maintains financial information required by law, such as the details of income upon which tax must be paid.

Marketing department

▶ ensures that the organisation remains competitive by providing information about what products and services the market wants and what sort of prices it will pay;

Fig. 1.6 The work of company departments

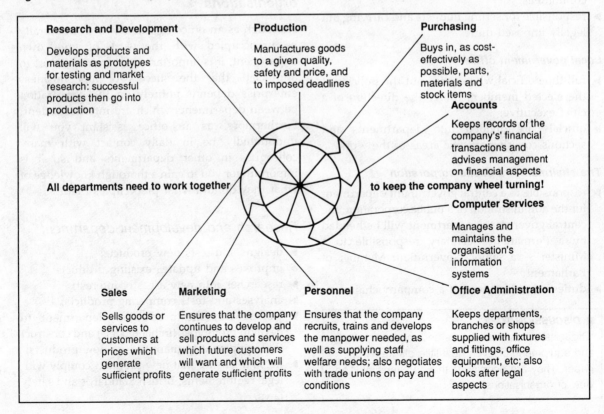

Research and Development

Develops products and materials as prototypes for testing and market research: successful products then go into production

Production

Manufactures goods to a given quality, safety and price, and to imposed deadlines

Purchasing

Buys in, as cost-effectively as possible, parts, materials and stock items

Accounts

Keeps records of the company's' financial transactions and advises management on financial aspects

All departments need to work together **to keep the company wheel turning!**

Computer Services

Manages and maintains the organisation's information systems

Sales

Sells goods or services to customers at prices which generate sufficient profits

Marketing

Ensures that the company continues to develop and sell products and services which future customers will want and which will generate sufficient profits

Personnel

Ensures that the company recruits, trains and develops the manpower needed, as well as supplying staff welfare needs; also negotiates with trade unions on pay and conditions

Office Administration

Keeps departments, branches or shops supplied with fixtures and fittings, office equipment, etc; also looks after legal aspects

▶ maintains a market research function to explore new markets and new product opportunities; monitors the success/failure of its own products and competing products;

▶ works with R & D and production departments in the design of attractive and 'sellable' new products, as well as the updating and improving of existing ones;

▶ designs and develops advertising materials and campaigns aimed at increasing sales;

▶ monitors local and national trends in consumer demand or industrial marketing needs;

▶ provides advice on the termination of existing products and the introduction of new ones at appropriate intervals; in large companies, maintains computerised models of markets and uses them to predict what will sell.

Sales department

▶ prepares an annual sales plan which breaks down how many of what type of product will be sold at what profit in the year; divides the plan up into regions, districts and branches, or sales representatives' territories;

▶ supplies point-of-sale material and advice to customers to help sell products;

▶ monitors discreetly the sales of competing products in customers' outlets;

▶ supplies market intelligence to the marketing department on current sales activities; sales representatives provide weekly sales reports to senior sales department personnel;

▶ aims to secure new business with new customers and to increase sales with existing customers on a given target basis.

Personnel department

▶ ensures that the organisation has the human resources needed to achieve its aims;

▶ coordinates employee selection, promotion and termination; supervises appraisal schemes;

▶ provides a staff training and development service;

▶ maintains the organisation's employee records, including pension, sickness benefit and superannuation payments;

▶ supervises industrial negotiations on pay and conditions of work with trade unions and associations;

▶ provides a confidential employee counselling service and runs welfare and social activities in many instances;

▶ monitors personnel activities in competing companies so as to avoid key staff being lured away by increased offers on pay and fringe benefits etc.

Office administration department

▶ provides a service for other departments in areas such as centralised purchasing of stationery and office supplies, and advice on what equipment to purchase for office use;

▶ coordinates the internal or external design and printing of forms and schedules;

▶ oversees a centralised reprographics service for bulk photocopying/printing for other departments;

▶ provides word processing/desktop publishing/ text production services, if required;

▶ maintains the organisation's insurance requirements;

▶ monitors any leasing arrangements;

▶ where an organisation has dispersed branches or retail outlets, supervises their administration with the help of branch inspectors.

Computer services department

▶ acquires and maintains company computing equipment;

▶ secures or creates computer software needed by all departments: in larger organisations many computer functions are supplied via custom-designed software;

▶ maintains computer records of organisational information and archived data: large companies have a single database of information which is constantly extended and updated and accessible according to security clearance: back-up duplicate records are essential!

▶ coordinates and supports national and international computer-based communications on behalf of staff;

▶ maintains a watching brief on new developments in information technology to ensure competitiveness and efficiency;

▶ may run staff training schemes for new staff in various computer/data-processing functions;

▶ installs new/updated versions of software as they

are released; ensures hardware is able to match growth in company's activities and increased use by staff.

Transport department

▶ coordinates the organisation's transport needs, from directors', managers' and sales representatives' cars to acquisition and maintenance of fleets of lorries and/or vans;
▶ keeps service records and renews insurances, vehicle registrations etc;
▶ designs cost-effective delivery routes via computer for delivery fleets;
▶ negotiates purchases and leasings with car/HGV dealers;
▶ provides training as needed.

Note: Some business organisations have separate purchasing departments and training departments, while some amalgamate marketing and sales. They may also have a press or public relations office to promote their company image and publicise the company's products in a general way, perhaps by sponsorship of a sports event. Generally, the larger the organisation, the more specialised departments it is likely to create. Remember that the number of departments and the work they do depends directly upon the nature of the organisation's activities, its size and the degree to which it can afford to employ specialist as opposed to generalist employees and managers.

EMPLOYEE RIGHTS AND RESPONSIBILITIES

The school or college leaver of today naturally takes for granted the many benefits and protections which society provides in terms of treatment for ill-health, state education, community policing and so on. By the same token, the rights of an employee engaged in full-time work for a company or public service are often given little thought or consideration until an incident occurs affecting an individual personally.

Yet many of the rights we take for granted today came about only after many years of struggle and lobbying by our forbear members of trade unions and members of parliament.

The following checklist illustrates some of the major rights to which employees are currently entitled:

The right to:

▶ a specific contract of employment in writing (to be made available within 13 weeks of commencing work);
▶ be protected by an insurance scheme taken out by employers in case of industrial injury etc;
▶ sick leave during which one's job is kept secure. (Details of statutory sick pay are to be found in the 1978 Employment Protection (Consolidation) Act.);
▶ work in conditions and locations which are safe and not injurious to health;
▶ equal opportunities for appointment, promotion and advancement whether male or female, and the right to equal pay for doing 'like work';
▶ freedom from racial discrimination or harassment at work;
▶ freedom from sexual harassment;
▶ maternity leave, while one's job is held open;
▶ belong to a trade union or professional association (and the right not to—'closed shops' used to exist in which every employee had to belong to a particular trade union);
▶ strike/withdraw labour. (While an employee may in principle enjoy such a right, it is today hedged around with extremely complex employment legislation, including the postal balloting of trade union members in advance, and reinstatement is by no means guaranteed.);
▶ protection from victimisation and unfair dismissal: all employees are entitled to a fair hearing under established grievance procedures, and to take their case if need be to an industrial tribunal;
▶ redundancy pay according to length of continuous employment.

As you can see, this outline list of principal employee rights is impressive – and interpreting the various Acts of Parliament which underpin them is complicated. For this reason, among others, an organisation's management retains expert personnel staff to administer employer obligations, while full-time trade union officials provide guidance and representation to member employees.

Employee responsibilities

You may be forgiven for thinking that employment law is biased in favour of the employee but, as the following checklist indicates, an employee is also responsible for a range of obligations and conscientious practices while at work:

Responsible for:

▶ working according to the terms and conditions set out in his or her contract of employment;

▶ complying agreeably with any reasonable instructions from an employer or his representative manager (always provided that the instruction is not illegal);

▶ giving conscientious and honest service to the employer and producing work of a quality which is acceptable according to the skills and/or professional qualifications specified in the contract of employment and job description;

▶ his or her own safety under the Health and Safety At Work Act: all employees must ensure that they take all reasonable care with equipment and the safe maintenance of their working environment;

▶ respecting the employer's business confidentialities etc by working 'in good faith'.

In addition to the above essential responsibilities, employees may also be obliged to conform to specific company regulations, like not smoking in a no-smoking area (say in an oil refinery), or wearing a hard hat on a building site, or a hairnet in a food factory etc.

The employee's personal code of behaviour

No matter how well intentioned, no Act of Parliament or employment contract by itself can bring about a mutually satisfying and productive relationship between an employee and an employer.

While some jobs are (unfortunately) entirely governed by the mechanical demands of factory floor machines, most require an employee to:

▶ take on-the-spot decisions and use personal judgement;
▶ use initiative;
▶ use 'nous' or commonsense so as not to let the employer down or the organisation's image suffer;
▶ work conscientiously when unsupervised;
▶ be especially responsive to customers' requests and complaints etc.

This being the case, a bond of mutual respect and trust has to be forged between employee and employer if work is to be successful and the goals of the organisation achieved.

Moreover, it is in the best interests of all employees to develop personal standards of work practice and behaviour which will aid their career development and progression up the promotion ladder.

The following checklist identifies the major components which go to make up an employee's personal code of behaviour at work:

A personal code of behaviour is made up of

Being honest – with superiors and colleagues and with employer's property for which one is responsible.

Working with integrity – by acting according to conscience, within legal boundaries and moral codes accepted by society.

Keeping up a conscientious work rate – and not 'skiving' or gossiping when left unsupervised.

Doing a fair day's work for a fair day's pay – by arriving for work punctually and not finishing early each day.

Developing self-starting skills – by planning each day's work and reviewing tasks completed, by creating daily priorities and achieving them first.

Building interpersonal skills – such as cheerfulness, diplomacy and discretion, respect of shared confidences and sharing information.

Working effectively as a team member – by listening to and supporting the ideas of others, by trusting other team members and not letting them down.

Accepting instructions, advice and requests from senior staff – by acknowledging the experience and expertise of senior staff cheerfully and loyally.

SPECIMEN JOB DESCRIPTION

JOB DESCRIPTION

Date: 12 January 199-   Previous Review Date: 15 June 199-

Job Title   Personal Secretary to Deputy Sales Manager

Department: Homes Sales Department

Location: Company Head Office

Responsible To: Deputy Sales Manager

Responsible For: Work of WP Assistant and Office Information Assistant

Scope of Post: To provide secretarial services and informational support to the
Deputy Sales Manager and to assist in administering the activities of
the home sales force; to coordinate and supervise the work of the
DSM's word processing and office information staff; to liaise with
field sales personnel, according to DSM's briefings and requests.

Major Responsibilities

1   To supervise the opening of correspondence and to ensure its prompt
distribution according to house practices.

2   To transcribe and deliver as appropriate incoming fax, telex and Email
messages.

3   To accept, transcribe (using appropriate media) and dispatch DSM's
correspondence, reports, memoranda and textual messages.

4   To maintain the DSM's electronic appointments and scheduling diaries
efficiently.

5   To administer the DSM's paper and electronic filing systems effectively, and
to ensure the security of all computer-stored data.

6   To supervise the operation of office equipment so as to maintain efficient,
cost-effective and safe practices.

7   To make travel/accommodation arrangements for DSM and designated staff
as required.

8   To administer the sales force expenses payment system and to maintain the
DSM's office petty cash and purchases systems.

9   To maintain a cost-effective office stationery provision in liaison with the
company's office administration manager.

10   To receive visitors and look after their comfort and hospitality needs.

11   To supervise the work of the DSM's office personnel so as to maintain good standards and timely completion of delegated tasks.

12   To monitor office practices and procedures and to advise the DSM on possible improvements and modifications in the light of changing office technology and information systems.

13   To ensure that office security is maintained and that confidences are not breached.

14   To promote an alert approach to HASAW matters at all times.

15   To undertake any reasonable task from time to time at the DSM's request as may be deemed appropriate within the scope of the post.

Equipment/Systems Responsibilities

Office computer terminals for safe operations and malfunction reporting.

Office fax, CABX extensions, photocopying and printing equipment for cost-effective and safe operations and malfunction reporting.

Office-held computer files for safe keeping and prompt accessing and liaison with company DP manager for defect/malfunctioning reporting.

Education and Qualifications

General education to GCSE standard and vocational secretarial education to LCC Private Secretarial Certificate/NVQ Level 3.

Previous office information processing and secretarial experience essential; the post also requires developed interpersonal/communication skills and developed office applications software and telecommunications expertise as well as word processing proficiency.

Contents of a contract of employment

A contract of emloyment must contain details of:

▶ job role and job title: details of what the precise nature of the job is, and its title;
▶ pay: hourly, weekly or monthly rate and position on any scale or spine: circumstances in which overtime may be worked and/or details of any bonus or commission entitlement;
▶ working periods: normal starting and finishing times and total hours/week before any overtime may be claimed etc;
▶ paid holidays: the number of working days each year (excluding public holidays) of paid leave entitlement;
▶ sick leave and payment: details of the duration and nature of entitlement to sick pay, maternity leave etc;
▶ pension/superannuation scheme: details of the

contributory or non-contributory schemes the organisation offers;

▶ grievance procedure: clear details of the procedures in operation and the identity of the grievance officer;

▶ period of notice of termination of contract: the number of weeks/months of notice normally required on either side to effect resignation or termination.

In addition, the organisation will probably include in the employment contract package:

▶ a handbook of practices and procedures or code of behaviour expected;

▶ a schedule/booklet of regulations to be observed;

▶ particulars of any sports, recreational or staff welfare activities;

▶ an organisational chart relevant to the job role of the employee.

MAJOR FEATURES OF THE HEALTH AND SAFETY AT WORK ACT 1974

The HASAW Act, as it is popularly known, imposes statutory obligations and requirements upon both employers and employees alike:

Employers must:

▶ Ensure that working conditions for employees are safe and that their welfare and health are protected at all times.

In practice this means that:

▶ regular safety and maintenance checks are carried out on all plant, equipment and appliances;

▶ electrical wiring, cables, conduits and plugs/wall sockets are regularly checked;

▶ staff are trained in safety practices and how to prevent potentially dangerous situations – like trailing electrical cables, filing cabinet drawers left open etc;

▶ adequate arrangements are made for trained first aiders and first aid kit support etc;

▶ emergency and fire evacuation procedures and mustering points are displayed in working areas

and staff briefed at regular intervals; fire exits are kept open and free from obstacles;

▶ suitable protective clothes and equipment are available – e.g. glasses, goggles, steel-capped boots etc;

▶ suitable storage facilities are on hand to comply with the Control of Substances Hazardous to Health Regulations 1988 (COSHH). These may include cleansing detergents, carboys of battery acid, petroleum, bottled oxygen etc.

Employees must:

▶ Take care to ensure that their working environment is kept clean, safe and tidy.

▶ Ensure that potential hazards are reported directly and dealt with promptly.

▶ Be familiar at all times with emergency procedures.

▶ Make personal checks regarding the safety of equipment regularly used or under their charge.

▶ Ensure that subordinate staff are fully aware of HASAW procedures and practices.

THE EFFECTIVE USE OF THE ORGANISATION'S RESOURCES

It is important that everyone at work keeps a watchful eye on the organisation's precious resources of:

Time – both the time available to oneself and to any subordinate staff;

Money – which may be allocated to personnel in the form of: budgets for specific activities or purchases (e.g. PC replacements), stationery/office consumables, petty cash, advertising etc.

Materials – in the form of components, raw materials, spare parts, stationery, uniforms, cleansers etc;

Plant and equipment – like presses, lathes, copiers, PCs, lorries, vans, sales gondolas etc;

Energy – use of gas, electricity, water, oil etc;

Accommodation – shops, offices, stockrooms, cupboards, warehouses, factory floors etc.

How to control the use of resources

Time

Controlling one's use of time essentially requires forethought, planning and the discipline of keeping to a schedule or sequence of activities each day. The management of time, whether for oneself or of subordinate staff, is aided by the use of these 'tools':

▶ a day-at-a-time paper or electronic diary;
▶ an appointments diary;
▶ a bleeper or personal alarm (to provide a reminder time-check);
▶ a clock situated within eyeshot;
▶ placards to warn staff not to disturb: DEDICATED PERSONAL WORKING TIME FROM . . . TO . . .;
▶ a phone system capable of diverting calls.

People who manage their work time effectively:

▶ review at the outset of each day tasks which are unfinished, waiting upon information/action from others or newly required;
▶ create a priority job-list each day which puts the most urgent at the top of the list and which drops those completed in a daily roll-over process;
▶ block out fixed time periods each week which will be kept free for the completion of specific tasks; secretaries and colleagues are made aware of these slots;
▶ avoid time-wasting interruptions of staff dropping in for a quick word which then lasts 30 minutes, sales representatives calling in without appointments, intrusive telephone calls (secretaries are invaluable in filtering these out) etc;
▶ select carefully what they will read in depth, skim-read or pass on to other colleagues;
▶ monitor shrewdly what tasks they must personally undertake, what tasks are properly the responsibility of a colleague, and what may be safely ignored.

Further tips for improving time management include setting up a time-log, which is like a diary for each working day. The operator makes a note each 30 minutes of what activities he or she has been engaged upon – filing, telephoning, taking part in a meeting etc. At the end of the logged period, an

'People who manage their work time effectively monitor what tasks they must personally undertake, what is properly the responsibility of colleagues, and what may be safely ignored . . . .'

analysis is made of the way in which time has been spent and how it might be controlled more productively, say, by having incoming calls initially handled by an assistant.

Also, it helps to review periodically all routine tasks undertaken in case some are no longer necessary or could be combined.

Self-starting skills

Considering that each new intake of employees, of say, trainee managers, starts with a large firm on an equal footing and with exactly the same opportunities for advancement, why is it that after a few months some are shining and others are floundering? Given that all have met the essential qualification and entry requirements, the reasons must lie within their individual characteristics and work styles. And success for many new appointees lies in their ability to organise themselves – especially when working under pressure. The following section examines those factors which combine and are predominant in a self-starter. Measure yourself against the checklist below and identify which areas you will need to work at to transform weaknesses into strengths!

The self-starter's strong points!

▶ Makes a point of arriving at work in good time and being punctual for appointments.

▶ Maintains an orderly desk-top, where telephone message pads, addresses, telephone numbers, working papers, reference data and directories etc are always readily to hand.

▶ Keeps up to date a memory-jogging list of active jobs – tasks which have to be progress-chased or completed within set dates, either on a VDU or as a paper checklist. Checks and amends this list at least daily! Chivvies staff for due feedback and output accordingly.

▶ Ensures that appointments, meetings, deadlines, memory-joggers are recorded in an electronic or paper diary to which assistants or secretaries have access. Remembers to keep secretarial/support staff advised of freshly made commitments!

▶ Does not forget to carry out/follow up requests from the manager.

▶ Makes careful notes of any due deadlines of work assigned and devises a detailed plan of what needs to be done by when if the deadline is to be met. Gives support staff enough time to complete tasks delegated to them well before the deadline falls due.

▶ Checks the progress of a time-constrained task on a regular basis and at predetermined dates which support staff know about in advance.

▶ Makes sure that backsliding support staff meet deadlines and provides help if needed.

▶ Knows how to find out where the organisation's information resources are kept.

▶ Ensures that his or her work is backed up by a reliable management records/filing system. Takes trouble to remain fully acquainted with the location of files in case of late working etc.

▶ Keeps a constant eye upon security and confidentiality. Does not leave sensitive material on the desk for visitors and night cleaners to read and disseminate.

▶ Knows how to keep secrets and shared confidences.

▶ Is always alert for useful information – from colleagues, clients, competitors, neighbours, etc and makes sure senior staff are informed of potentially important items.

▶ Replies to letters, Email notes, phone calls, faxes, etc promptly sends copies to interested colleagues. Lists arising tasks in jobs checklist.

▶ Makes a point of nurturing relationships with colleagues and contacts who are in a position to provide help in emergencies, such as the reprographics assistant or office caretaker.

▶ Checks out with his or her manager any matter relating to an assigned task which is unclear or becoming problematical. Advises the manager early of any likely problems or tricky matters in the offing – does not 'drop the boss in it'!

▶ Is willing to share ideas rather than acting as an information hoarder and blocker.

▶ Does not duck a difficult decision. Involves colleagues and support staff in the decision-making process as part of an open-management approach to the work of the group. Has strength of will to stick to a decision – but also the nobler ability to admit to it when wrong.

While the above checklist is by no means exhaustive, it does illustrate some of the major skills and qualities which successful executives develop as they move up the career ladder and assume more responsibility for managing the work of others.

■ **GROUP ASSIGNMENT**

In groups of three or four, consider the following collection of attributes which a successful executive could be expected to possess. Allocate each item with a score of 1–5, where 5 signifies most important and 1 least. Then compare your scores with those of the other groups in your class and discuss the reasons which supported your rating of each attribute.

Able to meet deadlines
Respects confidences
Always punctual
Stands by decisions
Always open to suggestions
Does not hoard information
Does not pass the buck
Able to identify key priorities
Organises time effectively
Knows how to delegate

Meeting goals and objectives: targets and deadlines

Of course, the major reason for managing one's time effectively is that in the course of a business day many deadlines inevitably occur – to catch the post, to reach a client by phone before they go on holiday, to submit an advertisement for publication in the local weekly newspaper and so on.

The following list illustrates some of the most commonly occurring reasons for deadlines being imposed on organisations and their employees:

▶ the weekly/monthly payroll run – to ensure everyone gets paid on time;

▶ totalling the day's takings and running the final till printout, so that all retail branch takings may be totalled for analysis at head office;

▶ producing the relevant agenda, minutes and any papers for tabling before the next committee meeting;

▶ manufacturing a run of products for export in time to be containerised and loaded on board ship (and submitting the relevant export documentation);

▶ preparing the appropriate photocopies and allied papers about short-listed candidates for a job interview;

▶ working flat out before the month-end to meet an agreed sales target.

'But how does this affect me?'

Some organisational deadlines lie clearly within the ballcourt of colleagues. Nevertheless, each and every employee has a personal responsibility to assist rather than to impede the meeting of deadlines.

For example, stopping in the corridor to 'natter' to a friend while delivering the afternoon mail to the mailroom may result in its having to wait until the next day's collection. Careless filing may result in an urgently needed document not being available for an important meeting, thus preventing an urgently needed decision, while the failure to identify a priority task on a given day may mean that a publication date is missed and crucial publicity for an important event lost.

Using nous and thinking ahead

'Nous' is a very apt north-country word standing for common sense or practicality. Inevitably in busy and hard-pressed organisations, tasks with deadlines may become overlooked – as perhaps a more urgent and important activity looms large. For instance, your manager may be suddenly called to the MD's office to help out with a sudden crisis.

In such instances it may well be left to you to ensure that the day's deadlines and priority tasks are carried out, thus the ability to keep calm under pressure and to think ahead are very important.

For instance, if an irate client telephones during your boss's absence, not only is a careful message-taking job needed, but also the forethought which retrieves files and obtains answers from, say, other departments and colleagues so that a successful phone-call may be made by your manager to the client immediately upon his return.

How organisations set targets

We've all seen people lick an index finger and hold it aloft as a non-verbal communication signal for indicating that a decision is being made on a hunch rather than as a result of informed analysis.

Target-setting in organisations is, however, much more complex and sophisticated.

For example, a regular and crucial target which sales organisations undertake annually is to decide on the total income to be generated by sales for a coming financial year, and the levels of prices obtained so as to secure identified gross and net profit levels. The supporting data needed for such a decision is illustrated in the following examples:

▶ **Detailed estimates of likely costs**
of production of goods, their distribution and sales promotion, of items like total payroll and administration costs, so that an overall estimate of the cost of sales is obtained.

▶ **Details of the required net profit needed after tax and cost deductions**
which will enable a satisfactory dividend to be paid to shareholders and finance made available for future developments.

▶ **Estimates of likely increases in prices of goods bought for the manufacturing process and the**

degree of inflation likely in the coming year
since these will affect the costs of manufacture
and the amount of real profit obtained.

▶ **Details of the company's plans for growth and
development**
since the amount of goods sold (and at what
profit margin) will dictate how much money is
available to fund growth and expansion goals.

Having completed calculations involving the above
factors, a national or global figure emerges of sales
needed to generate the required gross and net
profits. Typically, this total is then broken down by
a national sales manager into regional sub-totals,
and regional managers then further subdivide it into
district or area totals. Then the area totals may be
again subdivided to provide a target either for an
individual sales representative or a retail branch.

Once agreed and allocated, such targets are
monitored – daily, weekly, monthly and quarterly
to measure 'sales to target'. And on this basis
bonuses and commissions are awarded.

Measuring performance

The world of business today is extremely
competitive. Companies have to respond to the
advanced technologies of competitors, to the cheap
labour markets of Far Eastern and Third World
countries and to increasing demands from
customers for high quality performance and long-
life products.

In order to meet such challenges successfully,
many organisations have introduced 'just-in-time'
manufacturing approaches, which gear the delivery
of parts and materials very closely to production
outputs so that money is not tied up in stock held
on shelves. They have also committed themselves
to 'total quality management' or TQM, in which
each and every employee strives to deliver a top
quality service, whether directly to customers or to
colleagues in house, say, for reprographic work
done or for accounting reports and so on.

In order to ensure that high standards of quality
are maintained, systems need to be in place to
measure all kinds of performance. For example, in
the computer services department of one major
multinational computer manufacturer a large
placard displays for each day and month what (if

any) time was lost because the computer was
'down' or not working.

Staff appraisal

Also, organisations need to monitor the
performance of their personnel. This function is
most commonly called staff appraisal. In order to
undertake a fair and effective process of measuring
an individual's performance, usually over the
period of a calendar year, the steps that need to be
taken are set out below.

How staff appraisal is carried out

1 Senior managers agree the overall performance
targets and objectives for, say, a department or unit
with the manager involved.

2 This manager then allocates the overall targets into
portions for each departmental section; for instance,
the annual stationery/consumables budget may be
divided among three sections. In a production
environment, output and wastage targets may be
allocated to various production centres. Similarly,
goals and objectives are broken down and allocated
to individuals.

3 One by one, the departmental manager will
interview his supervisors and staff to negotiate with
them what parts of the departmental targets and
objectives they will be responsible for delivering.
This interview will also bring about agreements on
what personal development the employee will
undertake and what areas of weakness or under-
performance he or she will work to remedy.

4 The targets and commitments agreed between
manager and personnel in such interviews are
written down and signed by both parties (rather like
a contract); then at intervals during the year the
manager will review the ensuing performance of
each staff member. At the end of the year a formal
interview takes place (the whole process acting as
a cycle) and the degree of each person's effectiveness
noted. To ensure impartiality and fairness all staff
have the right to have a difference of opinion
reconciled by a more senior manager.

Some organisations link performance appraisal to salary progression and or bonus payments. For example, each member of staff may receive the same cost-of-living increase, but a variable additional payment according to their merit rating on a scale which may range from zero to a thousand pounds. Also, the appraisal process may be linked to promotion and advancement.

■ **TALKING POINT**

Do you agree with the practice of linking job performance to annual salary awards?

Or should each employee receive the same pay for the same job done?

RESPONDING TO CHANGES AND DEVELOPMENTS IN AN ORGANISATION

When the historians in the next century start to record the happenings of the last quarter of the twentieth century, among the foremost will undoubtedly be the impact on daily and working lives of the second industrial revolution. Whereas the first brought about mechanisation and mass-produced cheap goods, the second transformed the ways in which information was handled and communicated as well as making possible new manufacturing techniques.

As a consequence, no one working in either the private or the public sector between 1975 and 2000 will be seen to have escaped the impact of such innovations as desktop personal computers (PCs), computer-operated manufacturing ('hand-made by robots'), out-of-town hypermarkets and shopping malls, instant computerised credit-rating checks, mobile and video phones and so on.

Indeed, the very pace of such change and innovation has caused journalists and industrial psychologists to coin the phrase 'innovational fatigue' to describe employees who find it hard to cope with:

▶ learning to operate a different manufacturing machine or process;
▶ mastering a different way of ordering goods/stock;
▶ having to use a PC to process text instead of a typewriter;
▶ having to digest an increasing flood of computerised and paper-based information;
▶ having to learn how to drive a new software package;
▶ having to learn an entirely new job because the present one has become obsolete.

Indeed, some industrial trainers and consultants

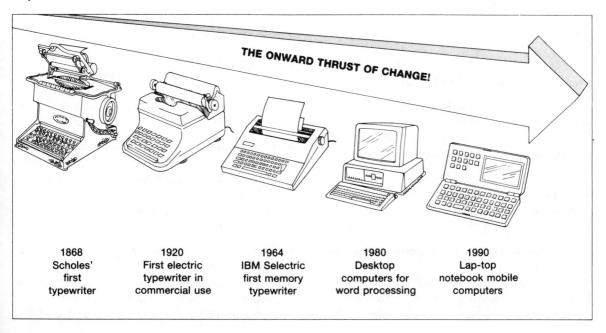

1868	1920	1964	1980	1990
Scholes' first typewriter	First electric typewriter in commercial use	IBM Selectric first memory typewriter	Desktop computers for word processing	Lap-top notebook mobile computers

believe that on average from now on an employee will undertake three or more entirely different kinds of job in his or her working life!

In a similar way, companies have completely changed their business activities as a result of shifts in technology or customer demand. For example, companies formerly only engaged in merchant and cruise-line shipping have diversified into house-building, and others from only selling motor cars into the hotel and leisure business. Such diversification as it is called helps to protect them from the dangers of having 'all their eggs in one basket'.

Coping with change as an employee

Before constant technological change became the norm in business and public service life, people could serve apprenticeships in, say, motor vehicle engineering, printing or shipbuilding confident that they would have a job for life because of the skills they had acquired.

Nowadays, however, each trade and profession requires its workforce to engage in a continuous process of updating and retraining in order to keep pace with developments. The following checklist illustrates some of the major actions you should take – throughout your career – to ensure that you can move comfortably along with changes and developments instead of being overtaken and left behind by them.

Undertaking a personal skills audit

One of the most useful activities to undertake as an individual in this regard is the periodic self-evaluation audit. This simply takes the form of a personal review of your abilities and skills in areas like:

▶ **Up-to-date knowledge of your organisation's products and/or services**
What new developments are you hazy about?

▶ **The range and degree of competence of personal operations skills**
Can you use word processing (WP), spreadsheet and database software competently? Are you fully familiar with the way your desktop

---

> ### Techniques for coping with change and developments
>
> 1 Accept and act upon the fact that learning and training are no longer restricted to teenage years, but take place at intervals throughout working life.
>
> 2 Take a genuine pride in keeping abreast of your specialist subjects by:
>   ▶ reading weekly/monthly articles and updates in the trade press and newspapers;
>   ▶ attending regional and national fairs and exhibitions showing the latest equipment and applications;
>   ▶ applying for relevant training courses and programmes in your field.
>
> 3 Make a special effort to 'bone up' on new processes, equipment and systems that are installed in your office or on your shop floor. It is all too easy to acquire the habit of shutting out the unfamiliar and avoiding loss of face by sticking to old and familiar ways and work habits.
>
> 4 Develop a listening ear and watchful eye for what competitors are introducing and employing to support their activities.
>
> 5 Make time to learn about new developments and techniques from visiting sales representatives or colleagues.

---

publishing (DTP) system works? Have you ever used the new graphics software?

▶ **Current expertise with your organisation's administrative systems and practices**
Are you fully expert with all the current procedures relevant to your present job – and to a degree with the job you aspire to?

▶ **Do you have a personal development plan?**
Have you ever sat down to draw up a checklist of the areas of knowledge and skill you need in order to develop the career you want? And then to plan consciously your own route to your goals?

▶ **Have you thought about where your organisation is going?**
All organisations have parts which are in the process of expanding and presenting opportunities, static or shrinking and shedding

personnel. Have you thought about where you should be in two to three years' time in this regard?

Job enrichment and job rotation

Many organisations have policies of job enrichment, which provide periods of varied work (usually within the same department or unit) so that employees acquire additional skills and know-how. Job enrichment helps firms to overcome problems of staff sickness, holidays and so on. Other organisations adopt a policy of job rotation, so that employees undertake associated but different jobs for varying periods. Such a practice increases significantly an employee's all-round ability and thus value, and job changes can refresh and re-enthuse.

Developing a positive outlook

The second industrial revolution is still unfolding. Cycles of expansion and recession still characterise the UK economy. And so, as the saying goes,

> *'The only constant is change!'*

This being the case, it is important that you determine to develop a positive approach to the new and unfamiliar at work. By accepting and adapting to change and development you will not only keep your job secure, you will also discover new avenues of job satisfaction and interest.

Reasons why change and developments occur in organisations

New laws or regulations are introduced

Example:

Car manufacturers and water boards are having to respond to new laws aimed at protecting the environment in many parts of the world

The wants and needs of clients and customers change

Example:

Today mountain bikes have become very popular among the 6–14 age range. As a consequence, tyre manufacturers had to produce new designs and drop old ones.

Living conditions and lifestyles alter

Example:

Working spouses and partners want to shop quickly and conveniently, so retailers have had to relocate out of city centres to parks and malls with easy access and car-parking facilities.

Competition proves too hot

Example:

So firms may decide to withdraw from one market and develop another – as happened to UK motor-cycle manufacturers in the 1970s.

Changes in living and population patterns

Example:

People move away from towns where large employers have closed down, thus affecting smaller businesses; everyone is living longer, thus creating increased demands for social, health and leisure services etc.

New technology makes existing operations obsolete

Example:

Manufacturers of ink-duplicating equipment had to move into entirely different lines when photocopiers entirely replaced their products.

THE ORGANISATION'S IMAGE AND ITS CUSTOMERS

Every organisation – whether it realises it or not – has a particular image among its customers and the proverbial man-in-the-street. A particular fruit shop may enjoy a reputation of always stocking first-class fruit at attractive prices, while another may be regarded as charging over the odds for tired and limp goods. Moreover, there is a close connection between the way in which a firm is regarded and its business success.

What makes up an organisation's corporate image?

In one sense, an organisation's corporate or total image is made up of the sum of all the experiences of the people dealing with it or working for it. Typically, however, a corporate image includes these features:

Appearance

The smartness and cleanliness (or otherwise) of: letterheads, logos, livery on vans and lorries, premises – forecourts, yards, shopping floors, offices, toilets. The uniforms or dress of: managers, executives, shop assistants, waitresses, forecourt attendants, drivers etc.

Products and services

The quality, design, durability and value-for-money of the goods or personal services offered for sale – including public sector services like refuse collection.

Customer services

The approach to customer complaints about products or services, the worth of warranties, the policies on exchange or replacement, the value of advice and guidance on technical matters etc.

Reputation as an employer

The track-record for caring and humane treatment of staff over a period of time in areas like career development pay policies, training and development, redundancy, dismissal and welfare.

Interface with the local community

To what extent the organisation nurtures its relationship with local community groups, including environmentalists, anglers and sailors, councillors and neighbouring residents.

Contributing positively to the corporate image

The term 'corporate image' sounds rather distant and formal, yet in reality it is made up of the thousand and one daily experiences of both customers and external contacts with the company or public agency.

Much therefore depends on each employee working to promote rather than to undermine the firm's image. The following checklist indicates the major areas which help to promote a good image:

Personal appearance

People rarely wish to interact with a firm's staff who appear unkempt, untidy and less than 'squeaky clean'. Care of personal appearance and hygiene is so central to promoting a good image as to be taken almost for granted – except that every day employees are encountered 'letting the side down'.

Courtesy and helpfulness

Whenever the phone rings or a customer addresses an employee directly, then that member of staff *is* the organisation as far as that customer is concerned. Thus an indifferent or impolite response and tone may adversely affect the customer's total view of the organisation for a long time to come.

So customer care – embodied in the watchword:

The customer is king!

should underpin each and every customer interaction.

Codes and norms of behaviour

Different types of organisation develop over time varying codes or norms of behaviour towards customers. A betting shop or family butchers may indulge in a friendly familiarity which would be out of place in a bank or GP's surgery.

Customers therefore come to expect – and demand – certain types of behaviour from various kinds of organisation. It pays therefore as a new employee to weigh up carefully the do's and don'ts of accepted behaviour and responses, and to adopt them cheerfully. For if doing so becomes a problem, then the chances are you will become a round peg in a square hole!

Knowing the ropes

This sailing ship term meant being experienced and proficient with the scores of lines and ropes needed to hoist, drop and adjust the sails of a ship of the line. Today it stands for possessing not only a good product knowledge, but also being experienced in procedures and practices – ways of doing things.

A major contribution, therefore, to corporate image making is to be really knowledgeable about the products, services or administrative aspects of your job and how your organisation works.

Familiarisation therefore with operation manuals, sales brochures, technical manuals and the like, makes the difference between someone who can talk with confidence and authority and someone who has to 'flannel' and bluff constantly, thus losing the customer's respect and damaging the firm's image.

In this context, the effective assistant:

▶ knows who in the organisation does what;
▶ is able to judge when to summon the help of more experienced colleagues;
▶ knows where to find relevant reference texts, sales literature or catalogues;
▶ supplies information which is up to date and accurate;
▶ is *au fait* with costs, guarantees and technical details;
▶ has enough 'gumption' when the occasion demands to protect the corporate image.

Consumer rights and protection

As well as promoting the organisation's corporate image, the effective employee should take pains to become familiar with the various Acts of Parliament and European Community directives which protect the interests of the consumer.

In the UK, two Acts in particular deal with purchasing transactions: The Sale of Goods Act 1893, and the more recent updating Sale of Goods Act 1979.

In addition, the Trade Descriptions Acts 1968–72 legislate for the advertising and merchandising of goods and services to ensure that the public are not misled. Further, consumers' rights are protected when purchasing goods or services on credit by the Consumer Credit Act of 1974.

Essentially, the 1979 Sale Of Goods Act requires that the seller describes goods for sale honestly, that he has the right to sell them and that they are of a merchantable quality – in other words, fit for the purpose for which they were purchased. If the knob immediately falls off a radio after purchase, rendering it untuneable, it is not of merchantable quality and so the purchaser is entitled to claim the return of the cost of the goods or their exchange. Importantly, the purchaser's contract is always with the immediate seller, and not with his supplier. Thus the purchaser should never be fobbed off with:

'You need to return it to the makers. I'll give you their address . . .'

Also, any warranty or guarantee provided with goods sold does not detract in any way from a consumer's rights under the Act.

The Trade Descriptions Acts are concerned to ensure that advertisements and sales tags etc provide honest and accurate descriptions of goods offered for sale. Where false claims are made, the seller is liable to criminal prosecution.

The Consumer Credit Act lays down specific requirements governing those wishing to sell goods or services by credit, who must be licensed. All credit agreement forms must meet very detailed regulations regarding their content and layout. Credit customers are provided with a 'think-it-over' period within which they can change their minds and cancel the agreement. All credit agreements must indicate clearly the annual percentage rate (APR) of the interest charged on loans given.

Customers are further protected against injury or death due to negligence while on business premises. This responsibility is called 'a duty of care' and extends to goods sold. A purchaser of, say, a jar of baby food which is found to contain fragments of glass upon opening it would have grounds for mounting an action for negligence.

Businesses today generally take out an insurance

policy to provide extensive financial cover in case of being sued by a customer seeking damages for a personal accident or the sale of defective products.

Agencies supporting consumers' rights

A number of agencies exist to help maintain consumers' rights and to maintain required standards of manufacture, advertising, cleanliness and so on:

Trading Standards Offices

These offices are run by local authorities and maintain a watchful eye on business practice as well as handling customer complaints. They may intervene, for example, to stop the sale of imported toys which do not meet EC safety standards.

The Advertising Standards Authority

This agency monitors all kinds of advertising (other than that broadcast) so as to ensure that it conforms to current legislation. It will also respond to complaints about specific advertisements. Radio and television commercials are monitored by the Independent Broadcasting Commission (IBC).

The Office of Fair Trading

This national agency acts as a kind of overviewing body to serve the public interest in trading matters. It supports trading associations in promoting good codes of practice and intervenes when fair and equitable trading standards are being ignored. It is also responsible for supervising all credit sale businesses.

The Monopoly and Mergers Commission

This agency is responsible for ensuring that the laws against restrictive practices are upheld and that no single organisation is able to create a market monopoly in, say, the sale of sugar, domestic fuel oil or newspapers.

The proposed acquisition of a business by an organisation which may result in the creation of such a monopoly is referred to the commission for a decision which is binding.

Public Health Inspectors

Such inspectors make routine visits to restaurants, hotels, cafés and so on where food is sold to check out the standards of cleanliness and sanitation. Offenders are liable to heavy fines and may even have their businesses closed until they conform to public health regulations.

The role of the customer services department

Large organisations selling goods or services employ a customer services department to attend to all the concerns, problems and after-sales services that their customers require. Smaller organisations are obliged to undertake customer services activities as part of the sales function, whether handled by the visiting sales representative or the ever-patient sales assistant.

As you will readily appreciate, no business organisation relishes becoming entangled with a public consumer protection agency over a customer complaint. It much prefers to handle the complaint itself and to err on the side of indulging the customer in order to ensure the continuance of his or her goodwill.

Thus all organisations tend to have developed procedures for:

▶ Dealing with a customer's complaint.
▶ Replacing defective goods or services.
▶ Handling goods returned under warranty.
▶ Providing technical support and assistance when complicated equipment is purchased.
▶ Trouble-shooting account payment disputes or errors.

Such procedures may require the completion of a standard report form listing purchasing details – names, dates, addresses, product manufacturing numbers etc. In addition an expert inspection of the goods may be needed for authorisation to be given for a refund or exchange.

Such transactions are stressful for both customer and sales assistant and so it is essential that the assistant keeps calm and explains in sufficient detail how the procedure will help speed the adjustment of the complaint.

Adjusting cheerfully and promptly a justified customer complaint is the most powerful means of promoting customer goodwill there is!

ACTIVITIES AND ASSIGNMENTS: *Working in an organisation: the work role*

■ *THE QUICK CHECK-IT-OUT QUIZ*

1 What is an organisational hierarchy?
2 What does an organisational chart depict?
3 Make a list of the different types of organisation you can identify.
4 Explain the responsibilities of:

a managing director;
a company secretary;
a county councillor.

5 What kind of work does a research and development department undertake?
6 Explain the difference between the work of a marketing and a sales department.
7 Explain briefly the employment rights of a young person starting a new full-time job.
8 What is a job description? What information does it contain?
9 What qualities would you include in a code of personal behaviour at work?
10 List the main components of a contract of employment.
11 Explain the duties of employer and employee under the Health And Safety At Work Act.
12 What are the resources available to an organisation that an employee must help to use wisely and cost-effectively?
13 What sorts of attitude characterise a self-starter at work?
14 Why are goals, targets and deadlines important in organisations?
15 What do you understand by the term 'performance appraisal'?
16 What can an employee do to cope with the demands of change at work?
17 What causes change and developments in organisations?
18 What is an organisation's corporate image? How is it maintained?
19 What rights and protections are available under the law to consumers?
20 What is the role of a customer services department?

Case study activities

These activities develop NVQ competences and awareness in:

* *identifying one's own position in the organisation;*
* *developing an understanding of organisational codes, norms and style;*
* *understanding organisational attitudes and behaviour;*
* *working as a member of a group in an organisation.*

Case study 1

RIGHT DRESS!

'Oh, Richard, would you step into the office for a moment, please.' Richard Williams, an eighteen-year-old clerk in the general office of Castle Insurance Company Limited put down his pen and strolled into the General Office Manager's office.

'Yes, Mr Pearson?'
'Ah, do sit down, Richard, there's something on my mind I want to discuss with you . . .'
'Is it the Kingston quotation? I'm working on . . .'
'No, no, it's nothing like that, it's your general

---

appearance that concerns me.'

'I'm sorry, I don't follow you.'

'You see, Richard, the company has a certain image to put across. As you know, we have a number of clients who call into the office regularly and staff are expected to look appropriately turned out at all times.'

'And you're saying I'm not?'

'What I am trying to say, Richard, is that your jean suit and open-neck shirts don't fit in with the sort of dress which I consider right. Then there's your hair. I know its the fashion these days for young people to adopt different hair-styles, but I think long, dyed hair is out of place in an insurance office.'

'I see. You think I'm some sort of disco freak, is that it?'

'No, not at all, Richard, I'd be the first to say that, given your – ah – style of dress, you always look fresh and cleanly turned out. It's just that what might be perfectly acceptable – even desirable – in a theatre or TV production team is out of place here. Look, I can see that you're taking this matter personally . . .'

'How else am I expected to take it? I really don't see that my clothes or hair are any concern of yours, provided I do my job properly!'

'Yes, well, that's an understandable response – from your point of view. Let me try to put it another way. You must have noticed that the female staff here always wear dresses or skirts and not trousers or the like. There has never been any compulsion in this regard on the company's part. I imagine that newcomers take their cue from the older, longer-serving staff. And I think the ladies look much more attractive and presentable in this – ah – mode of attire. So all I'm saying is that you would do well to make an effort to meet the expectations of the firm with regard to your personal appearance. You see, insurance is a field in which customers expect a certain reliability, solidity and, yes, even a certain amount of tradition.'

'So you'd prefer me in a charcoal, pin-striped suit with short back and sides? Does this mean that I may expect a salary increase to enable me to buy more expensive clothes?'

'Look, Richard, there's no need to adopt that sort of tone. If you'd just stop to think about it, I'm sure you'd realise that my bothering to take the time to talk to you about this – delicate matter – is because I have a high regard for you and don't want to see your career prospects hampered . . .'

'In other words, if I don't conform, I don't get on, is that it?'

'That's entirely a matter for you to consider. Now I've tried to put this matter to you in a helpful way, but I don't think you are prepared to see the problem *constructively* . . .'

'Well, I don't see that there *is* a problem! I think the whole thing is my own personal business. Perhaps you'd prefer me to resign, if, as you say, I don't "fit in".'

'I'm sorry you're taking this attitude, Richard, and I don't think any purpose will be served by prolonging this interview. I've told you what is expected of you. It's now up to you to reflect upon it and decide what you wish to do. Now, if you'll excuse me.'

Later that morning, in a sandwich bar:

'Well,' declared Patricia Roberts, a fellow clerk, 'I think old Pearson's taking a real liberty! He's just an old fuddy-duddy, who's failed to move with the times!'

'I don't know, though, I think he's got a point,' answered Peter Jenkins, 'he's got *his* job to do, and some of our customers are pretty fussy . . .'

'Well, I don't know *what* to do!' exclaimed Richard. 'It just seems an undue restriction on my freedom to dress as I please!'

■ *WRITTEN ASSIGNMENTS*

1 In class or in small groups, discuss the following aspects arising from the case study:

   a What would you do in Richard's place?

   b Do you think that Mr Pearson handled the matter effectively?

   c Do you think Richard's responses were justified?

d If you were a new female staff member, would you arrive for work after a few days wearing jeans or trousers? If so, why? If not, why not?

e Do you think it is justifiable for certain types of organisation to require staff to dress in a certain style? What justifications can you make for staff in certain organisations conforming to a certain type or style of dress?

f If firms do expect such conformity, should they make some provision for it in the salaries they pay? Can you think of any examples?

2 Assuming that the sort of dress to which Mr Pearson refers was made a condition of service for staff at Castle insurance, compose a paragraph to be included in the Staff Conditions of Service Schedule outlining the requirements, which would be applicable to both male and female staff members.

Case study 2

HE ONLY ARRIVED YESTERDAY!

Harry, Jim, Sue and Nicky all work as junior clerks in the office administration department in the head office of Electrix Motors Ltd. The company manufactures a wide range of electrically powered motors for use in industry. At present, all four are sitting round a table in the staff restaurant having their mid-morning coffee break.

HARRY: What do you make of the new feller then?

SUE: What new fellow do you mean?

HARRY: You know, the stuck-up, blond-haired feller who's just joined us in the office!

NICKY: Oh, him! *I* think he's rather dishy, actually! Wears his hair short, well-dressed, blue eyes . . .

HARRY: Yeah, that's the one! Right stuck up, if you ask me!

JIM: Well, what's he done to you, Harry? He only arrived yesterday!

HARRY: Fancies himself, that one! There I was, doing some collating for Mr Jenkins – a batch of sales instructions for the reps – I had all the sets of pages set out in numerical order. Anyway, he just walked by me and said he knew of an easier way to do it! I mean, I don't suppose he knows where the main entrance is yet! Telling me how to do my job!

SUE: I'm sure he wasn't, Harry. Perhaps he *did* know a better way, though. And even if he did, perhaps he was, you know, just trying to be friendly, to get to know you . . .

HARRY: Well, he's going a funny way about it.

NICKY: Who has he been assigned to?

HARRY: Miss Fox, I think. She'll soon sort him out, mark my words!

JIM: Well, I had a brief word with him yesterday afternoon – just after he had come out of Miss Fox's office. Didn't seem a bad sort to me. Bit sure of himself, perhaps. Still, it's bound to take him a while to fit in – find his way about.

NICKY: Does he play badminton by any chance? Perhaps I should see if he wants to join the Sports Club?

SUE: Well, I know someone he's made a hit with. And I reckon that someone will soon be having a spot of trouble with some collating, if I know that someone!

NICKY: Oh, be quiet, Sue. I'm only, well, just thinking he might be glad to join the badminton group, just to make a few friends here.

HARRY: Well, if that doesn't beat all! She'll probably be offering him my place in the team by next week.

JIM: Well, Nicky, here's your chance to ask him. He's just coming this way with a cup of coffee in his hand.

SUE: Go on, Jim, ask him to join us. I'm sure Harry's *dying* to get better acquainted.

JIM: No sooner asked than done . . . Hello, Peter, isn't it? Come and join us. This is Sue French, Nicky Wilson, Harry Jackson, and I'm Jim Thomas – we met briefly yesterday afternoon . . .

■ **DISCUSSION TOPICS**

1 Do you think Harry's initial response to Peter is justified?
2 How would you describe Nicky's attitude to Peter? Is she likely to make a sound judgement about Peter?
3 What would you say to Peter if you were Miss Fox, telling him about starting to work in the office administration department?

■ **WRITTEN ASSIGNMENTS**

1 Carry on writing the dialogue of the meeting of Peter with his new colleagues, until they go back to the office. Assume that Peter is anxious to start off on the right foot with the junior clerks.
2 Give an oral presentation to your class outlining the sort of problems someone is likely to encounter when joining a new group of fellow-students or work-mates. Suggest how such problems might best be overcome.

Case study 3

'I SHOULDN'T REALLY TELL YOU THIS BUT . . .'

Charlie Watson had worked for many years in the Office Administration Department of Britaware Cutlery Limited as a senior clerk. Hazel Perkins had been there almost as long and had worked her way up to central dictation supervisor. Not long after Mr Simon Walker, a young but able administrator, had been appointed Office Administration Manager at Britaware. Charlie and Hazel met in the staff restaurant:

'Afternoon, Hazel.'

'Oh, hello, Charlie. Come and sit down. How's the world treating you these days?'

'Not very often! Too busy trying to keep up with the new ordering system His Nibs has devised.

He must think I've got overdrive or something!'

'I'm not surprised. A real new broom by all accounts. A little bird just told me he wants to bring in some new sort of filing system. Though I daresay there's nothing wrong with the old one. Still, I expect you'll have something to say about that, Charlie.'

'Too right I will! Anyway, where d'you get that from? First I've heard!'

'Never you mind! Still, I thought you'd like to know. And, another thing. (Hazel leans across the dining-table to whisper into Charlie's ear.) Don't breathe a word of this, but Mabel – you know, works in the M.D.'s outer office – told me she'd heard that our Mr Walker left Dixon's under a bit of a cloud! Some talk of him and a dolly bird secretary who left just before he did. Not many weeks after their Christmas party! . . .'

'No! Well, well, well. The girls upstairs had better watch out then! Mind you, I'm not surprised. I've seen him and that Carole Waters looking – well you know – funny at each other come to think of it. Flighty piece if ever I saw one. You'll be keeping your eye on her, I'll be bound!'

'I've got her number, don't you fret! Listen, I shouldn't really tell you this but Mr Walker told me in confidence – now I know I can rely on you – that as soon as he's got time, he's going to introduce a new Saturday working rota system for the text processing staff. Something to do with the Works order book being full. I told him the girls wouldn't stand for it but he said it was all a matter of how it was put to them. Still, if the girls get wind of it, there'll be a right dust up, you mark my words! So don't breathe a word!'

'Course not! What do you take me for? Well, I'd better be getting back upstairs – see what else is new!'

Later that afternoon, Charlie wandered over to central dictation with a couple of cassettes in his hand and gave Susan Greenford the following instructions:

'Do this little lot soon as you can Sue.'

'I shouldn't really, Mr Watson. Miss Perkins doesn't really like us to . . .'

'Don't you fret! She's got other things on her mind at present. By the way, how's your boyfriend, Gary? Still mooning over each other every Saturday morning in Carlo's Coffee Bar? You tell 'im from me, he wants to make the most of his Saturday mornings!'

'How d'you mean Mr Watson?'

'Never you mind! You know what they say, ''Absence makes the heart grow fonder!'' '

'Oh, I haven't got the time to listen to your riddles Mr Watson, I've got work to do!' With that, Susan attacked her PC determinedly.

But Charlie's innuendo *did* form the last piece of the jig-saw that perceptive Susan Greenford had been assembling for some little time. And the picture she had pieced together did not please her at all . . .

■ **ASSIGNMENTS**

1 In groups, consider the above case study and then discuss the following questions:

  a What has the Britaware 'grapevine' to do with Charlie's and Hazel's conversation?
  b To what ends are Charlie and Hazel using the 'grapevine'?
  c How do Charlie and Hazel match up to your idea of senior departmental staff? Make a checklist of the shortcomings you think they display.
  d What do you see as the dangers of talking about departmental colleagues and business in the way that Charlie and Hazel do?
  e Can you envisage any ways in which the conversation could rebound on Charlie and Hazel?
  f What do you think might have prompted Charlie and Hazel to talk in the way they did?
  g What consequences do you see in indulging in 'grapevine gossip' and acting as a staging-post for grapevine rumours?
  Compare your group's views with those of other groups in a general group session.

2 Make a checklist of the qualities which all organisational employees ought to possess, which you think Charlie and Hazel clearly lack.

■ **FOLLOW-UP ASSIGNMENT**

In a general group discussion, explore the nature of the relationship between employer and employee, manager and subordinate. Try to establish a generally acceptable code of behaviour and standards which you think someone preparing for a career in business or the public service ought to stick to – through thick and thin, in good times and bad.

Activities to develop competence and confidence

The following activities develop knowledge and familiarity with important aspects of the work role in organisations and help to prepare you in producing NVQ evidence in your subsequent studies:

1 Design an organisational chart which clearly displays the organisational hierarchy of your school or college or for your work experience attachment organisation.

2 Carry out your research into **one** of the following and then deliver an oral presentation to your class on the subject for about five minutes:

The Health & Safety At Work Act 1974

The Trade Descriptions Acts 1968–72

The Consumer Credit Act 1974

3 By arrangement carry out your research and then design a job description for one of the following:

a your teacher;
b your departmental secretary;
c your work experience attachment supervisor.

4 You work in the personnel department of Radiant Lamps Limited, a company which manufactures a range of domestic and commercial lighting fixtures and fittings. Your manager is currently producing an induction manual for new staff joining the firm and has asked you to draft an entry entitled:

'Your Rights And Responsibilities As A New Member Of Staff'

Produce a suitable draft on not more than two sides of A4.

5 Carry out a personal audit of the knowledge and skills you already possess and what you need to acquire in order to be ready at the end of your course for your first full-time appointment. Compare your audit with those of others in your group and keep it under review as you proceed through your studies.

6 Research into the factors which have caused either your school, college or work experience organisation to change over the past two to three years and design a diagram to illustrate the main effects of the changes. Post your diagram on your baseroom noticeboard.

7 Arrange to interview two or three members of staff who have joined your school, college or work experience attachment organisation over the past 12 months. Ask them to describe how they felt in a new working environment and what experiences they found particularly memorable during the process of 'fitting in'.

In suitably anonymous terms, outline what you discovered to your class.

Work experience attachment assignments

1 With permission, obtain copies of two or three job descriptions of staff in different positions in your attachment organisation. Retain them in your file as specimens.

2 By arrangement, obtain a copy of your organisation's contract of employment. Compare it with those obtained by other students in your group.

3 Arrange to interview:

a manager
a supervisor
a secretary

and ask them to explain to you what techniques they employ to manage their time effectively. Make notes of your findings and share them with your group.

4 Interview the member of staff responsible for HASAW and find out what aspects he or she considers most important.

5 Make a checklist (after having discussions with relevant staff) of the major objectives, targets and deadlines current in your attachment department. Compare your list with those produced by other group members.

6 Find out how staff are appraised in your organisation and obtain a set of the forms used in the process. Share your discoveries with your group.

7 Make a checklist of the various components and features which you think go to make up your organisation's corporate image. Discuss these with your attachment supervisor to see if he or she agrees, and then share your findings with your group.

8 Find out how your organisation handles its customer services function. Establish what documents and procedures are used to support this activity and then give a briefing on your findings to your group.

Part *2*

Office support activities

OVERVIEW

A number of important office support activities are explained in this Part. These include: dealing with incoming and outgoing mail, filing and storing information, arranging travel for staff, setting up meetings and handling petty cash.

These activities centre upon administering the inward and outward flow of information, assisting busy staff and recording payments for small purchases on a daily basis.

Nowadays much importance is attached to quality assurance in organisations – so that everyone involved in the enterprise provides their very best work and attention for others, whether a customer or a co-worker. Everyone expects and deserves good support services, whether by ensuring his or her mail is handled efficiently, or by making foolproof travel arrangements for a business trip.

DEALING WITH INCOMING AND OUTGOING MAIL

Incoming mail

In large organisations incoming mail is received in a purpose-equipped mail room. Here skilled staff sort the mail into the separate stacks for delivery to departments or units. To do this effectively, the following equipment is commonly needed:

▶ an electronic letter-opening machine;
▶ racks, trays and pigeon-hole receptacles clearly labelled;
▶ trolleys and containers for distribution;
▶ tools and staple removers for parcelled items;
▶ manual/automatic date-stamping equipment;
▶ bins for waste wrappings etc;
▶ logging systems for incoming recorded/ registered mail and money orders etc.

Procedures for handling incoming mail vary from firm to firm, but the following are the important aspects to remember:

▶ Some firms open all non-confidential mail

centrally; others take it to the appropriate department for opening.

▶ Envelopes marked: PERSONAL or PRIVATE & CONFIDENTIAL or CONFIDENTIAL **are never opened by mail room staff**.

▶ Mail marked PERSONAL may only be opened by the named recipient.

▶ Some managers permit their secretaries/PAs to open private and confidential mail in the manager's office suite.

When dealing with incoming mail within a department or unit, the following are the steps to be observed:

▶ All non-confidential/personal mail is opened by the specified staff member (secretary, office assistant etc) and clearly date-stamped so that delays occurring in its delivery are picked up, and a record of arrival kept.

▶ The address is checked on each envelope before opening it so as to identify any mail received in error.

▶ Care is taken to ensure that every envelope is checked before being discarded for concealed items like cheques or enclosures. (Some companies have logging routines for incoming cheques/money orders to ensure security).

▶ Incoming cheques and associated correspondence are usually dealt with by a specified staff member.

▶ Then the mail is sorted into the stacks which relate to the department's organisation. For example, Sales, Purchases, Payroll etc, or according to named recipient.

▶ Discretion is needed to sort each stack into an order or priority such as:

- • • • • items marked 'urgent';
- • • • • letters from customers;
- • • • external letters;
- • • internal memoranda;
- • unsolicited advertising/sales material.

▶ Thus the most important items occur at the top of the stack and the least at the bottom.

▶ It is helpful to scan the letter-headings of correspondence to help in prioritising mail correctly.

▶ Letters with no named recipient are normally routed to appropriate section heads for processing by the departmental senior secretary. *Note:* Some mail-distributors staple letters and enclosures to keep them together and avoid paper-clips which can pick up and thus 'lose' other A4 sheets.

▶ Efficient staff have filing baskets or trays for incoming and outgoing mail in their working areas to avoid mail becoming misplaced and thus overlooked.

Recorded deliveries and registered mail

In some situations – whether to obtain a record of a mailed item having been received, or because of the valuable contents of an envelope or package – some mail is sent as recorded or registered post. Recorded deliveries are usually signed for by a mail room supervisor and registered mail by the recipient named on the envelope. All such mail is customarily logged in an Incoming Mail Logbook.

■ TOP ASSISTANT TIP

It is well worth the trouble to learn how to handle incoming mail efficiently. No one likes to receive mail which has been held up internally, or which, though confidential or personal, has been opened in error because of carelessness.

Also, if an item appears important, it helps to tell its recipient as promptly as possible:

'There's a registered item just arrived for you in Miss Pilkington's Office, Mr Milbourn.'

Outgoing mail

Outgoing mail is subject to similar in-house procedures. In some county surveyors' departments, for example, because most of the mail is legally binding, all outgoing mail is checked before dispatch and only senior staff are allowed to sign it.

In other organisations, staff are given more authority but circulate copies of letters to interested colleagues. Again, some departmental heads require to receive copies of all outgoing mail dispatched by staff.

The equipment to handle outgoing mail, whether

located in mail room or department is essentially:

▶ an electronic franking machine to imprint and record for Post Office billing the postage due;
▶ a set of scales for weighing bulky letters and parcels;
▶ wrapping and tying equipment;
▶ collators and folders for handling mail shots;
▶ reference books – e.g. the *Post Office Guide* – for details of postage costs and regulations;
▶ assorted stickers: FRAGILE, URGENT, AIRMAIL, NO HOOKS, etc;
▶ Dispatch forms for express and overnight services like Red Star and Datapost;
▶ Sacks and containers for holding outgoing mail.

Outgoing mail is collected usually twice each day – late mornings and afternoons – by the Post Office, and so needs to be assembled and processed in good time by the staff responsible. The following steps form helpful guidelines:

▶ Window manilla envelopes should be used whenever appropriate; they save time and money by avoiding the costs of retyping recipient and address details on envelopes.
▶ Pencilled indications – 1st or 2nd – on the top right-hand corners of envelopes are helpful to assist mail room staff in franking mail. Note: franking machines contain meters which record costs as mail is franked; meter reading totals are logged and costs paid to the Post Office at regular intervals.
▶ Envelope addresses should always include post codes and be set out in Post Office preferred formats (see the *Post Office Guide*.)
▶ Overseas mail should be correctly labelled 'AIRMAIL'; whenever possible lightweight airmail paper should be used to save postage costs.

Services for delivering urgent mail at home and abroad

Both the Post and private sector couriers provide fast-delivery services for letterpost and parcels:

Urgency
Letters may be dispatched, according to urgency in the following ways:

Inland
Motor-cycle courier
One-hour delivery guaranteed in larger towns and cities.

Intelpost
A fax-based Post Office service for fast document routing within UK or overseas; messages may be telephoned to the Post Office or handed in to a post office for onward transmission.

Datapost sameday and overnight
Another Post Office service for goods and documents; delivery is guaranteed within zones and overnight deliveries have a next day 10.00 am deadline across most of the UK.

Royal Mail Special Delivery
Here the Post Office operates a money-back next working day delivery guarantee for first-class letter packets provided they are given in by specific times.

Airway and railway letters
British Airways and some British Rail stations accept post for transmission to designated airports/stations for collection.

Overseas
Datapost International
The Post Office runs a service to over 90 countries worldwide – with a 'next-day' delivery to most of Europe and to New York. Items can be collected for dispatch. Contact Freephone Datapost.

Swiftair
Items may be given in at post offices or separately collected; delivery is scheduled for the day after posting to destination country.

Express delivery
Items travel by normal PO airmail services, but are given express treatment from destination post office.

Normal service inland
First-class Letter Post
The Post Office aims to deliver 90% by the next working day, provided items are posted before locally set deadlines.

Second-class post
Used for non-urgent items and the Post Office aim is delivery by the third working day.

Note: Increasingly, private sector distribution firms are offering highly competitive private sector services in the field of high-speed secure delivery.

Fig. 2.1 Post Office forms

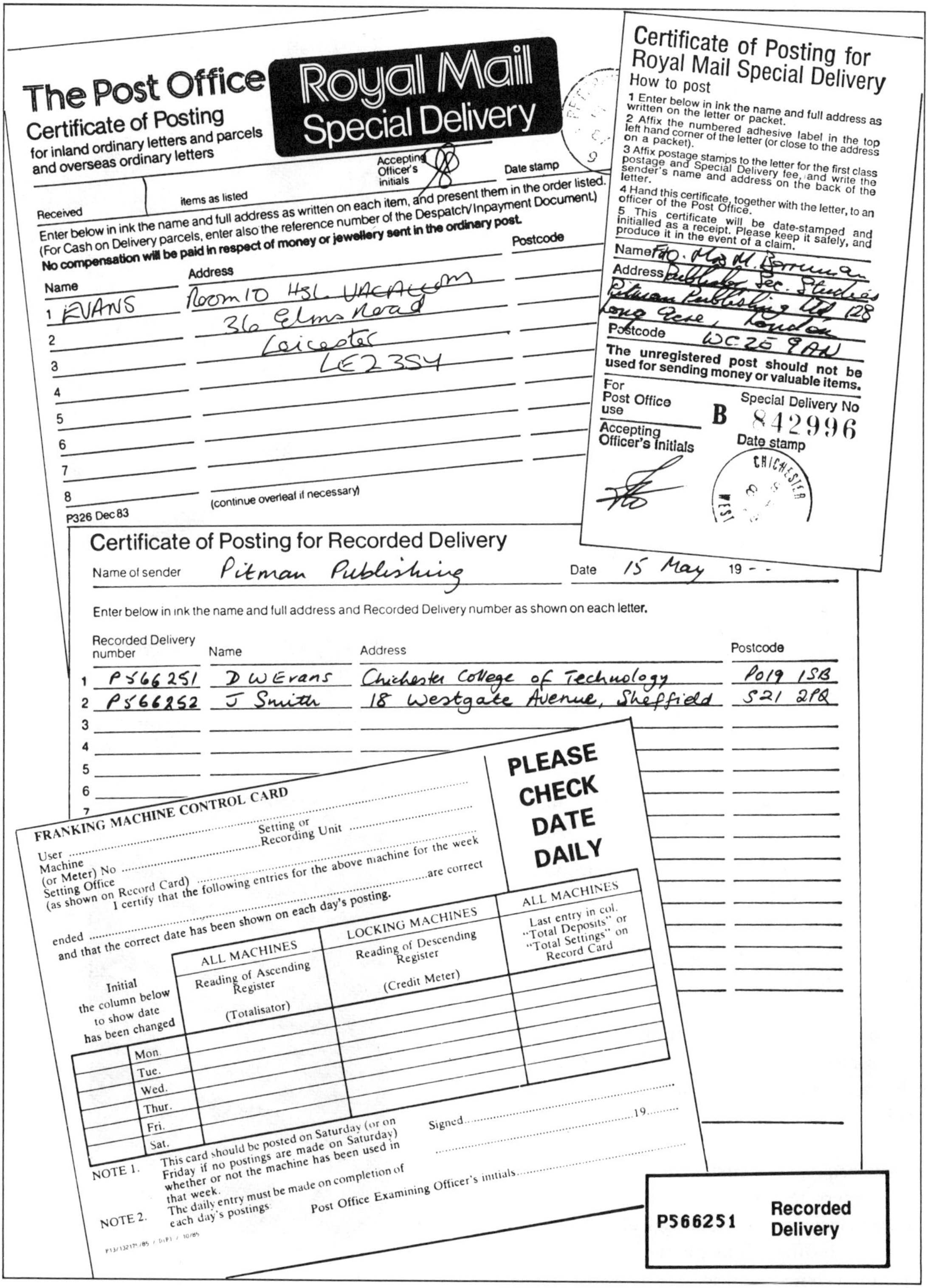

The Post Office — **Royal Mail Special Delivery**

Certificate of Posting
for inland ordinary letters and parcels and overseas ordinary letters

Accepting Officer's initials | Date stamp

Received | items as listed

Enter below in ink the name and full address as written on each item, and present them in the order listed.
(For Cash on Delivery parcels, enter also the reference number of the Despatch/Inpayment Document)
No compensation will be paid in respect of money or jewellery sent in the ordinary post.

	Name	Address	Postcode
1	EVANS	Room 10 43L UACALLAMS 36 Elms Road Leicester LE2 3S4	
2			
3			
4			
5			
6			
7			
8		(continue overleaf if necessary)	

P326 Dec 83

Certificate of Posting for Royal Mail Special Delivery

How to post

1 Enter below in ink the name and full address as written on the letter or packet.
2 Affix the numbered adhesive label in the top left hand corner of the letter (or close to the address on a packet).
3 Affix postage stamps to the letter for the first class postage and Special Delivery fee, and write the sender's name and address on the back of the letter.
4 Hand this certificate, together with the letter, to an officer of the Post Office.
5 This certificate will be date-stamped and initialled as a receipt. Please keep it safely, and produce it in the event of a claim.

Name F.A.O. Mr M. Borrman
Address Publisher, Sec. Studies Pitman Publishing Ltd 128 Long Acre, London
Postcode WC2E 9AN

The unregistered post should not be used for sending money or valuable items.

For Post Office use | Special Delivery No **B** 842996
Accepting Officer's Initials | Date stamp (CHICHESTER, WEST)

Certificate of Posting for Recorded Delivery

Name of sender *Pitman Publishing* Date *15 May* 19 - -

Enter below in ink the name and full address and Recorded Delivery number as shown on each letter.

	Recorded Delivery number	Name	Address	Postcode
1	P566251	D W Evans	Chichester College of Technology	PO19 1SB
2	P566252	J Smith	18 Westgate Avenue, Sheffield	S21 2PQ
3				
4				
5				
6				
7				

FRANKING MACHINE CONTROL CARD

PLEASE CHECK DATE DAILY

User .... Setting or Recording Unit ....
Machine (or Meter) No ....
Setting Office (as shown on Record Card) ....
I certify that the following entries for the above machine for the week ended .... are correct and that the correct date has been shown on each day's posting.

Initial the column below to show date has been changed		ALL MACHINES Reading of Ascending Register (Totalisator)	LOCKING MACHINES Reading of Descending Register (Credit Meter)	ALL MACHINES Last entry in col. "Total Deposits" or "Total Settings" on Record Card
	Mon.			
	Tue.			
	Wed.			
	Thur.			
	Fri.			
	Sat.			

Signed .... 19....

NOTE 1. This card should be posted on Saturday (or on Friday if no postings are made on Saturday) whether or not the machine has been used in that week.
NOTE 2. The daily entry must be made on completion of each day's postings.

Post Office Examining Officer's initials ....

P13/132171/85 / DrP1 / 10/85

P566251 **Recorded Delivery**

▶ Mail requiring a special postal service: Royal Mail Special Delivery, Datapost or Express Delivery must be accompanied by clear instructions for mail room staff.

FILING SYSTEMS

The following section explains the ways in which information is stored in both electronic and paper-based filing systems. Since virtually every administrative job involves storing and accessing information quickly and efficiently, it is important that you master the principles and practices in current use.

Manual, paper-based filing systems

Today the standard size of paper used in offices is A4 (297 mm deep by 210 mm wide) and A5 (same width, half the length). As a result, filing cabinets and wallets have been designed to hold this size of paper, though architects and drawing offices file plans and drawings in much larger storage drawers. Also, some accounting departments will have filing cabinets capable of storing A3 sheets (297 mm deep by 420 mm wide (double A4).

Vertical and lateral files

To accommodate A4 papers (often held in plastic or card wallets), two basic filing systems have evolved:

The vertical system – in which papers are stored in hanging V-shaped containers which are suspended from parallel tracks running from front to back of drawers which pull out of free-standing cabinets.

The lateral system – in which similar V-shaped containers are racked side by side, usually in open-fronted cabinets which are located around the walls of an office.

Both systems require the suspended or racked V-shaped containers to be clearly marked using a system which classifies the data logically, so as to aid the user in finding a specific file.

These filing systems include:

Fig. 2.2 Filing cabinet (vertical system)

Fig. 2.3 Filing cabinet (lateral system)

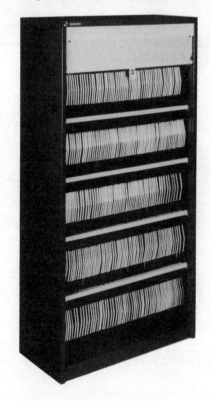

1 *Alphabetical order* A–Z (where names, titles, labelling references etc are used as identifiers)
2 *Numerical order* (e.g. 100, 200, 300 etc)
3 *Colour coding* to separate related items into groupings
4 *Chronological order* (e.g. from current day backwards in time)
5 *Geographical order* (say by a company's national regions and districts)

Each of these systems is explained in the following section:

1 Alphabetical order

Here files are arranged in a sequence which follows that of the A–Z order of letters. A number of protocols or rules for filing alphabetically must be committed to memory:

▶ **1.1** The alphabetical sequence must be strictly adhered to: abbess comes before abbot and Richards before Richardson.

▶ **1.2** Files or entries are sequenced letter by letter:

Dun
Dunn
Dunstable

▶ **1.3** Indefinite and definite articles (a, the) are ignored in entry titles.

▶ **1.4** Abbreviations are filed as written: Messrs Smith and Williams.

▶ **1.5** Abbreviated names like BBC, ITV, TUC, etc, are filed according to their abbreviated letter sequence.

▶ **1.6** St is filed as Saint and foreign versions like San or Sainte are filed as spelled. Some filing systems treat Mc, Mac or M' as quite different versions of 'mac' and file them according to their individual letter sequence; others treat them all as 'Mac'.

▶ **1.7** As a rule entries which are shorter come first:

Elizabeth
Elizabeth I
Elizabeth I, Queen of England

▶ **1.8** Personal names are normally filed surname first:

Richards, Jack
Richards, Dr John
Richards, Sir Gordon

Titles like Mr, Mrs, Dr, Prof, Sir etc, are ignored, save for forming part of the entry after the initial surname shown.

▶ **1.9** Where the same word occurs as a name, then the convention is to enter forename followed by surname, followed by corporate name, followed by name as subject:

Heather
Heather, Arnold
Heather Products Limited
Heather, British species

Advantages: Alphabetical filing enables files to be read and accessed quickly; the system is also readily expandable.

Disadvantages: Items within a named file require some additional system of classification – letters to an account client may need to be numbered or filed chronologically, making cross-referencing laborious.

Note: items 1.1–1.9 have been adapted from the British Standard on filing and indexing: BS 1749 specimen filing sequence.

2 Numerical order

Files may be numbered from 1 to 1000 and major sections may occur at regular intervals (100, 200, 300 etc.) as in the Dewey decimal system. Sub-sections within a file may be introduced by the addition of a decimal point: 100.1, 234.35 etc.

Advantages: Such a system is capable of infinite expansion and can cope with a very large number of sub-sections, sub-divisions and diverging branches of data.

Disadvantages: In order for the numbers to convey readily what they mean, it is necessary for an index to be created, e.g.:

600 Technology
  650 Business practices
  658 Management

This system is therefore more time-consuming to use than one in which each file is given an instantly identifiable name.

3 Colour coding

Colours may be used in any number of combinations to guide the eye quickly to a division or section within a filing system. Contrasting and bright colours are used, for example, in lateral filing systems as flags or markers to indicate the extent of files sharing a common identity:

BETWEEN YELLOW FLAGS, ALL WITH YELLOW SPINES:
All Account Customers in the North West Region

BETWEEN GREEN FLAGS, ALL WITH GREEN SPINES:
All Account Customers in Midlands Region and so on.

Colour coding is also used to identify copied documents in some organisations where pastel coloured copy paper is used in this way, for example:

WHITE PAPER: top copy – FOR DESPATCH

YELLOW PAPER: departmental copy – RETAINED FILE COPY

PINK PAPER: for information – DESPATCHED COPIES only, no action required

---

> ■ **TOP ASSISTANT TIP: FILING**
>
> It is good practice in maintaining a filing system to make a habit of:
>
> ▶ **Cross indexing:** making a reference in one file of related or helpful/additional data held in another file.
> ▶ **Noting files in use:** a file borrowed without a record of who has it, when it is removed from the filing system, etc, is a file lost! Make sure you have a 'file in use' set of slips to be filled out showing: user, date out, date due back, etc.
> ▶ **Maintaining security:** some files will certainly contain highly confidential data; make sure you control who may access what and keep a secure system for sensitive files.

---

4 Chronological order

Sometimes it is necessary to file items according to the day/date received – such as applications for permits or licences or the dates when vehicles in a company fleet were serviced:

May 19—
1 F195 BXP 30,000 service
2 E256 DFX 48,000 service etc.

Advantages: particularly useful when actions need to be taken on a cyclical basis – like relicensing sales reps' cars annually; good for cross-referencing – file on vehicle and relicensing date records quickly matched. Ideally suited to computerised database – all vehicles due for re-taxing on say 31 August 199– may be located and displayed on the VDU in a trice!

Disadvantages: Need for index and explanatory back-up system. Time-consuming to access data held in manual filing system.

5 Geographical order

Many organisations file data according to geographic region, area or locality, such as sales turnover by region or international sales division; public service departments hold many records in regional, county, district and parish council sections and sub-sections.

Advantages: Such a system enables statistics to be held in manageable and comparable units and also permits a large or 'macro' figure or total to be evaluated in terms of its 'micro' or component parts.

Visual filing systems

In addition to vertical and lateral filing designs, a range of visual systems exists, aimed at optimising ease of use and prompt location of data. Indeed the terms 'visual' or 'visible' are used to describe such systems, which include the following:

Rotary filing systems

Here files are inserted into free-standing, circular shelves constructed in columns which users can walk around. Visibility is good but they absorb a great deal of space.

Year planners and project charts

A variety of card or wipe-over charts are available either to pin or hinge to the office wall which display information like staff holiday rotas, key dates, branch visits, plant maintenance records, etc.

T-card slot indexes

This system takes the form of a large metal framework of slots – like rows of breast pockets – into which coloured cards shaped like the letter T are slotted: main titles or labels are written across the lateral bar of the T and more detailed data down its vertical bar which rests inside the pocket. Such T-cards may be moved around the frame and this system is popular in offices controlling projects or the work of personnel who move from job to job.

Strip indexes

Strip indexes often take the form of metal-edged frames with removable transparent inserts, beneath which a series of strips of card have been aligned in a particular sequence, each of which displays a piece of relevant information. For example, the displayed data may take the form of the names, addresses and telephone numbers of frequently used suppliers in a garage workshop to which mechanics may refer without greasing up a telephone directory.
Note: Sometimes such strip indexes are fixed around a central plinth as a rotary index.

Wipe-over whiteboards

Many office managers like to jot down memory-joggers and important information on wall-mounted whiteboards using coloured marker pens: while not particularly sophisticated this system is most effective in highlighting key information.

Desktop card indexes

Managers and clerical staff alike often insert frequently used information on card-indexes stored in small boxes or pop-up A–Z files encased in spring-loaded metal containers.

Micrographics

The miniaturisation of documents by photographing them and reducing, say, A4 normal size letters to approximately postage-stamp size is long-established. Both rolls of microfilm and postcard sized microfiches (which look like film negatives) are employed as filing media and used with optical readers in firms like insurance companies or design engineers, which need to hold thousands of records or drawings.

■ **TOP ASSISTANT TIP: FILING**

Computerised, electronic filing systems and their paper-based, manual counterparts are only as effective and reliable as the accurate and up-to-date information they contain. Therefore, no matter how busy you are, *always* make time to update or amend an entry upon receiving a change of address, job-title or telephone number, etc. This routine will pay handsome dividends when an office crisis occurs!

Guide to current archive retention practice

Agreements	12 years
Balance sheets	30 years
Bank statements	6 years
Cheque counterfoils	1 year
Correspondence files	6 years
Credit Notes	6 years
Customs & Excise VAT records	6 years
Delivery notes	1 year
Directors' reports	30 years
Expenses claims	1 year
Insurance claims forms	6 years
Expired leases	12 years
Licences for patents	30 years
Medical certificates	1 year
Expired patents	12 years
Power of Attorney	30 years
Prospectuses	30 years
Paying-in books	1 year
Purchase orders	6 years
Quotations, out	6 years
Royalty ledger	30 years
Sales invoices	6 years
Product specifications	6 years
Tax records	6 years
Share applications	12 years

This guide is reproduced by kind permission of Fellowes Manufacturing UK Ltd and Business Equipment Digest magazine

The advent of networked computers has given micrographics a boost by providing a high-speed retrieval system called Computer Aided Retrieval (CAR). This retrieval system is invaluable in situations where microform records, sometimes stored for many years, need to be quickly located and retrieved.

Electronic filing

Increasingly today office administrators are turning to computerised filing systems in their efforts to stem the tide of paper documents and also to take advantage of the high-speed features of electronic filing where, say, a retained file copy of a letter may be located in the hard-disk memory of an installed word processing package, displayed on VDU screen and a hard copy printed out if required all in a

matter of seconds. And, no matter whether the file copy is in the user's own desktop PC, or hundreds of miles away in the head office's mainframe computer!

The equipment needed for electronic filing

The equipment shown in Fig. 2.4 is linked together to provide an electronic filing system.

How to create electronic files

1 On floppy disks

As you will know, personal computers (PCs) with smaller memories operate by using two types of disk:

The DOS and software applications disks LOADED INTO DRIVE A

The disk on which working files are created LOADED INTO DRIVE B

Fig. 2.4 Electronic filing system

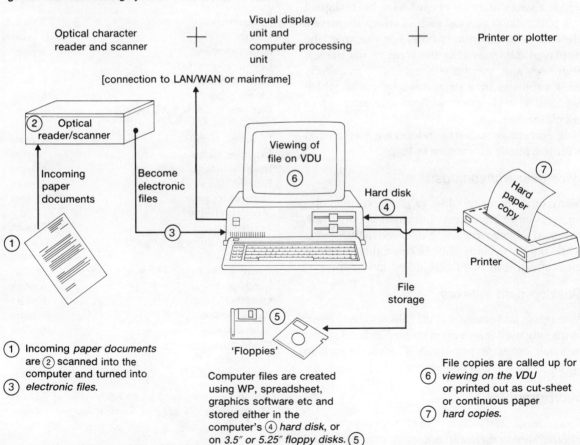

Optical character reader and scanner + Visual display unit and computer processing unit + Printer or plotter

[connection to LAN/WAN or mainframe]

(2) Optical reader/scanner

Incoming paper documents

Become electronic files

Viewing of file on VDU (6)

Hard disk (4)

(7) Hard paper copy

(1) (3)

Printer

File storage

(5) 'Floppies'

(1) Incoming *paper documents* are (2) scanned into the computer and turned into (3) *electronic files*.

Computer files are created using WP, spreadsheet, graphics software etc and stored either in the computer's (4) *hard disk*, or on *3.5" or 5.25" floppy disks.* (5)

File copies are called up for (6) *viewing on the VDU* or printed out as cut-sheet or continuous paper (7) *hard copies.*

When you use the FORMAT COMMAND of your DOS operating disk, your computer installs a set of electronic instructions on to your work disk which creates sets of tracks on both sides and divides both sides into sectors.

When you use the DOS/Software application command to create a work file like this: Document to open? [Filename] Can't find that file. Create a new one (Y/N)? then the computer's operating system will select a track on which to 'write' the file, using its 'read/write' heads. Each time you create a file on the working disk, its title will be added to a directory (which you may call up) showing how many bytes of memory the file has used up, and how many remain for future use.

SELECTING HELPFUL FILE NAMES

While computer technology is always in a state of hectic change, for the moment, most computer software requires its user to create file names using up to eight symbols before a dot (A–Z and 0–9, plus some qwerty signs) in various combinations, and up to three after the dot.

It is most important when devising such file names to build into them some clue as to what the file contains. For example, a letter to your organisation's bank would be easily recognisable when sought in the directory of files if it were called:

BANKLET

rather than:

XQT43J

Similarly, the three available symbols after the dot may be used as a numerical filing system, where BANKLET.1 is the first letter sent to the bank and BANKLET.23 the twenty-third and so on. Or, the three post-dot letters could be turned into a kind of calendar where the first is the month of the year, and the next two the days of the month. Thus BANKLET.812 would be a letter written on the 12 August to the bank.

Note: The letters .BAK at the end of a file name indicate that it is a saved, backed-up copy of a file for emergency access in case of the loss through erasure etc. of a working file.

2 On hard disk directories

In many ways, the organisation of files and software in a computer's hard disk is similar to that of a paper filing cabinet, where its drawers are the 'sub-directories' and the overall metal box holding them the root directory.

A computer's hard disk may be likened to an organisational tree, where the prompt C> immediately accesses the root directory, from which the command CD\ followed by the given name of an application package, summons it up from its sub-directory location:

STEP 1	<C:\>	root directory
STEP 2	<C:\>:CD\WS6	(WORDSTAR issue six) in its own sub-directory
STEP 3	<C:\WS6>WS	the addition of the 'WS' calls up the package's start menu on to the VDU and the process of creating files using Wordstar 6 can begin

Fig. 2.5 *How directories are created*

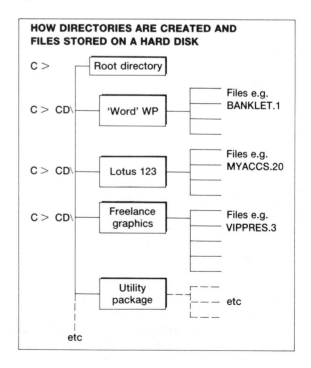

HOW DIRECTORIES ARE CREATED AND FILES STORED ON A HARD DISK

Note: Users of hard (Winchester) disks familiar with the MS-DOS hard disk directory system are able to create helpful sub-directories for storing not only software applications, like Lotus 123 or Word Perfect, but also what are called utility programs which help them use their applications more efficiently.

■ *TOP ASSISTANT TIPS*

The following tips will help you keep your blood-pressure low and aid your electronic filing effectiveness:

1 *Always* save your files at short, regular intervals when using application software! It is infuriating to lose several hours' work by inadvertently erasing unsaved files.

2 Give your files names which will readily trigger your memory about their contents.

3 Ensure you use the DISKCOPY and FILECOPY operations of your computer to copy files to security back-up disks.

4 Become a good housekeeper on your computer by erasing files which are no longer needed, and by saving the memory on your hard disk by storing your working files on removable floppies (unless it is organisational policy to keep all files in a central storage unit).

5 Label your floppy disks clearly with details of their contents. Experienced computer users create their personal directories for lists of files which record:

DATE OF CREATION	FILENAME	DESCRIPTION OF CONTENTS	LOCATION OF FILE (i.e. on what hard or floppy disk)

To do this requires self-discipline, but takes much less time than summoning up file after file on to the VDU to see if it is the sought-after one!

Files and databases

A database is the name of a particular software application package which is used to store information in a very logical manner. Databases are used in organisations to hold data on, say, account customer details, student or patient records,

specifications of products and parts, particulars of criminal activities, vehicle licensing data and so on. Indeed the ways in which databases may be used are endless. Yet they all share a common system for organising the information they contain, as the diagram Fig. 2.6 illustrates:

Note: The term 'file' when used in the context of database software takes on a meaning quite different from its common or garden one. A database file is the complete set of records which make up all the information held on a given subject area. For example, if the database were of patients' records, then a single 'file' might hold all the records for patients undergoing out-patient treatment for slipped discs. Another quite separate file might be for all patients currently in the intensive care unit, and so on. A database file holds a set of individual records which share a common classification. Thus the history of treatment for Mrs Anthea Foster's slipped disc would be entered on her individual record. And each record is made up of predesigned boxes or fields in which the information to be stored is entered as, for instance, full name, home address, telephone number, post code, sex, age, etc.

The remarkable feature of this type of electronic filing system is that any one field may be sorted through to display, for example, all patients who are male, or all over 60 years of age, or only those who have already experienced a heart-attack and so on. Moreover, such database systems are also capable of having the postal address details of selected people printed out for a mail-shot run. Each individual record may be updated at will and printed out as hard copy on demand.

Filing systems and good housekeeping

No matter how accurately information is set down in a file document (whether paper or electronic) it is of no value at all if lost, mislaid or misfiled. By the same token, if a file is taken from its cabinet (or if on floppy disk from its storage unit) without any record of its whereabouts being available, then frustration is bound to occur among other would-be users.

Therefore it is essential in operating any filing system to comply cheerfully with established in-

Fig. 2.6 Components of a database

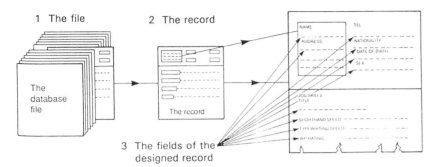

1 The file

2 The record

The database file

The record

3 The fields of the designed record

NAME · TEL · ADDRESS · NATIONALITY · DATE OF BIRTH · SEX · JOB SKILLS TITLE · SHORTHAND SPEED · TYPE WRITING SPEED · WP RATING

house procedures which are likely to include:

Centralised filing systems:

▶ completing an 'out-and-back' slip for the filing clerk;

▶ securing authorisation for handling a file with restricted access;

▶ obeying rules on not removing individual papers or copying if appropriate;

▶ returning files within specified time limits;

▶ taking on responsibility for the security of a confidential file while on loan to your office.

Decentralised/'Personal Responsibility' filing systems

▶ maintaining security locking of cabinets and/or VDUs when out of the office;

▶ maintaining filed papers in required order – e.g. most recent topmost etc;

▶ inserting copied documents in cross-referenced filing locations;

▶ monitoring index flags and labels to ensure they are accurate, current and undamaged;

▶ updating file entries methodically and regularly as required (e.g. on an electronic database, entering the newly renegotiated buying terms of an account customer);

▶ with supervision, shredding and/or erasing on a regular basis (according to statutory and in-house regulations) files which are no longer needed;

▶ maintaining regular back-up and security copies of all electronic files and disks, according to in-house procedures;

▶ administering an efficient bring forward system in which documents are either kept in an A4 diary (day-to-a-page) or reminders inputted into an electronic diary's alarm reminder system, so that on a specified future date these are brought to your manager's attention as requested.

Precautions against fire, theft and damage

Prudent organisations take a range of precautions to secure the safety of their precious customer accounts records, insurance details, sales orders and the like. These include the exchange of computer files between mainframes located hundreds of miles apart, storing paper files in fire-proof safes, keeping files in different media (paper/microform/electronic) on different sites and so on.

And where files are kept in their many thousands, extreme care is taken to install burglar and fire alarms as well as automatic sprinklers etc.

The Data Protection Act 1984

In organisations which keep on computer file particulars about staff, customers, students, patients or the general public, the law of the land obliges staff maintaining such personalised files to conform to a number of regulations which include the following:

▶ data must be collected fairly and lawfully and only held for specified lawful purposes;

▶ data must be accurate and kept up to date;

▶ data must be stored in an appropriately secure environment;

▶ data must, with very few exceptions, be accessible to those about whom it is stored – individuals have the right to see what detail is on file about them.

The Act also created a Data Protection Registrar with powers to ensure that the rights of the public are protected where information about them is being held on computer.

In a nutshell, the Data Protection Act obliges any organisation keeping identifiable data about their employees, customers or contacts to register the scope and nature of their computerised data records. Further, it gives individuals who suspect that data is being stored on computer by such organisations the right to inspect the 'Register of Data' kept by the appointed government Registrar's staff (in local offices, like the registry of births, deaths and marriages) in order to find out what is being recorded and how. Certain rights of confidentiality exist to protect the people who put the information on to computer but not so as to shield them from the consequences of any malpractice. Similarly, any data about people which is properly kept on computer file has to be protected by adequate security procedures. Some organisations – like the police – are exempt from the Act's requirements to give access to certain stored information if it is being held in the course of detecting crime.

The Act also makes a number of precise requirements of the user of computerised data and sets standards of integrity to be adopted.

HOW TO OPERATE AN IMPREST PETTY CASH SYSTEM

Virtually all departments in private and public sector organisations need to have direct access to modest sums of cash at regular intervals. The reasons are many and varied: to maintain a hospitality provision of coffee and biscuits, to make an emergency purchase of stationery between the regular supplier's visits, to pay for a junior member of staff's bus fare when delivering an urgent package across town and so on.

To meet such needs, the accounts department of the organisation provides a 'petty cash book' to each department which acts as an extension of the main cash book. The procedure for using the petty cash book is as follows:

1 The petty cash book is started up with an injection of cash from the firm's cashier. The amount decided upon varies according to the needs of the department which have been established over the year. The example below illustrates an initial injection or 'float' of cash of £50.00. The petty cash controller enters this amount in the 'Received' column and provides the cash book folio or page reference and date. The £50.00 thus provided is called an imprest, which means an amount of money forming part of an ongoing series of allocations.

2 As the petty cash controller meets individual requests for cash – whether to buy stamps, pay for fares or replenish milk, tea or coffee, etc – a voucher, numbered in sequence, is issued and signed for by the recipient of the cash so as to provide a written record. The controller then enters the description of the purchase and the number of the issued voucher (or receipt which is given a number) into the 'paid' columns (see the example on page 45). Additionally, the amount is entered into one of a set of analysis columns so that the various headings of outgoings may be brought together for the organisation as a whole in its accounts ledgers.

3 At the end of the petty cash accounting period – or as the petty cash imprest needs topping up – the various purchases are totalled and a balance is carried down representing what is still unspent from the original imprest.

4 The petty cash controller then obtains a further imprest, being the amount of cash needed to restore the imprest to its original sum. In the example, the second imprest needed amounts to £33.28, which transaction is also recorded in the firm's cash book, or in its computer system.

In this way, a petty cash controller or responsible office assistant is able to maintain a supply of small sums of cash for appropriate departmental needs for the duration of the financial year. As cash is

Fig. 2.7 Example of a petty cash book

'Injection' of an imprest of £50 to start the petty cash funds

Ledger page or folio number

A fresh imprest is drawn from the cashier in order to restore the petty cash imprest to its original £50 'float'. Thus £33.28 is needed.

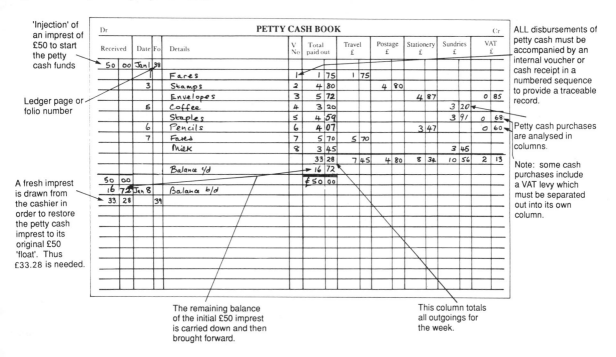

Dr			PETTY CASH BOOK							Cr
Received	Date	Fo	Details	V No	Total paid out	Travel £	Postage £	Stationery £	Sundries £	VAT £
50 00	Jan 1	38								
			Fares	1	1 75	1 75				
	3		Stamps	2	4 80		4 80			
			Envelopes	3	5 72			4 87		0 85
	5		Coffee	4	3 20				3 20	
			Staples	5	4 59				3 91	0 68
	6		Pencils	6	4 07			3 47		0 60
	7		Fares	7	5 70	5 70				
			Milk	8	3 45				3 45	
					33 28	7 45	4 80	8 34	10 56	2 13
			Balance c/d		16 72					
50 00					£50 00					
16 72	Jan 8		Balance b/d							
33 28		39								

ALL disbursements of petty cash must be accompanied by an internal voucher or cash receipt in a numbered sequence to provide a traceable record.

Petty cash purchases are analysed in columns.

Note: some cash purchases include a VAT levy which must be separated out into its own column.

The remaining balance of the initial £50 imprest is carried down and then brought forward.

This column totals all outgoings for the week.

Fig. 2.8 Example of a petty cash voucher

Such vouchers will be issued when staff request cash from the imprest system in order to make small purchases. The recipient of the cash signs for it and the request is authorised by the petty cashier.

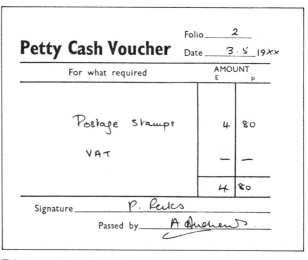

This transaction is recorded in the petty cash book.

Note: Retailer's receipts are also retained and used as petty cash vouchers in the same way.

involved, it is particularly important that due care be taken in maintaining the petty cash book and in issuing vouchers or obtaining receipts, so as to ensure that columns balance and that no sum of cash disappears from till or cash box which cannot be accounted for.

The imprest system and spreadsheet software

The recording of petty cash transactions is ideally suited to the computing and storing applications offered by even the most modest of spreadsheet packages.

The initial left-hand columns may be set up to record cash received, while the columns further to the right of the screen may be set up to detail amounts paid, voucher numbers and analysis columns in just the same arrangement as a petty cash book offers.

Additionally, the spreadsheet's ability to store numerical formulae used in repeated calculations enables the user to obtain running totals very simply and quickly. The process of carrying down and bringing forward is promptly keyed in and hard copies are available on demand, while the imprest may be speedily Emailed to the cashier for checking, along with a request for a top up!

TRAVEL SERVICES

Despite the world-shrinking effects of computer networks and telecommunications, managers still need to make trips out of the office, whether to UK or overseas destinations, because face-to-face communication still matters.

As a result, an essential plank in the raft of your administrative skills must be your ability to make travel arrangements for your manager which:

are completely reliable, having been meticulously researched and checked.

are not over-busy, and do not result in your manager suffering from nervous exhaustion or heat rash from trying to keep to the Olympian itinerary you designed!

look ahead and anticipate, by checking, say, the need for your manager to have preventive vaccinations or to obtain a visa.

provide in advance all the documents needed – while fax can work wonders, not every foreign country is oversupplied with transceivers!

Travelling in the UK by rail

A favourite slogan of British Rail in the 1980s was, 'Let the train take the strain!' and this is still good advice for the businessman with little time to waste, since a valuable opportunity is available for a final reading of papers or checking of figures from the comfort of a carriage compartment. A helpful reference here is BR's *Intercity Guide to Services*, published annually.

▶ Details of car parking and car hire at each destination, including Rail Drive Europcar.
▶ Prestel, Ceefax and Oracle page numbers and details.
▶ Traveline up-to-date information access details.
▶ Credit card booking telephone numbers by region.
▶ How to make reservations.
▶ BR's Business Travel Service details a comprehensive service to businesses which includes hotel bookings and executive ticket service, covering all linked travel elements and 24-hour free parking, etc.
▶ Intercity Pullman, Sleeper and Motorail services.

For travellers who are able to avoid the peak times of intercity journeys (notably Fridays), BR offers its Intercity Saver tariff of fares, through which up to a third of normal costs may be saved. Intercity Savers are always available to Scotland.

Keep in mind also BR's facilities for you to make reservations in advance (for a small extra fee) by credit card and to stipulate first-class, non-smoker, etc. On long journeys, also ensure you check that the train has at-seat dining, restaurant or buffet facilities. Remember to double-check departure and arrival times for inclusion in any itinerary you are asked to produce. Also, note that a useful service on some Intercity trains is BR's trainphone, which takes standard BT phone cards or credit cards.

Travelling in the UK by air

Many executives today accept the higher costs of air travel because of the saving in time. The UK enjoys a developed network of regional airports – East Midlands, Birmingham, Manchester, Leeds, Glasgow, Teeside, Belfast, etc – in addition to the Greater London airports of Heathrow, London City and Gatwick. Passengers are also able to fly to many European and more distant destinations from the major regional airports.

Tickets are available from local travel agents, airline desks (bookable by telephone and supportive credit card number in advance) or from service companies specialising in business travel. Air travellers may also take advantage of car valeting services (parking and securing a car during its owner's absence) within the airport complex. Additionally, a number of UK airports have Business Centres where executives are able to make use of sophisticated fax, telephone and secretarial services as well as private conference rooms – all for hire on a membership basis. Nor is the secretary overlooked! Some leading international airline companies run executive secretary clubs which offer expert administrative help, hotlines and updating bulletins as well as social events for secretaries whose managers are regular air travellers.

Airline tickets for the UK and overseas may be reserved in either smoking or non-smoking areas and window seats may be requested. Some planes may also carry the Skyphone telephone service. Generally in the UK, baggage is restricted to one piece, not exceeding 22 kg and a single small cabin bag as 'hand luggage'.

■ TOP ASSISTANT TIP

While stand-by and similar cheap flights are a welcome saver for tourists with plenty of time, always ensure that you book UK or overseas flights as *scheduled flights*. No manager can afford to take the risk of arriving late for an important meeting. The extra costs of scheduled flights are justified by their advertised and usually maintained departure and arrival times and secure reservation facilities.

Hotel reservations in the UK

Generally, hotels will accept telephoned reservations supported by a credit card number. Otherwise, the hotel usually requires a written confirmation of booking – as evidence of intent (and for charging) if the traveller does not turn up. Alternatively, fax or telex may be used to make and confirm a booking. Today, many companies negotiate special deals with hotel chains and may have all bookings for their employees made through a single centralised account. Indeed, some national hotel chains employ staff full-time to service such accounts and business needs. Needless to say, the ever-ready 'plastic money' credit card is most widely used to secure hotel accommodation and allied facilities. Several major hotel groups operate their own credit cards with built-in attractions like: guaranteed reservations held for 24 hours, 'best room available on booking', express check-in and out, bill forwarding for checking, extended late check-out at no extra cost, cheque encashment, etc.

The facilities which hotels offer business travellers naturally vary, but larger hotels will have fax and modems available, as well as room and telephone services, early morning call and newspaper ordering, clothes and shoe valeting, secure car parking, private suites for hire, sports and leisure facilities, from sauna to surfboarding, all supported by computerised billing and reservations systems.

Checklist for making a hotel reservation

1 **Before you start,** make quite sure you have definite details of: estimated arrival and departure times, duration of stay, particulars of any special requirements – dietary, telecommunications, reprographic, etc.

2 **Write down the major features you wish to book before telephoning** and go through them with the receptionist. This way you won't forget any.

3 **Check acceptable mode of payment with receptionist** – no manager likes to be embarrassed by, say, proffering a credit card not accepted by the hotel.

4 **Check car-parking arrangements** – Secure parking is essential in most localities. Imagine if your manager has to park on the highway overnight and finds the car vandalised at the start of a busy day!

5 **Make written notes of your negotiated arrangements** – particularly of a guaranteed reservation and either fax, telex or confirm by letter so as to create a written record. Ensure a written note with clear details of major aspects of the reservation(s) is included in your manager's travel pack.

For the busy secretary, some national chains operate centralised booking services through which a number of hotel reservations may be made at one time to cover a manager's business route.

Travel services and IT

The travel industry, like banking, makes extensive use of information technology to provide a faster, more reliable and sophisticated service, so make sure you update yourself regularly about:

▶ Prestel and viewdata information and booking services, from air travel to theatre tickets.
▶ ISTEL/TRAVICOM/ABC Corporate Services databases for instant advice on facilities, itineraries ticket issue, etc.
▶ Branch up-to-the-minute computerised reports on items such as exchange rates, snow reports, industrial disputes, hotel availabilities.
▶ Computerised convergence to scan multiple airlines for next available flights, and to effect EFTPOS payments, etc.

Foreign travel

A wise man once observed that: 'There are two kinds of knowledge, the kind you have to carry around in your head, and the kind you need to know where to get when you need it!' Nowhere is this truer than in the field of foreign travel, which is, in itself, a demanding and complex specialism. It pays, therefore, to foster a good relationship with a local or company-approved travel agency which will provide you with the following areas of service and specialist advice:

Travel agency services

▶ Making reservations for air or sea travel.
▶ Arranging for car hire at destination airport.
▶ Making worldwide reservations in approved (good quality) hotels and advising on their telex, fax and cable addresses, leisure facilities, and price tariffs.
▶ Providing personal, valuables and baggage insurance.
▶ Advising on public holidays, customs and procedures of foreign countries and also on vaccination and visa requirements.

▶ Working out in advance optimum travel routes and economic costs for travellers using various airline routes between countries and continents.
▶ Securing tickets (including rail or coach tickets) and other documentation for collection or onward posting and accepting (by arrangement) payment on account or by credit card.
▶ Obtaining traveller's cheques and foreign currency for clients.

As the foregoing checklist indicates, travel agencies provide a range of support services which are designed to save the busy assistant's time and energy. Travel agency staff rely extensively on directories like those produced by *ABC Corporate Services Worldwide Hotel Guide, ABC Guide To International Travel* and *ABC Air Travel Atlas.* These are updated on a monthly basis and comprise encyclopaedic details of airline companies' current scheduled flight costs, worldwide hotel facilities and costs, airline routes and connections and a further range of advice and requirements on vaccinations needed and recommended medication to carry, etc.

Airline reservations are generally made through either ISTEL or TRAVICOM, two companies which provide a network of computers in travel agency offices operating a 'real-time' booking system. This means that the operator can check the 'up-to-the-minute' extent of a scheduled air flight's bookings and add a further number of seat reservations there and then. This process may be conducted while operator and secretary are connected by telephone and confirmed upon supply of a credit card number or central account number.

Checklist for making foreign travel arrangements

Start well in advance and avoid haste; set up a file and create a list of the jobs to attend to; then prioritise them.

Essential documents (to be checked out early)
- ▶ Valid and current passport (note that regular travellers can obtain 90-page passports for visa stamps, etc).
- ▶ Valid **visa** and certificates of vaccination; remember to allow enough time for the doctor to undertake these and for the after-effects to wear off (check with the travel agency for the latest requirements).
- ▶ Current driving licence, international driving licence and **Green Card insurance**, if driving and/or taking a car abroad; consult AA/RAC handbooks for individual countries' vehicle and equipment requirements.
- ▶ Form E111 for free medical treatment in EEC countries (available from the Department of Health).
- ▶ Travel tickets and hotel reservation(s) confirmations.
- ▶ Business documents for the trip, including itinerary and factsheet(s) for each country to be visited, itemising the main features of political/social life, customs, religious practices, etc. Also checklist of names, job designations, addresses, fax and telephone numbers of all principal foreign contacts. Note: Don't forget to list home office fax, telex and other contact numbers!
- ▶ Travel guides and leaflets from the Department of Health.

Money and financial resources
- ▶ Foreign currency(ies), Eurocheque card and cheques.
- ▶ UK cheque book and Visa/Mastercard-based credit card and international cards (American Express, Diners Club, etc).
- ▶ Any **bankers' drafts**, or international money orders.
- ▶ Details for cabling money from UK in emergency, etc.

Personal travel resources
- ▶ Advice on appropriate clothing for season (remember heat plus humidity factor in many countries), travel iron/valeting kit, handy dictating machine and cassettes, notebook computer, batteries and disks, calculator, foreign language dictionaries and phrase books, first-aid/medication kit, books for light reading, etc.

International travel arranging: health checklist

The following checklist illustrates the major arrangements and precautions which need to be organised before a business trip abroad:

1 **Check of countries to be visited** in terms of what preventative vaccinations need to be given. *Note:* the Department of Health's brochure *The Traveller's Guide to Health* (T1) provides a helpful listing.

   Medical appointments may need to be made several months in advance of the journey for some vaccines to be effective, so forward planning is essential!

2 **Drinking water:** local drinking water is unsafe in a number of countries and so advice as to the purchase or inclusion of bottled mineral water in baggage needs to be included in itinerary notes.

3 **Taking medicines abroad:** regulations exist in some countries regarding the import of medicines: advice is available from the relevant embassy.

4 **Medical insurance:** Completion of Form E111 will cover NHS-type medical treatment in any EC country for UK/EC nationals. This form is available from local DoH offices.

   Otherwise comprehensive medical insurance is essential for international travellers; taking a UK NHS medical card on such trips is often helpful.

5 **Local situations:** in some foreign countries rabies, for instance, may be currently raging; embassies and consulates provide advice and it is always worth checking for any particular local health hazards and highlighting these on travel briefings.

■ *DISCUSSION TOPIC*
What sort of training programme would you devise for office assistants who frequently have to arrange overseas business trips for their managers?

Passports and visas

An essential part of any international travel arranging is the checking out of passport and visa particulars. For example a one-year EC traveller's passport may not be valid for entering other countries, which require a full British passport. Similarly, a full passport on its own will not satisfy those countries which require entry- and exit-type visas which detail the reasons for a visit and in some cases the areas to be visited.

Visas are issued through the embassies and consulates of the countries involved. In some instances it can take several weeks to obtain a visa and so last-minute rushes are to be avoided.

Summary of free baggage allowances

1 **Internal UK flights**
   2 pieces not exceeding 62 inches (combined length, height and width)

2 **USA and Canada**
   2 pieces not exceeding 32 kg per bag

3 **Rest of world** Economy Class: 1 piece
   First/Club Classes: 2 pieces
   Concorde/First Class: 40 kg
   Superclub/Club: 30 kg
   Economy: 23 kg

All plus a single piece of hand luggage

Source: British Airways Travelwise Baggage Information

Details of a typical airline reservation slip

The illustration indicates the information needed to secure a computerised airline booking:

Fig. 2.9 Airline reservation slip (Courtesy of Hogg Robinson (Travel) Ltd)

The travel itinerary

The word 'itinerary' derives from the Latin word for journey. Today it stands for a printed schedule which details:

▶ the days, times and dates of a projected journey;
▶ the locations to be visited;
▶ the people who will take part in the journey, e.g.

multinational company colleagues, overseas customers, politicians or diplomats;
▶ brief explanatory details of what is due to happen, where and when.

Illustrated is an extract of a specimen itinerary to show its structure and format; but bear in mind that these are not fixed, but rather for you to design to best effect.

Fig. 2.10 Itinerary

ITINERARY

SIMPLEX BUSINESS SOFTWARE LIMITED

Export Sales Visit to Japan, Australia & New Zealand

Visiting Sales Team:

Susan Peters, Export Sales Manager
David Richards, Financial Consultant
John Dickinson, Far East & Australasia Sales
Coordinator
Pietra Zybieski, Chief Programmer and Technical
Advisor

Tuesday 23 May 199-

   1630 Arrival Heathrow, Terminal 4, Check in
     at British Airways Desk & Executive Club

   1730 Scheduled departure time
     Stopover: Anchorage

Wednesday 24 May 199-

   2015 Arrive Tokyo Haneda Airport
  (local time)
     Chris Harrison, Japanese Sales Agent
     will meet Team and escort to Eastern Dawn
     Hotel

Thursday 25 May 199-

 0900 - 1200 Travel Recuperation Period
        in Hotel Solarium/ Swimming Pool/
        Beauty Salon/Complex

 1215 - 1500 Welcoming Reception & Lunch

        Tokyo Chamber of Commerce Delegation:
        President Mr Ahiro Akaihito
        (approx 25 delegates: see travel
        pack listing company representation)

        Hotel Lotus Blossom Suite

 1500 - 2000 Visit to Head Office of Taniko Computer
        Company, Tokyo to meet Directors and
        Senior Managers

Fig. 2.11   International time chart

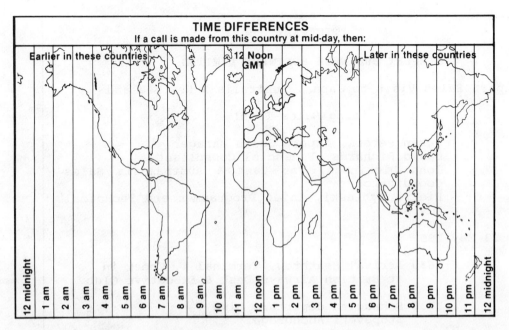

TIME DIFFERENCES
If a call is made from this country at mid-day, then:

Earlier in these countries   12 Noon GMT   Later in these countries

| 12 midnight | 1 am | 2 am | 3 am | 4 am | 5 am | 6 am | 7 am | 8 am | 9 am | 10 am | 11 am | 12 noon | 1 pm | 2 pm | 3 pm | 4 pm | 5 pm | 6 pm | 7 pm | 8 pm | 9 pm | 10 pm | 11 pm | 12 midnight |

(Reproduced by kind permission of British Telecom)

Make time for a time check!

Don't forget the time zone differences across the world – or British Summer Time, etc. Remember that airports, railway stations and ferry/port timetables always show *local* times which may be as much as twelve hours ahead of or behind UK times. Also, make it a habit to check your office time chart before telephoning San Francisco or Sydney, only to raise the overnight cleaner or caretaker! And of course, international times must be closely checked when producing an itinerary for an overseas visit.

Taking money abroad

While it is possible to pay before departure for travel and hotel costs etc, all international travellers need to take money in some form or other with them for entertainment, out-of-pocket expenses and so on. The following major options are listed below:

Foreign currency

Easy and simple in terms of pay-as-you-go abroad, but may prove costly in countries with rampant inflation, where the purchasing power of cash decreases daily and cash has been purchased at home some days in advance; also, cash is easily lost or stolen.

Some countries put a limit on how much of their currency may be taken in and out by foreign travellers.

UK clearing banks charge a percentage of the currency ordered for providing the service, and advance notice (check the bank) is required for less popular currencies.

Travellers' cheques

All banks supply travellers' cheques, say, in pounds sterling or US dollars in denominations of sums like £20, £50, £100 etc. The customer puts his signature on the top half of each cheque in the presence of the Overseas Transactions Cashier, and then again when encashing the cheques in a foreign bank or hotel, so as to prove rightful ownership.

All travellers' cheques are numbered and by keeping a record, a traveller can claim back the amount of any stolen or lost cheques. The banks at both ends of the transaction make a charge for the service.

Eurocheques

Many EC/European banks and shops accept Eurocheques. These are processed just like UK cheques and are available from UK clearing banks. Details are recorded in the local currency and the issuer's home current bank account debited in due course at the prevailing rate of exchange.

Money orders

Some business travellers take money orders for large amounts (say, to pay for a business deal) which are arranged in advance between banks which guarantee the payment of the sums involved.

Travellers abroad who become 'financially embarrassed' can obtain funds quickly by asking the overseas bank to contact the home bank in order for them to 'wire' a money order directly. Again, this is a form of guaranteed exchange of credit and debit between banks, so that the penniless traveller is once more in funds!

Credit cards: Visa, Mastercard, Access etc

Many countries around the world accept payment for goods or services through the medium of the plastic credit card – used just as it is in the UK. Receipts are signed and copies provided on the spot. The charges appear some weeks later on the credit card statement back in the UK. Foreign currency can also be obtained with a credit card, but interest is charged on the transactions by most companies from the day of purchase, so it can prove an expensive way of obtaining instant cash!

Establishing a bank account

In situations where personnel work abroad over extended periods of time, it makes good sense for their organisations to arrange a banking account for them with the local branch of a bank connected with their UK company bank. In this way, the full facilities of the overseas bank become readily available, and costs prove cheaper over a period of time.

Making booking arrangements for travelling executives

The busy export sales representative, for example, will have no time to spend on sorting out travel arrangements once embarked upon an exacting sales trip overseas.

The organiser of his itinerary, therefore, must take pains to ensure that bookings are confirmed and accepted *in advance*.

Some overseas organisations such as hotels or car-hire firms will accept a faxed confirmation of a telephoned booking. But some require a letter of confirmation which details:

▶ Name(s) of person(s) purchasing service
▶ Dates and times of arrival/departure
▶ Details of services purchased e.g. type of room, access of travellers to business office in hotel, type of car to be hired etc
▶ Details of agreed charges and confirmation of method of payment (by prior agreement)

Some credit card companies provide such a service as part of their international travel provisions. Hotel chains and airlines sometimes make additional charges for confirmed bookings, but they are a godsend when a weary traveller arrives at an airline desk and finds his flight overbooked. He will receive priority!

Large companies negotiate, say, with the International Hilton group of hotels, for their staff's bookings to be made centrally between respective accounts departments. Less fortunate travellers need to have their itineraries booked and means of payments agreed with individual hotels.

Budgeting for overseas travel

Many large organisations with considerable numbers of staff regularly visiting or residing overseas produce tariffs or costing schedules which set defined limits on what may be spent per 24 hours on hotel accommodation, meals, transport and out-of-pocket expenses etc. Staff making booking arrangements have to comply with such tariffs, which are regularly updated.

Returning travellers are required to supply receipts as far as possible and to complete an expenses return for their accounts department, which is checked against the current tariff.

ARRANGING MEETINGS

Supporting the work of managers often requires arranging meetings for them, either between in-house colleagues, or the firm's managers and external visitors. There are three essential phases to take into account when arranging meetings:

1 The pre-meeting planning/ communication phase

This may last many months (in the case of organising a large conference) or 2–3 weeks for a smaller, more informal meeting, depending on how full are the diaries of those concerned. Thus the first and indeed most important task is *to fix and communicate clearly and in good time:*

▶ the day/date;
▶ the start and finishing times;
▶ the precise location of the meeting;
▶ a listing of all those involved with job titles etc;
▶ details of the various items of business to be transacted at the meeting (perhaps in the form of an agenda).

This information should be communicated courteously in advance using letter-mail, fax, or Wide Area Network (WAN) Email (see page 107). Also, it is helpful to provide visitors with district and site maps and to indicate where parking is provided. If visitors are to arrive by train, it is customary for them to be met by a member of staff and driven to the meeting place.

Before the meeting is confirmed, it is always prudent to make provisional bookings of conference rooms and audio-visual equipment, and so on, so as to be sure of their availability.

2 Preparation of the meeting room and documents phase

For a meeting to go well, careful preparations must be made to set up the room or suite in which it takes place (*see* checklist below). Common sense dictates that checks are made on lighting, temperature and circulating fresh air. No one can work effectively in gloomy or glaring light, feeling chilly or hot in airless surroundings. Similarly, the arrangement of seating is important so that the meeting's leaders have a prominent place where all participants can see them clearly and each member is easily visible to everyone else. Thought needs to be given to status and people's self-esteem in seating plans – hence the popularity of circular tables for meetings.

Effective meetings provide a kind of place-setting for each participant, with ball-points, pencils, notepaper and, in high-status meetings, personalised name plaques, wallets or binders for papers etc. Adjacent glasses and carafes of water and/or soft drinks, accompanied by refresher mints are usually provided at longer meetings.

Nowadays most meetings are supported by a range of audio-visual aids (AVA), and it is the duty of the meeting organiser to ensure that these are in good working order, with spare bulbs, overhead transparency foils, whiteboard marker pens, flip-chart paper, substitute (copied) computer floppy disks etc on hand in case of need. Murphy's Law states that if any piece of equipment is going to fail, it will do so at the most important psychological moment, such as the climax of the Managing Director's presentation. It is therefore wise to have a technician and spares on stand-by for all high-level meetings!

The documents which are used at meetings vary according to the purpose of the get-together. Part 5 provides extensive guidance on notices, agendas, minutes, and resolutions, and Part 6 similarly on reports. Good practice – whatever the type of document involved – requires that spares are available for those participants who forgot to bring posted sets etc. Papers to be 'tabled' at a meeting (without members having seen them beforehand) are normally neatly arranged at each place-setting.

3 The post-meeting tidy up phase

Whoever acted as secretary to the meeting is responsible for producing reports, minutes or action notes, but it is often left to the meeting arranger to ensure that the suite or conference room is cleaned and tidied. Most important is to ensure that no confidential papers have been absent-mindedly left on tables or crumpled in waste-paper bins. In government cabinet meetings, even ministers' doodles are promptly shredded after each meeting!

Equipment should be checked for any failures or damage before being returned to its storage location and any used bulbs should be replaced directly. A short 'thank you' note to helpful caretakers or other support staff always helps to oil the wheels for asking favours when arranging subsequent meetings.

'I didn't bother with an agenda this time – you know how awkward they get when they come prepared . . .'

Pre-meeting servicing checklist

Ask yourself the following questions, and make sure you have the right answers, in the run-up to the meetings you service:

1 Has every member received the notice, agenda and any supportive papers for the meeting?

2 Has a list of apologies for absence been made out for the chairman?

3 Has incoming correspondence been copied for chairman and treasurer? Should all members be given a copy of an important letter at the meeting?

4 Are sufficient spare copies of agenda, minutes of the last meeting and any supportive papers available for members who forgot to bring their own?

5 Have reserved parking spaces been properly 'signalled' with name-plaques of members? Do caretaking staff know start and finish times of the meeting?

6 Does the foyer receptionist have details of the meeting so as to direct members to it? Is it posted on the electronic noticeboard?

7 Have appropriate arrangements been made for refreshments? Are these limited to serving coffee and biscuits on arrival or does the chairman need to be prompted about adjourning the meeting for a served meal?

8 Is the venue properly prepared? Note the importance of a personal check shortly before the meeting of: lighting, room temperature, ventilation, seating and table layout (this can be square, oblong, round, U-shaped etc). Is each 'place-setting' ready: blotter, notepaper, water glass, name-plaque, set of any tabled papers, ball-point pen, etc?

9 Are all the documents and papers to hand which the chairman will need: chairman's agenda, copy of the minutes of the last meeting (or minutes book) for signature, copies of correspondence received, list of apologies for absence, reminder note to welcome new members, copies of papers to be discussed, etc?

10 If audio-visual aids are to be used at the meeting, such as an overhead projector with foils, slides or video-cassettes, have these been checked and equipment tried out by a technician before the meeting? Is microphone equipment required if it is a large meeting?

11 Final checks by the secretary: Minutes book or file to hand in case reference is made to a previous minute. Spare copies of documents, minutes notebook, spare pens/pencils, spare writing-paper, personal and manager's diaries available. Checklist of names of all members for reference and to check arrivals. Refreshments on hand. Assistant notified of likely absence from office and location of meeting in case of urgent messages, etc.

12 Post-meeting: pick up and dispose of papers left by members – post on to them as appropriate. Arrange for room to be tidied, switch off appliances.

ACTIVITIES AND ASSIGNMENTS *Office support activities*

■ *THE QUICK CHECK-IT-OUT QUIZ*

1 List the most important items of equipment used in a mail room.
2 What actions should be taken to ensure that mail is opened and distributed efficiently?
3 How can an organisation ensure that important mail is delivered to a named recipient?
4 What mail services are available when deliveries are urgent?
5 What are the procedures for processing outgoing mail?
6 What equipment is needed to deal with outgoing mail, and how is it used?
7 Explain briefly the difference between vertical and lateral filing.
8 What rules are applied when filing in alphabetical sequence?
9 Describe four methods of filing *other than* alphabetical.
10 What is meant by the practices of cross-indexing and cross-referencing?
11 Describe briefly three visual methods of filing data.
12 Explain briefly how an electronic filing system works (you may wish to draw a diagram).
13 List what you think are the most important steps to take in order to store electronic files safely.
14 Explain how directories and files are organised on a computer's hard disk.
15 How is information stored on a software database package?
16 Detail good practice for handling files in a centralised filing system.
17 What is the Data Protection Act for?
18 Describe the operation of an imprest petty cash system.
19 What major services are available on British Rail intercity trains?
20 List the benefits to a businessman of an airline's shuttle service.
21 Describe briefly the different ways a traveller may take money abroad.
22 What health precautions should a visitor to, say, central Africa take before departure?
23 List the services which a competent travel agency branch provides.
24 What information should a good travel itinerary contain?
25 List the actions an effective meeting arranger should take to ensure the success of a meeting.

Case study activities

These activities develop NVQ competences in:

arranging travel: references, information etc;
supplying information for a specific purpose;
information processing – using a database;
telecommunications and data transmission: Email.

Case study

HAVE WORKSTATION, WILL TRAVEL!

You work as an assistant to Richard Keys, deputy office administration manager of Industrial Pumps Limited, at their head office in Milton Keynes.

Industrial Pumps Limited is a UK company employing some five hundred staff – manufacturing, sales, marketing and administrative personnel – to make and sell a wide range of electrically powered pumps. The pumps are used in a host of different ways – to pump water into irrigation canals in Third World countries, to control the movement of chemicals and fluid products in manufacturing processes, to assist in land drainage, and so on. Indeed, it is difficult to think of a pumping situation for which IPL has yet to design a suitable pump! For example, they also manufacture valves which surgeons insert into human hearts to restore their pumping capabilities.

As a result of years of ingenious design work, excellent craftsmanship and resulting reliability, IPL pumps are selling at an ever-increasing rate all over the world. The export sales department staff has doubled in size over the past five years and today there are 20 export sales executives who devote most of their time to travelling across the world to sell IPL pumps to government installations, hospitals, chemical plants and so on. Additionally, IPL employs a home sales force of some 25 sales executives to sell their products throughout the UK.

Hitherto, the home sales executives have tended to make their own travel arrangements, according to their sales itineraries and then to submit monthly expenses for petrol, hotels, meals and so on. As a result, there has been no real underlying organisation of their needs, and IPL is spending money it could save by making agreements with national hotel chains, for example, and securing a group discount. Also, claimed expenses have come to be paid 'on the nod' with little monitoring.

The export sales executives have usually made their travel arrangements with the help of two clerical assistants, Julie Halliday and Carol Parker, who have developed close links with the local branch of Global Travel Limited, a nationwide travel agency chain. The counter assistant they usually like to deal with is called Sally Owen. However, the Global local branch has become increasingly busy over the past six months, partly as a result of a sharp increase in the influx of retired businessmen and their wives, who have the money for foreign holidays and plenty of time on their hands to seek the most detailed guidance and advice from the Global staff.

As a result of these developments, there has been a rash of mistakes and errors over the making of travel arrangements, both at home and overseas. Hotel bookings have not been confirmed and arriving executives have been turned away. Two export executives recently missed their flights as a result of typing errors on their itineraries, and one had to postpone an important sales visit to India because of a slip-up in vaccination arrangements.

'Start right, stay right'

This morning, Mr David Searle, office administration manager, called you into his office and briefed you as follows:

'The MD is pretty fed up with the problems he's been hearing about over faulty travel arrangements and the steeply rising cost of our UK and overseas sales teams' travel expenses. He wants us to tackle the problem and has delegated its solution to me.

'This is how I am proposing to solve it – or at least to improve matters substantially. I want to second you for three months to develop our own internal travel services unit. I've arranged to have Julie Halliday and Carol Parker transferred from export sales to work for the unit full time.

'I think that what is needed here at IPL is an integrated approach that arranges all travel, home and overseas. So, assuming you are in agreement . . . (*You nod!*) . . . I'd like you to produce your ideas on equipping a travel office. I've made room

C231 available.' (*It is some 5 m wide and 6 m long and fully 'plumbed' for LAN/modem communications and PABX phone extensions, etc.*)

'Draw up a layout for me that you think would be most appropriate, and let me have your list of reference books and materials and any communication facilities you think you will need. Essentially, the MD wants us to speed up the travel arrangements process, cut out these vexing mistakes and look to running our sales team's travel needs as cost-effectively as we can, not forgetting our image as a world leader! He says he doesn't mean us to try to take on the travel agencies at their own game, but to see how we might help them to help us do it better.

'I need you to give this one your best shot – the MD's pretty fired up! If you like what you've created, we can talk in three months' time about whether you want to stay with it, or return to being Richard's secretary. Oh, and by the way, just in case you said 'yes', I've set up a desk and phone and so on in room C231, and Richard's allowing you to start straight away! There's an old proverbial expression we engineers like to quote: 'Start right, stay right!' and I'm sure it is true of this new travel servicing venture!'

■ *CASE STUDY QUESTIONS*

1 What advantages do you think are likely to stem from the setting up of the travel services unit?

2 What routine procedures would you establish to help the unit:
   a To make UK travel arrangements efficiently?
   b To make overseas travel arrangements efficiently?
   Are there any forms which might be designed which could aid these processes?

3 What management information systems (IT based) would you want installed in room C231? And what software applications packages to do what tasks?

4 What books, directories, guides and timetables, etc, would you select as part of your reference/information database in room C231?

5 In what ways would you like to liaise with Global Travel's local branch? Can you suggest any new procedures which might improve their service – bearing in mind that IPL are very good customers of Global?

6 How would Julie and Carol be most efficiently employed in the unit? What individual tasks would you allocate to them? They can both process text and data on the firm's LAN workstations and operate fax and telex equipment.

7 How would you 'sell' the new travel services unit to IPL's sales teams and their departmental office administrative staff?

■ *ACTIVITIES*

1 Design your proposed layout for the travel services unit office in room C231.

2 Produce your initial list of reference source books and guides, etc.

3 Design a software database file (or form), for making travel arrangements for export sales executives shortly to travel abroad for periods of one to two weeks. Your form should seek to assemble the essential information needed to allow a clerical assistant to make the basic arrangements for the visit.

4 Having carried out your research, compose a memorandum to the office administration manager, outlining how the travel requirements of the UK sales force could be organised so as to save money and avoid the passing of excessive expense claims.

5 You can assume that all sales team personnel use IPL's electronic mail system. Compose an Email message to *either* the UK or the export sales executives which provides instructions on how they should take advantage of LAN/WAN networks to

communicate their planned work schedules in advance so as to enable your unit to make any needed reservations and bookings and to confirm them back to the executive(s) concerned.

Activities to develop confidence and competence

The following activities develop NVQ competences in:

* *storing and supplying information;*
* *maintaining an established filing system;*
* *supplying information for a specific purpose;*
* *making travel arrangements and booking accommodation;*
* *arranging and setting up meetings;*
* *information processing;*
* *processing records in a database;*
* *making and recording petty cash payments.*

Incoming and outgoing mail

1 By arrangement with your teacher, assume the responsibility for one week of collecting the mail for the Department in which you are studying (or to which you are attached for work experience).

You should follow both standard and in-house procedures for opening, date-stamping, sorting into priority and distributing the incoming mail, having regard to confidential and personal mail, and to procedures for recording registered mail etc.

2 Also by arrangement, supervise for one week the Department's outgoing mail, having particular regard to:

correctly signed documents, correctly headed and addressed letters and envelopes, clearly indicated postal rates (first, second, registered, etc) shown, enclosures secured, parcels securely sealed, logbooks maintained and security procedures adopted; if possible, seek to obtain evidence of competence in use of franking equipment.

Filing systems

3 Within an office or simulated training office environment, demonstrate the ability to file documents correctly, having regard to alphabetical and numerical systems and correct indexing practices.

4 Use a database software application to achieve the following task, having secured permission from your Head of Department and members of your group:

Your Head of Department wishes to undertake a pilot scheme involving the transfer of student records from a paper to a computerised system. You have therefore been requested to set up the following information on a computerised database:

The following information is requested about your class group (or a minimum of ten members):

1 Full name
2 Postal address
3 Age
4 Sex male/female
5 Last school/college attended

6 Enrolment number/code
7 If any European foreign language studied YES/NO
8 Which language? State: e.g. French/German/Spanish
9 If previous experience using word processing software YES/NO
10 If able to touch-type YES/NO

Your HOD wants to be able to retrieve records as follows:

1 Number of students in group by age and by sex.
2 Ratio of males to females in group.
3 Percentage with some foreign language skills.
4 Breakdown of who has study experience of which European foreign languages.
5 Ratio of members in group with previous experience of using wp software.
6 Ratio of members in group able to touch-type.

Design a database record with fields which will produce the information required and demonstrate your ability to obtain the information required in *1–6* above.

5 Use a word processing software application to set up the following files:

1 A letter from your Course Tutor to Business Textbooks Limited requesting an inspection copy of *Business Administration in the 1990s.* Your Course Tutor's name is: Helen Jackson.
2 A memorandum from Helen Jackson to Paul Simpson, College Librarian asking for *Using A Local Area Network* by Gordon Dennison to be reserved for her.
3 A circular letter to the parents of members of your group inviting them to attend a parents' evening on Wednesday 14 October 199— 7.30–9.00 pm in the Parkwood Suite at your school/college to discuss progress and attainment etc. A reply-slip is required to be returned to Helen Jackson.

Demonstrate your ability to retrieve each created document (a) to VDU screen and (b) as a printed out hard copy.

Also demonstrate your ability to copy item *3* to another formatted disk. Satisfy your teacher that the filenames you have created are practical.

Making and recording petty cash payments

6 Use a preprinted (or electronic) petty cash book to record the following transactions for the week commencing 12 February 199—:

	£	
1 Opening Cash Received Balance:	55.00	
2 Stationery: 1 × box of staples	4.99	inc VAT
3 Replacement Jar Coffee	2.25	
4 Taxi Fare (courier delivery confidential papers)	7.59	
5 Postage (urgent docs)	3.34	
6 Plant Feed for Office Plants	2.99	inc VAT
7 Pack of A4 White Envelopes (ran out)	3.49	inc VAT
8 Weekly Milk (w/c 5.2.9—)	2.44	

Also, complete a petty cash voucher for items *2* and *7* above. Item *2* was purchased on 15 February, and item *7* on 13 February. Your teacher can act as your office supervisor.

Arranging foreign travel

7 Your manager, Dr Julian Manston, is the export sales manager of Biotechnics Research Limited, a company which specialises in developing products which promote the growth and yield of a range of cereal crops. He has just finished fixing up a sales trip to a number of Far Eastern countries to promote a new product which improves the yields of rice crops. He plans to be away for a fortnight and to give sales briefing seminars in Singapore, Hong Kong and Seoul. He needs to convey a first-rate corporate image as he will be dealing with top-rank government officials and company executives. The MD has therefore authorised first-class travel and first-rank hotel accommodation.

In groups of three, carry out the following (researching as appropriate one country and destination each):

a Produce an itinerary giving Dr Manston a minimum of three days in each centre. He has a preference for flying with UK airlines whenever possible.

b Find out the costs of his air travel.

c Decide which hotels you will book him into and provide details of facilities, etc, with costs.

d Produce a factsheet for each country and centre to brief Dr Manston, who has never before travelled to the Far East. He will be travelling in July.

e List any helpful guidelines for Dr Manston about arrangements he will need to make before his visit, any items he should take with him, and helpful advice regarding his journey.

8 You work as assistant to Mrs Fiona Hezeldine, Sales Manager of Tendresse Cosmetics Limited. She has to travel to Edinburgh (alternative location: Bristol) next week to meet regional sales personnel in order to brief them on the launch of a new product, a range of lipsticks manufactured from animal-friendly ingredients. Mrs Hezeldine requires hotel accommodation for three nights, Tuesday, Wednesday and Thursday. She wishes to be booked into a single room with full *en suite* bathroom, shower and wc facilities; also, she would prefer a hotel near the city centre and with sauna and swimming pool facilities if possible.

Use your school/college's Prestel system to make a simulated booking, having perused the Prestel pages on likely hotel accommodation in either Edinburgh or Bristol.

Arranging a meeting

9 Your firm, National Security Systems PLC, sells and installs a wide range of home and business burglary and fire alarm systems. Your head office is situated in Birmingham's Bull Ring complex, and your boss, Peter Richards is the national manager for installation and customer services. On Thursday of next week, he is due to hold his monthly meeting with his seven Regional Service Managers, each of whom is responsible for a team of mobile technicians who install, service and trouble-shoot equipment.

The Regional Service Managers are:

Mr Steward Ferguson, based in Glasgow	Scotland
Mrs Jean Fosdyke, based in York	North-East
Mr Andrew Davidson, based in Manchester	North-West

Ms Gillian Patel, based in Coventry	Midlands
Mr Barry Masters, based in Bristol	South-West
Mr Lawrence Winston, based in London	London
Mrs Kirstie Worley, based in Guildford	South-East

Customarily the monthly meetings take place in the company's Conference Suite on the third floor (Room 320), commencing at 11.00 am and finishing at 3.00 pm. Lunch is normally served in the company's staff restaurant on the fourth floor (1.00 pm–1.45 pm).

The main items of business at the forthcoming meeting are:

Regional Reports: Technical Problems With The NSS Mark III Burglar Alarm System.

The new conditions proposed for overtime working of company technicians.

Regional Quality Assurance Reports on ratio of customer complaints to installations.

Discussion on what vehicle to specify as national fleet service van (current leasing contract is up for renewal).

Tasks

1 Produce a memorandum from Peter Richards to his Regional Service managers to call the meeting.
2 Draft a suitable agenda.
3 Produce a memorandum to the company's Communications Manager, Jackie Rivers to book the suite and to specify the AVA equipment you anticipate will be needed.
4 Make a suitable entry in Mr Richards' diary.
5 Draw up a checklist of the items which will be available to each participant at his/her table setting.

Work experience attachment assignments

1 By arrangement, spend one or two days in your organisation's mail room. Seek to try out as much equipment as possible and make your notes on how and why it is used. Find out what sources of reference and informatiion are used in the mail room (e.g. *Post Office Guide*) and make a list for future reference. Also, find out what procedures govern the handling of money coming in through the mail.

Report back to your group on your experiences and discoveries.

2 Make arrangements to interview clerical assistants and secretaries so as to create a checklist of the range of filing systems and practices the organisation employs. Make sure you understand the principles of each, and set down your findings in clear notes, so as to be able to share your findings with your group.

3 With permission, find out how the organisation uses:

scanners, database software, WP software, integrated package software, hard-disk directories etc, to set up and use computerised filing systems for information.

With suitable examples, brief your group on what you discovered.

4 Find out whether your organisation uses any microform media (roll-film, microfiche, computer input/output microform etc) to store data and retrieve it. If so, ask for a

demonstration, and make notes of what you find out. If possible, obtain a microform record to show your group.

5 Ask to see how the organisation handles its petty cash and the way in which petty cash payments and receipts are recorded in the main account ledgers.

6 Ask for a demonstration of the spellchecker feature on the WP software used by the organisation and how it aids proof-reading of documents prior to printing.

7 Conduct a series of interviews with selected staff so as to ascertain how the organisation arranges foreign travel for its staff. In the form of a numbered sequence of points, make notes of how the arrangements are carried out. Share your findings with your group.

8 Make arrangements to talk to the manager of the Overseas Transactions Department of a local clearing bank, so as to find out what services the bank offers its customers travelling abroad. Make notes of your findings and report back to your group.

9 Arrange to interview two or three senior secretaries/PAs so as to find out how they organise meetings for their managers. Make notes of your findings in the form of a set of guidelines for staff having to arrange meetings for managers.

Part *3*

Information technology applications

OVERVIEW

Today, information technology applications are interwoven in almost all the activities which organisations undertake in the course of a working day – accounts, office administration, sales, production and so on. And so this book has referred to various applications in each Part, as appropriate.

Nevertheless, a part which concentrates specifically on the ways in which databases, spreadsheets, photocopiers, printers and facsimile transceivers work, and which also provides an overview of current IT trends in office work will help you to become familiar and confident with those IT applications which are commonly employed in business administration.

NVQ references

This Part covers the following BTEC First Diploma in Business And Finance and ABC/NWPSS competences:

BTEC First Diploma:

Business Support Systems 1:

Competences: 7, 8 and 9 Producing alphanumeric information in typewritten form, identifying and correcting errors, updating records in a computerised database; 15 producing copies from original documents using reprographic equipment

Business Support Systems 2: .

Competences: 7, 8 and 9 Processing records and information in spreadsheets; accessing and printing hard copy reports, summaries and documents

ABC/NWPSS

Level 2:
Unit 7	Reprographics
Unit 13	Information processing: databases, spreadsheets, hard copies
Unit 16	Text processing a variety of business documents

Level 3:
Unit 2	Researching and retrieving information
Unit 5	Preparing and producing documents presenting graphic and tabular information

---

WHAT HAS I T ACHIEVED SO FAR, AND WHERE IS I T GOING?

So far . . .

In 1981 the government introduced the theme of 'Information Technology Year' to raise people's consciousness about the revolution led by computers in all walks of life, and particularly in the world of business. At that time, PCs were the exception rather than the rule in offices and word processing units 'stood alone', working on primitive and restricted memory systems. Fax was in its infancy, ink duplicators were as common as photocopiers and local area networks hadn't been developed.

Indeed, the first commercially available silicon chip had been marketed by the American firm Intel only ten years previously.

Today, just over a decade later, it is amazing to review the extent and pace of innovation achieved in IT business applications.

The major developments and systems include:

▶ intercommunication via desktop terminals over local and wide area networks (LANs and WANs) using electronic mail and file exchanges etc;

▶ open systems integration (OSI) by which people using different makes of equipment and operating systems are able to 'talk' to each other;

▶ global messaging in seconds thanks to satellite telecommunications and fax/WAN Email;

▶ true-to-life, high resolution colour on VDU screens, colour printers, copiers and plotters;

▶ sophisticated in-house printing and graphics using desktop publishing systems;

▶ software applications based on Graphical User Interchange (GUI) where icons or pictures are used in conjunction with a computer mouse as a highly effective means of issuing commands to activate software applications – like opening a file, sending an Email note, exporting a created file from one package to another and so on;

▶ computerised telecommunications systems which enable IT hardware equipment (phones, fax, PCs, notebook computers, printers etc) to exchange messages in seconds across continents.

Where IT is going . . .

It is hard to predict what the IT 'whizz-kids' of California and Japan will introduce next, but these are likely candidates on the list of IT innovations waiting in the pipeline:

▶ First and foremost (like the alchemist's stone which would turn lead into gold) voice input of data into computer systems; now in its infancy, but soon to, send keyboards into science museums!

▶ Video-phones: already developed and being trialled and test-marketed; users will employ communication modems for voice messaging while seeing their contact on their VDU screen, which will also embody TV circuitry.

▶ Truly mobile videophones working on the same principle and hooking into transmission networks for world-wide telecommunication.

▶ Voice-operated software systems: *'Display the spreadsheet with next year's sales target please. Now print the column totals as a three-dimensional bar-chart with this heading . . .'*

▶ Electronic, computerised 'books' created by optical disk technology, which combine video film, textual, audio and graphic information and which may be browsed through or specifically referred to by using computerised search and sort commands; these interactive disks are already being marketed for educational and training uses.

THE ARRIVAL OF THE LOCAL AREA NETWORK (LAN)

By the early 1980s computer and telecommunications technology had overcome the problems of developing a circuit or network and allied computer components which were capable of transmitting data or electronic messages from terminal to terminal connected together in a kind of ring or circuit. To look at, the ring of the LAN appears very much like the coaxial cable which is familiar in every living room. The LAN ring, on to which each terminal – whether PC workstation, printer or scanner – is hooked, is continuously sending a 'token' around the ring on to which electronic messages may be attached and routed to their chosen destination, which, if the message is in Email, would be another terminal, or if text for printing, would be the network printer. Thus one type of LAN is that of a 'token ring', or means of loading electronic messages on to a sort of continuous conveyor-belt for off-loading wherever instructed. (Actually, each workstation looks at each message with extreme rapidity and if it is not for that terminal, passes it on to the next – much faster than an operator can be aware of – until the rightful destination is reached.) Note: some LANs operate by means of 'bus' or 'star' interconnections.

Major attractions of a LAN

The attractions of a LAN for larger offices – say spread over many floors of a multistorey building – are as follows:

▶ ease of intercommunication between users,

Fig. 3.1   Interconnection of a LAN

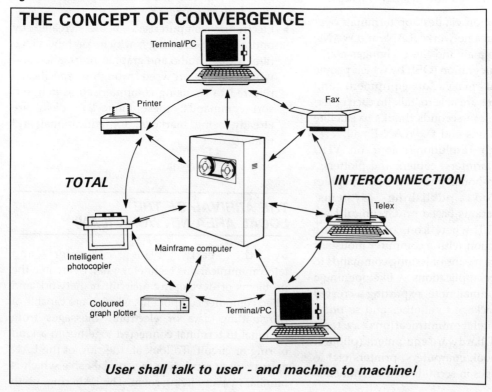

THE CONCEPT OF CONVERGENCE

Terminal/PC

Printer

Fax

TOTAL

INTERCONNECTION

Telex

Intelligent
photocopier

Mainframe computer

Coloured
graph plotter

Terminal/PC

User shall talk to user – and machine to machine!

Fig. 3.2   LAN 'Tapestry' – the home screen

File for creating
and sending
outgoing Email
messages

The Home Screen

Gateway access to
telecommunications
facilities e.g. telex

File containing
incoming
Email
messages

29 November   •HOME SCREEN•   Friday 7:56pm

In Tray   Out Tray   Communications   Telephone

Pathway to all software
applications packages
available for use on
the network

File Manager   Shared Cabinets   Network Printers   Applications

1 Help 2 Lock Up 3 Logout 4 Customise 6 Server Manager

'Personal'
files handling
facility

Storage and access to
files shared with
other LAN users*

Provides access
to network's
printer(s)

*as specified by
pre-agreement

The tapestry user accesses the home screen directly after logging on.
The network's facilities all begin here.

▶ speed of message/data transmission and feedback confirmation of receipt,

▶ very high standards of user security – even during the shared access of software packages,

▶ availability of secure personal filing 'cabinets' within hard disk storage system,

▶ organisational savings – only *one* printer or scanner needed for extended cluster user groups on network,

▶ instant access to a worldwide network of telecommunications services and to other LANs via modem interfaces – hence links to wide area networks (WANs),

▶ access to international computer databases via gateways in, for example, Prestel's viewdata service,

▶ access to up-to-the-minute and real-time computerised data and records stored on the organisation's central mainframe computer,

▶ capability of each PC terminal to act as a stand-alone desktop computer using floppies or built-in hard disk drive,

▶ user-friendliness: icon menus and window overlays enable the user to consult several application packages at a time on the VDU and to transfer work from one package/file to another.

As a result of increased international cooperation, standards for LAN designs have been agreed by major authorities to ensure problem-free transmission across the world.

WORD PROCESSING APPLICATIONS

The technique of computerised word or text processing was the earliest to emerge from the IT revolution of the 1970s. Early word processing machines were 'stand alone' with limited memories and capacities. Today's WP packages, like Word Perfect, Wordstar, Word for Windows etc are extremely powerful, providing a number of support features in addition to their ability to process text:

▶ **Spellchecker:** a means of checking the spelling of every word keyed into a file.

▶ **Thesaurus:** a reference section to offer alternative words and phrases so as to aid style and variety of expression.

▶ **Import/Export:** the ability to accept and position files created on other software e.g. a spreadsheet table or graphics diagram; and likewise to copy WP files to other software applications.

▶ **Mailmerge:** a feature which integrates names and addresses and personalised sentences/ paragraphs into standardised letters, sales brochures etc.

▶ **Database:** usually a simple form of database used for storing the names, addresses and key information about the user's network of contacts, customers and associates and so on.

▶ **View:** the opportunity to see how several pages of text appear in miniature on the VDU screen prior to printing – a kind of DTP layout design feature.

▶ **Communication features:** many WP applications today support the sending of text as Email, as faxes or as telexes, thus avoiding the need for the WP operator to key in text more than once.

▶ **Outline idea organisers:** a support feature to enable the user to create skeletal structures and headings for a first draft of a report or sales brochure, and so on.

▶ **Windows/graphics user interface (GUI):** all the leading WP software houses are now providing editions of their packages which work with Windows, manufactured by Microsoft – a kind of overlay or 'shell' which enables the PC's disk operating system to be driven by icons – pictures of command functions such as: create a file, save a file, print etc represented by icons of filing cabinets or printers and so on. When touched by a mouse-driven cursor, the icon activates the DOS command in just the same way as keyboard commands.

▶ **File organiser:** this feature enables the user to design a filing system for created files according to whatever particular classification is needed.

New features and add-ons are continually being marketed as parts of WP packages nowadays and, as the above checklist illustrates, current word processing packages are very powerful communication tools.

How a word processing package works

Many volumes have been written upon this subject, but undoubtedly the best way to discover how a WP package works is by hands-on experience and trial and error! Nevertheless, this overview will provide you with the main principles and features to proceed from in your own WP explorations.

From electronic page to printed letter

Essentially, word processing is a computerised system for:

a creating a text-based document on the VDU screen;

then

b editing and amending it on screen until satisfied with its accuracy and appearance;

and then

c by a series of print commands, transferring the electronically displayed screen version into a printed-out counterpart on paper, all by courtesy of an obedient printer linked to the PC or LAN terminal.

Creating a file

Files for word processing are created by using the customary file creation procedure employing up to eight letters followed by a dot and a further three letters (or numbers):

FORMLET.123

Current file creation operations employ drop-down window menus or icon command sequences instead of keystroked commands.

The diagram in Fig. 3.3 illustrates the file creation operation of Wordstar 6's word processing package.

Customising the package and formatting the page

Before files are created or text entered, the user customises the package according to personal preferences. For instance, colour VGA screens may be given appealing or restful colourings depending upon the choice of colour for background screen, drop-down menus, help lines and so on. Again, the WP software needs to be informed about the type of printer which will be used – dot-matrix, ink-jet or laser, and what make, Canon Bubblejet, Hewlett-Packard etc.

In the same way, preset rules for page size, resident font (which typeface will be used as first choice), size of print (point size), right and left page justification, default page numbering (unless switched off) and so on, may be installed into the software loaded on to the PC's hard or floppy disk.

During the process of creating a document layout, features may be accessed by pulling down the menu of available alternatives, which will include:

▶ page length;
▶ text width via right and left margin settings;
▶ head and foot margins (white space at top and bottom of paper sheet);
▶ tab settings (for indenting and tabular work);
▶ character line length (the number of letters which can be typed continuously across the page on one line);
  etc.

Producing a word processed document

Once the file has been created and given its unique name, the WP package displays a kind of electronic blank page on the VDU which is topped and tailed by:

1 confirmation of the drive in use e.g. C in the case of a hard disk PC;
2 the given name of the file e.g. FORMLET.123;
3 confirmation of the page being displayed e.g. 1, 2 or 3 etc;
4 the same confirmation of the line at which the cursor is currently located e.g. 6, 12 etc;
5 and as well, the column across the page (usually between 01 and 80, depending on the preset page width).

Most packages also display the operations titles, such as:

File Edit Go To Window Layout Style Other

which may be accessed either by mouse or keystroke command in order to summon up help, save a file, move a block of text and so on.

Between these two sets of helpful information is the blank page on to which the document will be keyed from the qwerty keyboard.

Entering the text

Once the page layout has been selected and the file created, the user is ready to key in the desired text.

Fig. 3.3 Creating a new document file with Wordstar 6.0 (Reproduced by kind permission of Wordstar International Incorporated)

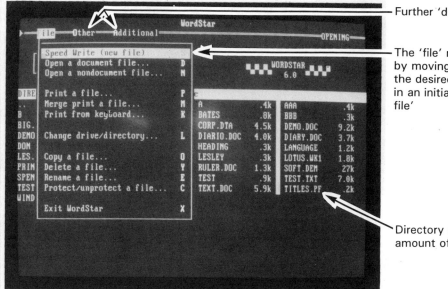

— Further 'drop-down' menus

— The 'file' menu options accessed by moving the coloured 'bar' to the desired command or by keying in an initial, e.g. 'P' for 'print a file'

— Directory of created files showing amount of memory used

The cursor

The flashing cursor always indicates where the next letter or number will be entered. As it moves about the page, so the numbers at the head of the screen change to indicate the precise location of the cursor in terms of line and character.

The process of entering the text works in just the same way as the familiar qwerty typewriter – as each key is depressed, so the letters appear on the screen, separated by spaces entered by the space bar.

The electronic rubber

What is so appealing about WP technology, however, is its ability to wipe out or erase whatever is keyed-in incorrectly, or whatever form of words seems awkward or ill-chosen, simply by 'rubbing them out' with the backspace or delete keys, or by using commands which delete whole lines or paragraphs!

Moving blocks of text

Even more remarkable is the WP package's ability to move whole pages of text around a long document by means of block operations. The selected piece is bracketed by markers and then repositioned by means of another marker. In this way, the user can rearrange the sequences of paragraphs or pages at will.

Highlighting key text

Key headings, phrases and words may be emphasised in the text by:

▶ expanding the height and length of characters;
▶ emboldening;
▶ italicising;
▶ reverse printing (white letters in a black box);
▶ using contrasting fonts for key headings.

All such features involve keying in instructions around the specific text to be highlighted which act as commands to the printer when the document is being printed out.

Text support features

In addition to style and presentation features, WP packages include facilities to support the production of academic and scientific documents which may require:

▶ tables of contents;

- indexes;
- footnotes and page references in superscript (small numbers set just above the end of a word);
- scientific symbols and formulae signs;
- mathematical function signs;
- foreign language letters and accents;
- automatic page numbering;
  etc.

■ **TOP ASSISTANT TIPS ON SUCCESSFUL WORD PROCESSING**

1   Before starting work, make sure that your working file will be created on the correct drive or floppy disk. Avoid creating files among the software application files of a hard disk drive for instance, or on the wrongly inserted floppy, where they will quickly become mislaid.

2   Remember to give your file a filename which is logical and aids memory recall at a later date.

3   Get into the habit of inserting this filename unobtrusively upon the document you have created, so that someone using a hard copy printout can quickly call up the file if need be.

4   Always save your work at short and regular intervals. It is extremely frustrating and time-wasting to key in several pages of A4 text only to lose them for ever because a single key was wrongly struck!

5   When using your desktop PC/terminal, always keep the need for security at the front of your mind. Get into the habit of saving your text and locking up your screen if you need to leave your PC in the middle of a task. You never know who may be peeking while you're out of the office!

6   Don't be shy of exploring the many features of your WP application. Avoid the temptation to use only those parts of the package that get you by. Investing time in WP exploration will undoubtedly make you more efficient and creative in your work.

7   Don't forget that spell checking facilities cannot tell whether words such as principle or

principal are being used correctly. Only you can do that! So always make time to proof-read and check over your draft work.

8   Always take care with the 'good housekeeping' of your WP work. Remember to back up files in use regularly and to store your floppy disks out of sunlight and away from electromagnetic fields which may exist around other electronic equipment. Always ensure that your floppy disks are fully labelled with format dates, summaries of contents and subject classifications etc. Valuable time can be wasted in scanning through the directories of several disks searching for a much needed but elusive file! So make a habit of creating logical sub-directories if storing files on a hard disk, or sets of floppies labelled according to area of use or work done for individual staff etc.

9   Develop a personal routine at regular intervals for ensuring that your word processing equipment is functioning correctly. Run a print test for example on your printer, and call up files from your sub-directories or floppies to check that all is well. Report any faults immediately to your supervisor. Always keep HASAW in mind, and check that plugs are still safely wired and that cables are not dangerously trailing.

10 Lastly, take a pride in your WP work. Once a document has left your desk, it will inevitably be vetted by colleagues or customers for its quality and appearance.

Fig. 3.4 How Microsoft's word processing package 'Word for Windows' works (using GUI) (Reproduced by kind permission of Microsoft Ltd)

Styles can save you time and help ensure consistency throughout a document - or throughout a company. Simply save the paragraph formats you've created, then apply them instantly anywhere in your document.

Icons make character and paragraph formatting faster and easier. Use the Ribbon to perform basic formatting, like boldface or italics, at the click of a mouse.

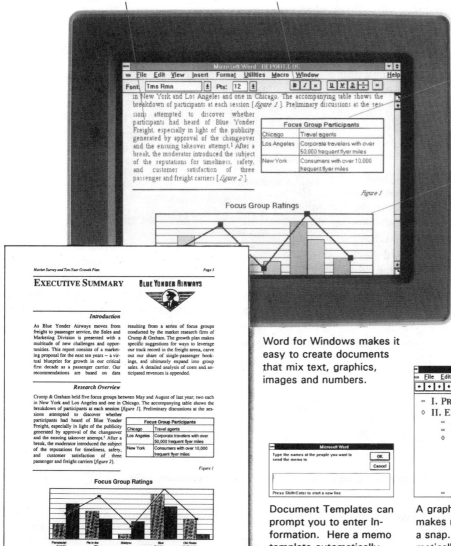

You can anchor an imported chart, table, or graphic image any-where on your page, then automatically wrap text around it.

DDE links allow you to update information from other programs automatically.

Word for Windows makes it easy to create documents that mix text, graphics, images and numbers.

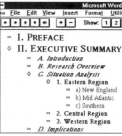

Document Templates can prompt you to enter In-formation. Here a memo template automatically asks who to send the document to.

A graphical outline processor makes reorganising any document a snap. An outline is auto-matically created when you use styles to format headings.

WYSIWYG lets you see - and edit - all character and paragraph formats on screen; you'll know exactly how your document will look in print.

WORKING WITH SPREADSHEETS

Just as WP software proved a boon to secretaries and copy-typists in the 1970s, so spreadsheets became a godsend to accountants, bookkeepers and in fact anyone who needed to manipulate numbers. Early spreadsheets (like WP packages) were 'stand alone', but today they are much more easily integrated into other software applications through the import and export of files, either within a single PC, or around linked LAN/WAN systems.

How a spreadsheet works

The term 'spreadsheet' arose because of the central feature of this software which enables its user to create numerical files in different areas of what is in effect a large electronic work sheet. The computer's VDU screen can only display small 'windows' of this large sheet by scrolling up, down or sideways. Fig. 3.5 illustrates what the starting point or home screen of a spreadsheet looks like.

As the diagram at Fig. 3.6 illustrates, a spreadsheet is divided into thousands of cells – A1, B3, C5 etc. Into each of these cells number values may be inserted as shown in Fig. 3.6.

Figure 3.6 also illustrates a simple spreadsheet task, which is to list and add the sales totals by region in the first quarter of the year and to compute both regional totals and an all company total. This is made possible by using the spreadsheet's formula for adding and totalling as follows:

$$
\begin{array}{llll}
\text{B3} & \text{C3} & \text{D3} & \text{E3} \\
+\ \text{B4} & +\text{C4} & +\text{D4} & +\text{E4} \\
+\ \text{B5} & +\text{C5} & +\text{D5} & +\text{E5} \\
=\ \text{B6}+ & =\text{C6}+ & =\text{D6}+ & =\text{E6}=\text{F6}
\end{array}
$$

In this task, the spreadsheet is given a command like:

$$*@SUM(\ B3.B5)\ ENTER$$

to enter the combined total into the cell B6.

In its simplest operation, a spreadsheet task such as the one above is achieved by instructing the spreadsheet to add together three sets of cells – B3, 4 and 5, C3, 4 and 5 and D3, 4 and 5 and to display the resulting respective totals in cells B6, C6 and D6.

Further, commands are keyed in to add together the totals of B6, C6, D6 and E6 and display the result in F6. At this point, one might be forgiven for thinking that a spreadsheet is a very expensive form of pocket calculator! But this would be wrong and hasty, because the above table illustrates what a spreadsheet can do at the very threshold of its capabilities.

Fig. 3.5 Diagram of the home screen of a spreadsheet

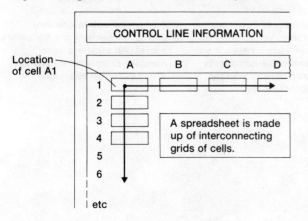

Fig. 3.6 Spreadsheet cells

	A	B	C	D	E	F

CONTROL LINE INFORMATION					
A	B	C	D	E	F
1	Sales	by	region:	1st	Quarter
2	North	South	East	West	
3 Jan	17593	15282	14396	11564	
4 Feb	16348	16976	16202	12692	
5 Mar	19467	17654	15143	14329	
6 Totals	53408	49912	45741	38585	187646
7					
8					

Fig. 3.7 *Key features of each spreadsheet cell*

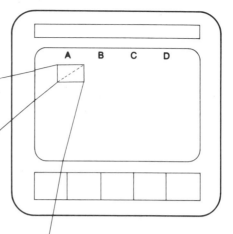

THE CELL: THE KEY TO SPREADSHEETING

Key features of each spreadsheet cell

1 Each cell provides a unique address for the data it contains − e.g. B14, AA21 etc. This 'one-off' address is essential for moving information around the large expanse of the spreadsheet's grid. Thus each cell provides a single grid reference or 'postal address' on what amounts to a very large 'map'.

2 A cell can be formatted to span several default columns in order to accommodate long names or titles.

3 Each cell may have written into it: either text, or a number, or a spreadsheet formula − e.g. +B4*C4 may be written into cell D4 to provide a multiplied total. The D4 cell will display the total calculated from the formula concealed in the spreadsheet's memory.

4 Cells and the data they contain may be copied to other cell addresses across columns and down rows anywhere on the spreadsheet.

5 Blocks of cells may also be copied or moved around the spreadsheet.

6 Any cell may be allocated a prepared formula or a macro function (which could be a complicated calculation) previously stored on the spreadsheet and called up with a single keystroke. Such macro (large/extended) commands save time when installing often-used formulas.

7 Each cell may be protected so that the key data or formula it contains cannot be inadvertently erased.

8 The data contained in sets of cells may be transformed into a graphic display such as a pie-chart, line graph and so on, by using associated commands built into the software package.

9 Files made up of the interlinked data of the created cells may be exported to other applications packages (or sections of an integrated package) such as word processing or graphic presentation by means of the command system built into the software.

10 Any part of the spreadsheet may be printed out at will.

Spreadsheets and their ability to interconnect tasks

Not only can a spreadsheet display columns in which the arithmetic functions of adding, subtracting, multiplying, dividing and percentaging may be undertaken, it can also recalculate in the wink of an eye fresh subtotals and final totals if a single entry (or several) is changed in a specific cell. For instance, if in the above table the operator had made a mistake and the correct figure for C4 was 15,432 and not 16,976, then, upon entering the correct figure, the total in C6 would be amended instantly to 48,368, and the total in F6 to 186,102.

Thus the ability of a spreadsheet to maintain a network of links or relationships between cells makes it far more powerful than the modest pocket calculator. It saves precious time for, say, the retailer who needs to increase the VAT calculation on goods he sells from 15% to 17.5%, or for the payroll supervisor in an organisation to implement salary increases for certain staff and obtain the resultant increase cost of the total payroll.

Again, cost accountants in manufacturing firms can quickly work out the effect on profits of an increase (or decrease) of the cost of buying in certain parts used in making a product. Not only can a spreadsheet recalculate formulas for related cells displayed on a single screen, it can also update the calculations carried out for quite a different task (entered on another part of the spreadsheet) which has imported or employed data from a separately created file. For example, if a marketing manager is engaged in working out effective sales prices for a range of goods on one area of a shared

Fig. 3.8 Example of the screen layout of a spreadsheet

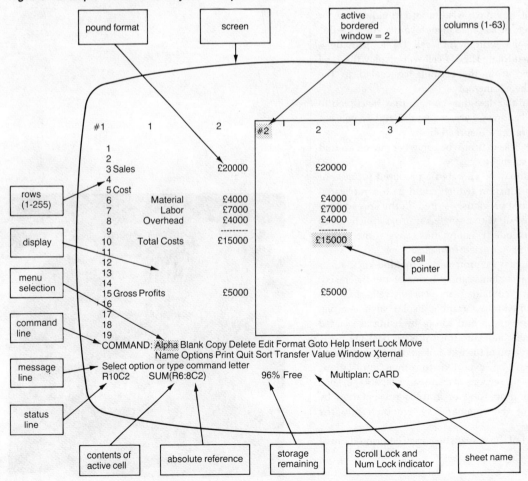

spreadsheet, his working totals and figures may be automatically revised and updated as a result of the work of the production-line cost accountants, who update the costs of manufacture for certain products on their part of the shared spreadsheet. In this way, executives working on complex business operations benefit by having access to the latest and most accurate calculations and data.

Fig. 3.9   Example of Microsoft's spreadsheet 'Excel for Windows' which uses graphical user interface (GUI) icons and mouse to speed creation and display operation (Reproduced by kind permission of Microsoft Ltd)

One-step styles. Click to apply different formats to your worksheets. Microsoft Excel automatically chooses appropriate styles for different level subheadings.

One-step formulas. Double-click on the auto-sum button to add ranges of numbers automatically, either horizontally or vertically. Microsoft Excel intelligently chooses the correct range for summation.

One-step formatting. Click the bold and italic buttons to apply these formats to cells you've selected. Use the alignment buttons to justify your data right, centre or left.

One-step drawing tools. Click on the rectangle, oval, arc or line button to draw attention to important numbers.

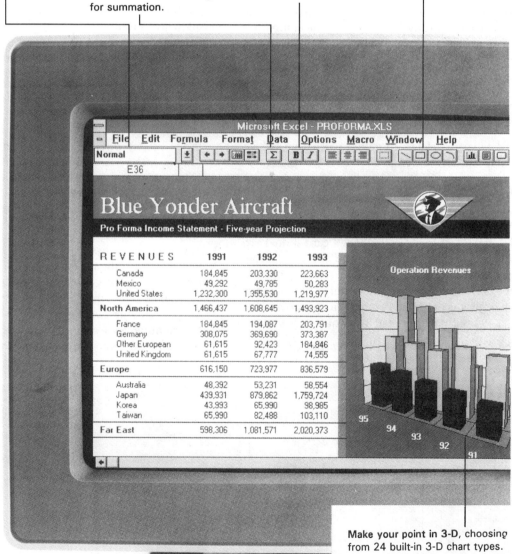

Make your point in 3-D, choosing from 24 built-in 3-D chart types. Just click the chart button on the Toolbar to create charts automatically, then customise the chart format.

HOW A DATABASE PACKAGE WORKS

The term database simply stands for an assembled collection of information or data, parts of which may be sorted or classified into desired lists and sequences. For example, an employment agency may have at any one time 200–300 temps on its books available for either top-flight PA, junior secretarial, WP operations or clerical assistant work. By entering key particulars about each one – name, address, phone number, skills, qualifications, foreign language proficiency, competence in which WP software package, etc, the agency manager can – extremely quickly – interrogate the company's database of registered personnel so as to extract and match a short-list to an employer's requested job needs or particular specification.

Database structure

A database package contains a program which enables its user to design a kind of electronic card-index system which may be illustrated as follows:

A database consists of three major components:

The file: which represents the collection of records (like the set of cards in the boxed card index). To be of any use in the orderly world of the database, a file must comprise records of the same design and type, say, all head office personnel, all items in the export product range, all examination records of the 1992–93 full-time enrolled students.

The record: which sets out the recorded data about one of the persons or items which go to make up the file. In the case of the above employment agency's temps, the record may contain all the recorded information on Angela Gibbons, bilingual secretary.

The field: at the heart of the way a database works are its fields. Each file is the sum of a number of records where each and every one has been designed upon an identical template. This electronic master form is itself made up of a series of fields. Again, using the temps file example, Angela Gibbon's record – and everyone else's – will have been compiled by filling in preconstructed blank boxes which are the record's fields. For instance, Angela's record will comprise in part her full name, correct postal address, telephone number, nationality, date of birth and sex. In addition, it will include field boxes to list skills, equipment experience and so on.

The great value of the database lies in its ability to locate, in a twinkling, information which lies waiting in each record's filled-out fields. Thus the employment agency is able to scan its temps file and extract from its 346 records the particulars, say, of each of five registered temps whose fields reveal that:

1 they are postgraduates;
2 they are currently available;
3 they speak fluent German and Spanish;
4 they can handle competently the WP package the prospective employer uses;
5 their remuneration requirements are in line with what the employer will pay, and so on.

Fig. 3.10 Components of a database

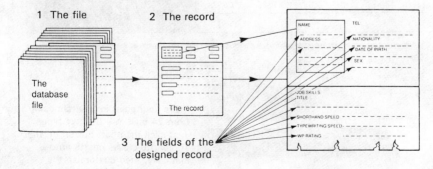

In this way, a properly compiled database can save hours of searching for specific sets of data on what could be thousands of records. But, it is important to note that, while individualised information can be entered on each record, only the information which has been entered into the predesigned fields in a standardised way can be searched, sorted and displayed as indicated above. Thus it is crucial in designing an effective database for the user to have tested it out in pilot form first, so as to ensure that the fields as set up will be able to deliver the desired data across the entry range of predetermined sorts and searches. Otherwise a painful and time-consuming reorganisation of assembled data is unavoidable.

Some major applications of databases

▶ personnel training/pay/promotion/disciplinary etc records
▶ account customer particulars
▶ staff specialisms/qualifications
▶ fleet servicing records
▶ product specifications and standards
▶ insurance and pension records
▶ mailing lists
▶ price lists
▶ product design records
▶ branch/property maintenance data
▶ patient records
▶ sales call records
▶ training materials
▶ scientific research abstracts, etc

OFFICE REPROGRAPHICS

Printers

Electronic printers

The advent of the widely distributed desktop PC in the late 1970s meant that users either needed access to an adjacent personal printer or the opportunity to share a faster, more sophisticated and more powerful one. And to complicate matters, while office DP managers were seeking to provide a prompt and easily accessible service to managers,

secretaries, clerks and WP operators, printer manufacturers were busy developing four quite different major types of electronic printer, known as thermal, dot matrix, ink-jet and laser. Each has its advantages for use in many different types of office application and the thoughtful assistant will ensure she knows which type of printer offers the best cost-effective approach for various tasks.

The dot matrix printers

This printer's name stems from the way in which it imprints characters on to paper. Early dot matrix printers possessed a print head made up of nine pins which struck an inked ribbon in various patterns so as to imprint, say, the letter A, the number 2, or the percentage sign %. A close

Fig. 3.11 Photocopying

examination of 9-pin dot matrix printing reveals the rather ragged outline made in this way:

Fig. 3.12 An example of dot matrix printing

THE DOT MATRIX PRINTER CREATES
CHARACTERS FROM DOTS

The use of nine pins meant that each character was in effect nine dots high and text was printed by the printer running bidirectionally – left to right then right to left for consecutive lines of text. The 9-pin dot matrix printer could print at roughly 100–200 characters per second (cps) in what is called now draft quality typescript – that is to say with a print quality only suited for internal consumption and not up to letter quality. Dot matrix printers at the upper end of the market operated at both *draft quality* (DQ) and *near letter quality* (NLQ). The NLQ speed is appreciably slower because the print-head passes twice over each character in a slight skew to fill out its ragged edges. An additional feature of the dot matrix printer is its ability to print graphs, charts and other computer-originated diagrams. The computer directs the printing operation (as it does in the case of all electronic 'on line' printers, i.e. printers which accept their instructions from the computerised software program).

In 1985 some 85% of the electronic desktop printer market in Europe was dot matrix; however, the arrival of ink-jet and laser printers at more affordable prices caused dot matrix printer manufacturers to look to their laurels as users demanded a higher quality of print appearance – up to letter quality standards. As a result, a 24-pin dot matrix printer was developed by leading

Fig. 3.13 An Epson printer (Reproduced by kind permission of Epson (UK) Ltd)

manufacturers. This offered a much enhanced print appearance of letter quality and offered speeds of some 400 cps in draft mode and 50–60 cps in letter quality mode. Current upper end of the market dot matrix printers embody several different types of fount (or font; a design of typeface) and can also accept single, cut-sheet paper inserts without tractor-fed continuous stationery having to be removed. Also, some modern dot matrix printers can accept a colour ribbon add-on and so print documents in different colours – i.e. vary the colour in which consecutive lines of text are printed. Thus a use of different typefaces and colour at low cost makes it possible to produce appealing sales leaflets and house magazines, etc.

While the low purchase and running costs of dot matrix printers makes them attractive, the noise of their impact printing is much less so and a market for accoustic covers to limit noise soon arose, and users need to balance low-cost with impact printer noise levels.

Ink-jet printers

These printers operate within a quite different technology. Ink is drawn up from a cartridge into a series of tubes which focus on to a central printing point. An electrical pulse ejects the ink on to the awaiting paper page which has been electrostatically treated so that the ink sticks to those parts which carry the text. The ink dries almost immediately.

While less ragged than draft quality dot matrix printed text, ink-jet text does not always convey the same high quality of appearance of either daisywheel or laser printed text. However, the quality of an ink-jet printer depends on its price and the one with 32 jet nozzles at the more expensive end of the market acts like the 24-pin dot matrix counterparts and upgrades the text to NLQ at a typical speed of 100 cps.

Like the dot matrix printer, the ink-jet can take continuous fan-fold paper and cut-sheet paper and generally possesses both tractor and sheet feed options. It will also accept roll paper.

Both types of printer are able to print text in the following ways:

emboldened, underscored, proportionally spaced, expanded, double height, double width and italics

all effected through keyed-in computer commands.

Ink-jet printers are cheap to acquire at their lower market range and can accept normal office paper. They operate at a much quieter level than impact printers. Typical speeds are: draft quality using 10 pitch – 200 cps, and near letter quality – 75 cps.

Ink jet printers are currently finding a growing market as portable printers linked to notebook computers, battery powered and about 50 cps at NLQ.

Laser printers

The laser printer is generally regarded as the very best of the electronic printers. Its technology uses a concentrated laser beam of light to transmit the computer's printing instructions (the text or image for printing) on to a cylindrical drum as a line of text or a line of a photograph or image in the making. The drum or roller moves over the sheet of paper on to which the text/image is to be printed. Those parts of the drum which have not been exposed to the laser beam's light accept the toner (black carbon dust) from a loaded cartridge and become the black printed letters or shades of black and grey in a photograph or drawing. The print resolution of laser printers is very high – 300 dots per inch, or 90,000 dots per square inch! As a result, text and images look crisp and sharp and of very good letter quality.

Also, the laser printer's print speeds are high compared to those of their counterparts. Some specialist (professional printing) laser printers can print at a rate of 200 A4 pages per minute. Typical office desktop laser printers operate at about 8–10 pages per minute, or about one A4 page every 6–8 seconds! However, this speed drops appreciably if the page for printing is complicated and includes several images or graphics.

In addition to high quality appearance, laser printers are extremely versatile – some have as many as 40 different print founts inbuilt with the facility to access others from slot-in electronic cards. Such printers provide a virtual printing house in the office!

Like its counterparts, the laser printer not only offers a very wide choice of founts, it also prints in the variations indicated above – italics, emboldened, proportional spacing, subscript and superscript, etc, and, because of its high resolution facility, can print type from very tiny sizes (printers would refer to 'four point' type) to very large sizes – say, 'seventy-two points' in printers' jargon. The term point is a measurement of print height and width.

The laser printer tends to use A4 cut sheets stacked in a feeder and some models accept multisize stacking trays and can switch from A4 to envelopes or to labels directly. It also tends to be used by larger firms to produce their own forms and stationery cheaply, and its memory can retain the design of an extensive number of forms and schedules.

Line printers

It is worth noting that a high volume printer called a line printer is used in large organisations to produce computer DP printout in collated and bound report form.

Printers and paper

All the above printers will accept A4 cut sheet paper if appropriate feeders are fitted to them. Depending on their width, they will also accept continuous stationery up to some 400 mm or 16 inches in width. Dot matrix and ink jet printers accept most types of office paper, but laser printers require high quality bond paper for best results.

Printers and costs

As you might expect, there is with electronic printers a direct relationship between quality output and cost. The following factors affect such printing costs:

▶ Capital cost of leasing cost of the printer.
▶ Cost of maintenance contract (can be significant).
▶ Renewal costs of: toner cassettes, cartridges and laser drums or black/colour ribbons or print wheels.
▶ Cost of electricity to drive the printer.
▶ Cost of paper used and amount used per month.

Note: some printer and photocopier suppliers levy monthly charges based on the number of pages/copies printed.

When costed out at an all-in price per sheet, such costs vary considerably depending on the above factors and type of printer employed, with laser printers proving most expensive to run.

Photocopiers

Choosing the right copier for the right job

At present there are some 175 different types of photocopier on the market and larger organisations will employ a family of photocopiers for different purposes and applications. These range from the small, personal desktop machines for very low volume 'one-off use' through middle or departmental copiers which may produce some 6,000–20,000 copies monthly, up to systems machines which are used in a central reprographics unit or print-room and may copy as many as 200,000 pages per month. In this situation it is important for the office assistant to be fully aware of the comparative costs of copying on a small copier as opposed to a systems machine – large print runs are made much more economically on large, purpose-built photocopiers and runs of 20–50 copies are very expensive by comparison on a single-sheet feed copier. Office managers tend to pay little heed to copying costs, and expect their work to be copied instantly – by any machine available. Efficient office support staff control and route such reckless copying demands!

Low volume desktop copiers

The low volume desktop copier works slowly, but is reliable and cheap to buy. It is designed to handle occasional copying needs such as making a copy of an incoming letter three to four times to circulate to section heads, or to copy internal memos, notices or bulletins a few at a time.

Such copiers operate at approximately 8–15 copies per minute (CPM) and will only copy on one side of the paper at a time – to copy the reverse of a sheet requires reinsertion. The low volume desktop copier generally incorporates these features:

▶ hand-feeding of single sheets (a laborious process)
▶ light–dark adjustment to compensate for good/poor originals
▶ toner level indicator – to warn when toner is becoming used up
▶ paper jam indicator
▶ simple trays to hold paper passing through the copier before and after the process.

Fig. 3.14   The Minolta EP 870 photocopier (Reproduced by kind permission of Minolta (UK) Ltd)

The mid-range or departmental copier

Such copiers are becoming increasingly popular since they occupy little space – not much more than a desktop – yet provide a very much larger range of features, while the cost of the modest single sheet copier is a few hundred pounds, the middle range copier (sometimes referred to as a departmental copier) will cost anything from £2,250–£12,500. As with all office equipment, the buyer tends to get what he pays for. The following checklist illustrates some typical features of the mid range copier:

▶ Able to copy from A6 postcard and A5 to A3 paper sizes.
▶ Automatic enlargement and reduction.
▶ Automatic document feed – for copying sets of different originals.
▶ Bypass feed to do a quick single-sheet copy in the middle of a long job.
▶ Automatic exposure control – to adapt to originals of varying quality.
▶ At least a 10-copy stacking bin which automatically collates copies into sets of reports, minutes, etc.
▶ User control system – either a security lock or insertable type of credit card which meters copies made.
▶ At least two automatic paper feed trays (A4 and A3) Note: some models automatically activate the appropriate paper 'cassette' tray according to the size of original.

- Capacity to hold at least 1 ream (500 sheets of copy paper) – many will hold 2,000 sheets or more.
- Automatic enlargement and reduction features – both by predetermined ratios (according to paper sizes A5, A4, A3, etc) or by percentage – from, say 50% to 150% of original by single percentage steps – sometimes referred to as 'zoom magnification'.
- Emergency override switch to halt the photocopying process in the event of a mistake or machine fault.

Such is the pressure of competition to sell photocopiers – a market leader sold over half a million worldwide last year – that even the above range of features in the middle tier of copiers is being increased by such sophisticated facilities like:

- **Editing board and stylus** – rather like a computer's VDU and light-pen, this additional equipment enables the user to edit existing originals on a screen electronically and to blank out unwanted portions (image overlay), to join together parts of different originals without tell-tale lines showing and to adjust margins for right- or left-hand sheets in a bound document.
- **Automatic double-sided copying** (sometimes called duplexing) – a feature which prints simultaneously on both sides of the paper from two originals placed side-by-side (tandem copying).
- **Colour printing** – the incorporation of red, blue, sepia, etc, colours one to a single sheet (not to be confused with full-colour copiers which can reproduce colour photographs) at the touch of a button.
- **Copying of three-dimensional objects,** such as jewellery for insurance purposes and bound books without showing dark areas where light has been let in.
- **Automatic electrical power saving mode** operated when the machine is not in active use (to save electricity and costs).

Given the present pace of copier design development, such features and facilities are being extended and improved virtually every month as a new or upgraded model is introduced. Therefore the effective office assistant will take steps to become fully proficient on the equipment the organisation employs and keep an eye on incoming sales leaflets and office equipment magazines to stay up-to-date and *au fait*. Local exhibitions of office equipment mounted in hotels, etc, are very useful in this respect.

The systems photocopier

The systems photocopier or print-room model will copy at speeds of 40–200 cpm and handle an output of millions of sheets per year. Such copiers will carry out all the above applications and will also:

- accept the continuous fan-fold paper for computer data copying;
- adjust to various specialist modes for, say, converting colour photo originals to black and white with good clarity;
- collate, staple/bind extensively paged documents and insert coloured chapter pages and front/back covers;
- conduct complex enlargement, reduction and automatic document reversal operations;
- handle a wide range of paper sizes – A5 to poster size from automatic feeder trays and effect runs up to 9,999 copies long without stopping.

Colour copiers

Recently a wide range of full-colour photocopiers have been marketed which bring exciting design and presentation within the reach of the office manager in medium-size to large organisations.

Such machines can reproduce colour photographs and paper copies of original photographs with remarkable faithfulness, and one market leader's model can provide up to 64 tones of each major colour! Such machines operate on the laser principle and are revolutionising the quality of in-house document and quick-response sales brochure standards. Such copiers work at about 5 cpm.

Photocopying costs

The factors which go to make up photocopying costs are very similar to those for electronic printers. Most office administratioin managers circulate offices with regularly updated costs per sheet according to machine used, paper size, type of copying and volume etc.

Photocopying paper varies widely in cost and the assistant with a stationery buying role should take care to select copying paper which can accept print on both sides, will not cause jams, for example, because it is too light in weight, and which is problem-free from insert to collation stage for ream after ream.

In terms of recurring photocopying costs, it is worth remembering that, while the photocopier with more automatic facilities may cost more to buy or lease, it will undoubtedly save money each month in saved personnel time – compare the time taken to hand-feed single sheets with a fully automated feeding and collating operation which may be left unattended.

Photocopiers and the future

The next phase in photocopier development is already under way with one leading Japanese manufacturer marketing a copier which is also a fax and telex transceiver and scanner! Such multifunctioning equipment is only made possible by the extensive use of reliable microprocessors and clever design.

In addition, copier manufacturers will undoubtedly want to develop further the editor board and stylus operation which resembles the kind of page creating and modifying ability fast becoming popular with users of desktop publishing equipment (*see* below).

We can certainly expect to see a rapid introduction of 'intelligent photocopiers' in offices with LAN/ WAN systems so that text may be originated at an individual's desk and networked to the office copier for automatic duplication according to copy commands which the user keys in at the end of the text and which instruct the copier accordingly, much like existing computer print commands. Equinox, for instance, is a new electronic system for combining the function of a photocopier, word processor, laser printer, fax, modem and document scanner, with a desktop publishing system, and is also IBM compatible.

DESKTOP PUBLISHING (DTP)

Desktop publishing (sometimes referred to as electronic publishing) has been one of the fastest growing IT developments of the 1980s. Its rapid uptake was the result of a number of factors and influences, principal among which was that the equipment was already in existence – PC desktop computer with hard disk, laser printer, scanner and mouse. What was the vital additional ingredient was of course the software to do the creative job.

In a nutshell, a desktop publishing system provides its user with the means of producing page-by-page and document-by-document highly attractive and well printed copy – that is a mix of:

▶ **text** in a wide variety of typefaces and sizes,
▶ **photographs, drawings, graphs and charts** all capable of being enlarged or reduced to fit a predetermined space,
▶ **lines, rules, shading, cross-hatching and frames** which either make reading easier or create visual appeal as part of the overall page design,
▶ **imported artwork from the DTP software** which can be quickly positioned on to a given page.

Previously, such printed matter had to be given to a printing house to set and print. The development of DTP, however, has had a profound effect upon the production of organisational documents and the presentation of information, as it has brought the printing house – with many of its visual and graphics devices and effects – right into the heart of office information processing.

How desktop publishing works

Perhaps the best way to view DTP is as a kind of

Fig. 3.15 The screen on this desktop publishing unit shows graphics and text combined on the Aldus Pagemaker system with mouse cursor control in the foreground

enhanced word processing and visual image combining system. Desktop publishing creates an electronic page of text on the PC's visual display screen using aspects of the mix outlined above. The text for this mix is usually originated by means of a current commercial word processing package and, in a similar way, previously devised charts and graphs, etc, may be installed into the DTP system from a graphics software package. Photographic or drawn images are installed by means of a scanner. Once all the desired ingredients have been 'loaded' into the DTP system, the process of designing each page of the document may commence.

Desktop publishing: step-by-step

1 The mock-up phase

A mock-up of the desired page or document is created which provides the DTP editor with a clear idea of such aspects as the nature and required size of illustrations – quarter page, 3 cm × single column etc, and the way in which text is to be displayed – in simple paragraphs, in columns divided by rules, with emboldened paragraph titles, or with a reversed white text in a black box, etc. The mock-up will also show the size of any required headline for eye-catching effect and will provide the required data on margin sizes etc.

In organisations where DTP is established, the mock-up phase will also include a choice of typefaces (technically known as founts) and the respective sizes of typefaces for use in different areas of the page. The sizes of different founts varies considerably – just think of the size of some newspaper headlines and the small print of some books and documents – and is measured in points (a printer's term). The illustration on page 86 provides a clear idea of the range of fount sizes between 6 and 30 points and newspaper banner headline founts are even larger.

Fig. 3.16 Desktop publishing kit

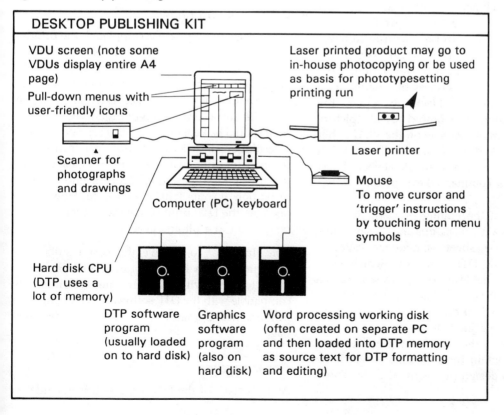

DESKTOP PUBLISHING KIT

VDU screen (note some VDUs display entire A4 page)

Pull-down menus with user-friendly icons

Scanner for photographs and drawings

Computer (PC) keyboard

Laser printed product may go to in-house photocopying or be used as basis for phototypesetting printing run

Laser printer

Mouse
To move cursor and 'trigger' instructions by touching icon menu symbols

Hard disk CPU (DTP uses a lot of memory)

DTP software program (usually loaded on to hard disk)

Graphics software program (also on hard disk)

Word processing working disk (often created on separate PC and then loaded into DTP memory as source text for DTP formatting and editing)

2 The text/graphics installing phase

The text (often called 'copy' for desktop publishing) is usually produced in organisations by departmental secretaries – as the wording for an advertisement, a handbook to set out a product's specifications, items for the organisation's house journal or as a sales brochure, etc. This copy may be produced via hard or floppy disk.

Where the text producer is familiar with the organisation's DTP system and its software is compatible with the WP package in departmental use, the WP copy may be given format/editing instructions to assist the subsequent DTP editing process, but it may fall to the DTP operator to work on the word-processed text in order to make it suitable for DTP editing (this may involve taking out underscoring or emboldening instructions if the DTP page is to be reformatted from scratch). Such a process is called 'flooding in' the text.

3 The editing phase

The text and graphics having been installed into the DTP system, the editing process may begin. In order to design each page – employing the mix of typefaces and graphics outlined above – a mouse is used as the DTP's control mechanism to move the cursor rapidly around the screen. It can pull down (bring into play or activate) various DTP menus of instructions – such as the shading of a space, the reversing of black on white, the 'cropping' or cutting to a required size of a picture or the enlargement of the page on the VDU either to see it as a whole or to see a magnified portion of it. In addition to the mouse, the PC keyboard may be used with its command keys in the editing process.

At the outset of the editing process, the DTP operator will check the mock-ups and, to save time, will select a style sheet (sometimes called a template) from the DTP's memory which most closely resembles the desired page design. Such a sheet is a kind of skeletal blank page with, for example, the rules and columns already set, and margins already specified etc.

The operator may then 'pull down' the various menus which contain the instructions which he wishes to use to design the required page. These menus include:

File for loading data on to the page and subsequently storing it – simply the setting up of a file in the normal way.

View to provide enlarged or reduced displays and to check illustrative material.

Page to add page sequencing and numbering features, to set up right-hand and left-hand page alignments and to set the ongoing page structure, etc.

Frame to insert lines, rules, boxes to a desired size.

Graphic to add illustrations on to page designs.

Type to enable the operator to select the chosen fount or typeface and its size.

Note: Various DTP software applications have similar functions grouped in similar menus, and provide an extended range of instructions which the operator can select or 'tag' in order to build up the page with the desired typeface, graphics and layout. Also, for ease of use, icon 'tool kits' are available for selection by mouse to draw lines, circles and move items around the page, etc.

4 The printing phase

When the editing phase is completed, the printing process via laser printer is begun. The laser printer with its high quality end product and ability to print in an extensive range of typefaces (founts) and type sizes (points) is what makes DTP so incredibly versatile and useful in larger organisations. Even so, it should be kept in mind that a laser printer with a resolution of at least 300 dots per inch cannot compare for print quality with professional printing by the phototypesetting process in which a resolution of some 1,100 dpsi is used. However, if need be, the DTP print command sequence can be relayed on to a phototypesetter.

Note: In order to achieve the best results, it is important that a high resolution VDU screen is used, together with a laser printer which is fully compatible with the DTP software – changing laser printers will change the format of the designed page.

Proof-reading

At each stage of the DTP process it is essential to

proof-read copy carefully. The nearer one approaches the end product, the more difficult and time-consuming it is to correct errors of spelling or layout.

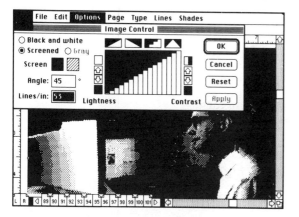

Fig. 3.17 Examples of Aldus Pagemaker screen layouts

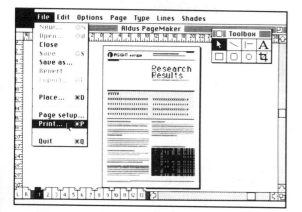

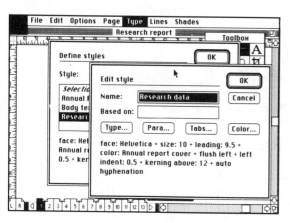

Founts and presentation

While individual secretaries (say in an advertising department or working for a senior manager) may become expert regular users of a DTP system, it is more likely that they will originate text on their own desktop PCs for installation into the DTP unit which will be operated by a specialist member of staff working full-time in the organisation's reprographics centre. Nevertheless, it is very important for everyone working in an office environment to become informed and aware of elements of page design and the visual impact of different kinds of typeface and type size.

Introductory glossary of desktop publishing terms

The advent of DTP has brought into more general use a specialised, technical set of terms and expressions from the world of printing and typesetting. Here are some of the more commonly occurring terms to start your own personal checklist:

Automatic page numbering; automatic table of contents; running headers and footers: DTP programs allow the user to give the commands for the automatic sequencing of instructions throughout a document.

Automatic text flow: allows copy to move across pages when a multipaged document is being designed.

Clip art: some DTP packages include sets of artwork/graphics – say, a hand in the 'stop' gesture of a policeman to convey graphically 'Don't . . .!' – which may be included in a design at will: clip art provides quick graphics for in-house documents, sales literature, etc.

Cropping: adjusting the size of an illustration so as to fit it into a given space.

Kerning: adjusting the space between letters to improve clarity and visual appeal.

Leading: a term for the spacing of text line by line and the spacing between titles and paragraphs.

Left and right justification: columns or paragraphs of text may be left ragged or justified as desired.

Pica and point: are both measurements of print size: a pica is 0.1660 inches and a point is a twelfth of a pica.

Fig. 3.18 Desktop publishing enables you to use a large variety of type styles and sizes (Reproduced by kind permission of Headway Computer Products)

LePrint & JLaser

from

Headway Computer Products

LePrint will enhance any text and is suitable for use with Wordstar and any WP that can produce an ASCII file.

Characters can be varied in size
from 4 point to 700 point (nearly 10 inches high).

A large range of Type Styles is available.

This is 12 point Old English... and this is Prestige.

Here is the Courier type style.

LCD gives a futuristic look to your documents.

All this is achieved by the use of dot commands within the text, which are recognised by LePrint. The capability of the system is further enhanced by Headway Computer Products JLASER board.

LePrint is the low cost alternative to a shelf full of font cartridges. It runs under MS DOS on IBM's and compatibles and utilises the power and versatility of the Laser Printer. LePrint will also function with a wide variety of Dot Matrix printers.

Contact HEADWAY today for more details or a demonstration of

LePrint and JLaser

This document was produced using LePrint and JLaser and printed on a Canon Laser Printer.

HEADWAY COMPUTER PRODUCTS
Headway House, Christy Estate,
Ivy Road, Aldershot, Hants. GU12 4TX.

Tel: 0252 333575 Telex: 859518 Fax: 0252 314445

Fig. 3.19 Hewlett Packard LaserJet printer

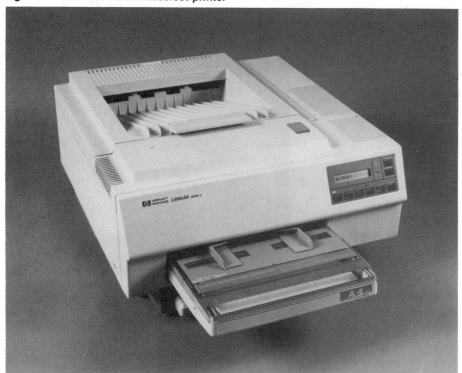

Vertical rules: lines inserted between columns of text to aid the eye in easier reading.

Widows and orphans: terms for the very short lines of text at the top or bottom of a page: an orphan is an isolated word or short bottom line and a widow is a short top line; DTP can sometimes avoid the problem by modifying text spacing.

WIMP: Windows Icons Mouse Pull-down Menus – a term to describe the 'tools' used to edit in DTP.

WYSIWYG: What You See Is What You Get – a term used to explain that a VDU page of data is exactly reproduced by the printer.

Note: A newcomer to DTP is bound to find the specialist terms and jargon expressions somewhat bewildering. But remember that, as with all IT technologies, everyone is in the same situation and the people who get on are those who are prepared to 'have a go' at grasping new ideas and techniques quickly and readily.

Applications of desktop publishing

Already DTP has revolutionised the speed and quality of in-house created documents such as:

■ Reports ■ Price lists ■ Bulletins ■ Notices ■ Posters ■ Social Club Announcements ■ Catalogues ■ Training and Technical Manuals ■ Circular Sales Letters ■ Leaflets, Brochures, etc ■ AVA Foils and Handouts.

So acquiring an informed overview of desktop publishing techniques and the ability to produce WP text suited for DTP installation are essential items on the training agenda of today's office assistants!

■ DISCUSSION TOPIC

'All these manufacturers seem to think about is designing and selling systems and equipment which end up giving the poor old manager and secretary ever more data to read, react to and remember! Far from simplifying office life, IT's just making it much too complicated!' How far would you agree with this hard-pressed manager's cri de coeur?

FACSIMILE TRANSMISSION – FAX

While universally known as fax (or telefax in the EC), the full name for this messaging medium explains its function, since a facsimile is an exact and faithful reproduction of text, photographs or graphic images.

Essentially, a facsimile transceiver works as follows. It accepts printed paper documents and passes them over an electronic scanner which encodes every least printed item – text, numbers, logos, photographs, etc – into electronic signals. Either immediately, or after a timed interval (to secure cheaper transmission rates) the transceiver will transmit the set of signals representing the letter, leaflet or diagram to the fax address entered as part of the transmission process. The address, of course, is that of another fax machine located almost anywhere in the world served by telephone lines, cables or radio/satellite networks.

The receiving fax machine decodes the set of signals back into precisely the same pattern of text or images of the original and prints it out onto a specially treated paper which is loaded in a roll into the machine and guillotined into an appropriate size.

Delayed transmission

In order to save costs or avoid busy peak transmission times, most fax systems allow the user to 'stack' a number of messages for onward transmission until a predetermined transmission time – say overnight UK time. At the appropriate moment a timer is activated to set the transmission sequences into operation. This function is usually set up at the end of the office day when no further messages are to be sent by normal means.

Status reports

A very useful feature of fax transmission is the intermittent (say after 50 transmissions) issuing of a status report which lists the number of calls made, their date, time and transmission duration, their destination and the number of pages transmitted. This provides a means of monitoring the fax bills when they arrive.

Fig. 3.20   CF 50 facsimile machine (Reproduced by kind permission of British Telecommunications plc)

Fax is particularly user-friendly and simple to operate and seems destined to oust the less flexible telex system. Today's fax machines are highly sophisticated. They can store as many as 100 abbreviated addresses, send multiple copies out to, say, account customers; ensure confidentiality by requiring a keyed in password at the receiving end for a designated recipient to access an incoming fax; send batches of fax overnight and during low-cost periods; receive incoming faxes automatically and stack them for collection; monitor all transmitted faxes and provide regular status reports and costs to date, etc. While the quality of printout hitherto has been only adequate, the latest fax equipment can be connected to laser and ink-jet printers.

As an office assistant, you should take the trouble early in your studies to become thoroughly conversant with fax technology and operating systems. Undoubtedly fax will figure in your working life from day one. Fax equipment is becoming cheaper and one telephone company already guarantees a connection to anywhere in the world within two minutes! Indeed, so popular has fax become that mobile lap-top versions are proving highly successful, and indispensable to globe-trotting executives.

■ *TALKING POINT*

Is IT taking us down the 'scenic route' to Big Brotherdom?

Fig. 3.21   Three routes for fax transmissions (Reproduced by kind permission of Muirfax Systems Ltd)

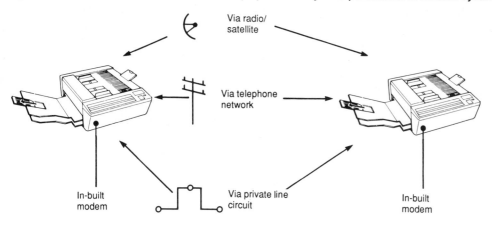

TELEX

The telex system preceded facsimile transmission and it is not unusual, therefore, that it should embody features which are similar in many ways to those of fax. For example, message receivers are contacted over the telephone wire and a 'ready to receive' confirmation known as an 'answerback code' is confirmed by the receiving teleprinter –

both fax and telex machines employ a kind of 'handshake' system to tell one another that they are ready to communicate. Also, telex employs many fax-type facilities such as retrying busy numbers, logging and reporting on calls and sending telexes to multiple recipients.

As by now you will have come to expect, the advent of IT gave a large boost to telex communications systems and current telex equipment resembles a desktop PC, rather than the

Fig. 3.22   Specimen telex message

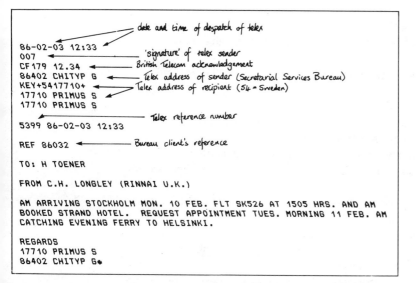

This message was despatched by a Secretarial Services Bureau on behalf of a client.
Reproduced by kind permission of Select Office Services, Chichester and Mr C H Longley (Rinnai UK)

outsize, heavy typewriter appearance of earlier teleprinters. Indeed, the user may either opt for a dedicated telex terminal or may incorporate a telex facility into a networked computer terminal. For the present, a major advantage of the telex system lies in the large number of telex terminal/system owners throughout the world. Nevertheless, the advent of fax has brought about fierce competition and telex is unlikely to continue for much longer in its present form.

Telex operations

By employing electronic text preparation and editing techniques, telex messages may be prepared, edited and checked prior to transmission by means of VDU or LCD display and microprocessor memory systems. Using features very much like those of fax transceivers, such messages may be kept on electronic file until a later transmission time and then dispatched automatically. Having prepared the text of the telex, the user makes contact with the recipient by typing the telex number, obtaining a confirmatory answerback code response and providing sender identification (i.e. the user's own answerback code). The telex may then be dispatched. Once the message has been delivered, the telex system immediately resumes a message acceptance mode, ready to receive incoming telexes, and will provide a series of printout message status reports.

ACTIVITIES AND ASSIGNMENTS Information technology applications

■ *THE QUICK CHECK-IT-OUT QUIZ*

1 Explain the meaning of the following:
   LAN WAN OSI GUI DTP FAX
2 What are the major advantages of installing a local area network for IT operations in an organisation?
3 In what ways could Email be used to cut down on the issue and circulation of paper documents?
4 Explain what 'icon-driven' and 'windows environment' mean.
5 What features are currently offered by current major WP packages in addition to producing text-based documents?
6 What features of a laser printer are available to enhance and vary the appearance of the printed word?
7 How does Microsoft's Windows software improve a computer's DOS operation system?
8 Describe briefly how a spreadsheet package works.
9 Give three examples of work-based situations in which a database applications package would be helpful, and explain the reasons why.
10 Explain simply the basic differences in operation of: (a) a dot-matrix (b) an ink-jet and (c) a laser printer. For what sort of business documents would each of these printers be used most effectively?
11 Explain briefly the differences between: (a) a low volume (b) a departmental and (c) a systems photocopier. For what sort of work is each most suited?
12 What are the cost components which go to make up the photocopying costs of a single side of A4? How would you go about ensuring that your department's photocopying requirements were undertaken cost effectively?
13 Explain briefly the major stages in producing a document using a desktop publishing system.

14 What are the features of current facsimile transceivers (fax machines) which have made them so popular with busy business executives?

15 Explain briefly how a fax system operates, and how it may be used most cost-effectively.

Case study

'OPEN ALL HOURS!'

Arun and Lata Patel's lives had been 'open all hours', ever since they first bought their business – a minimarket in a suburban shopping precinct – some five years ago. Then, the 150 houses on the Westbury Park development had been only half completed and business had been slow and hard to build. Thanks to the Patels' relentless hard work and willingness to rise at the crack of dawn and retire well after midnight, the minimarket had prospered, as the Westbury suburb of Grafton, a busy industrial town, had rapidly expanded. The store, called the Minimax Grocers & Newsagents, was in the middle of five shops in a parade lying back from a busy through-route to the A6. The Patels, with their 16-year-old daughter, Sonal and 10-year-old son, Naresh, occupied a flat over the store.

Minimax had started out as a run-of-the-mill general store, specialising in those small order items which local shoppers had forgotten to buy at the supermarket or did not want to make a special journey for. With a bus service into town stopping just opposite, and room for parking out front, Arun quickly realised, however, that there was ample scope for selling newspapers, magazines and sweets, etc. Before much longer, he was employing six newspaper delivery youngsters. They also picked up orders for home-delivered groceries, which Arun delivered mid-mornings around the adjacent estates in his elderly but trusty van. The delivery side of the business expanded rapidly to a point where Arun had to stop taking on new customers – much against his will.

About a year ago, with the completion of the upmarket Westbury Park development, customers who had acquired a taste for exotic micro-oven ready meals, gave Arun and Lata the idea of making room for another open freezer which would stock the spicy and different dishes which innovative food manufacturers were marketing under Chinese, Indian, Mexican and Indonesian brand names.

By this time, the Patels badly needed more helping hands. As luck would have it, two of Arun's nephews moved into the district looking for work in Grafton's textile industry. Both in their early twenties, they were just the trustworthy help that the shop urgently needed. Nor did they need much persuading, when Arun outlined his longer term plans for acquiring additional outlets. Ramesh, the elder brother took over the newsagency and confectionery side, while his brother Raj delivered the grocery orders and with his easy humour and persuasive ways quickly extended business.

Soon after, an incredible stroke of luck occurred – the butcher's shop next door came on to the market. The sitting tenant had been content to provide a mediocre service, and as a consequence could not afford the new lease's increased rents. Arun was quick to see his chance and had clinched the deal before the local estate agent had even displayed the particulars in his front window!

This time it was Mrs Patel who had her say. 'You know,' she had said, 'what Westbury needs is a really good fast-food takeaway!' Always with an eye to market trends, she had overheard snippets of conversation among teenagers and young married couples about the nearest fast-food outlet some two miles away which had a good reputation for ample portions and really tasty dishes. 'If they'll drive over there, they'll walk in here,' she observed shrewdly. 'We could also fit in a few tables for people who want to eat here, too,' she added. After meeting some demanding requirements, Arun obtained planning permission for the change of use and early in November, the grand opening of Arun's 'Tandoori Takeaway' took place, with Mrs Patel in charge!

* * *

Some eight weeks earlier, Sonal had started a two-year BTEC National Diploma course in Business and Finance at Grafton College of Technology. From day one, with business in her bones, she had never looked back. She seemed to devour the course material – especially those parts dealing with business information processing. She had a natural flair with software and had achieved a Grade A in her Business Information Studies GCSE.

One evening, having just finished an assignment, she poked her head round the door of her father's upstairs office in the flat. He was almost buried under paper! It bulged out of cardboard wallets, ring-binders and box files; it was festooned around the walls, suspended from rows of bull-dog clips, it littered his desk and window sills. Advice notes, invoices, handwritten orders, catalogues, price-lists, special offers and bank statements! It seemed as though Arun had kept every single piece of paper since the first day's trading. Sonal scooped up a handful and let it drop back on to the desk.

'Stop that you silly girl!' shouted Arun. 'Now look what you've done. I'd just sorted those invoices into sequence!'

'Daddy, look at you! You're drowning in a sea of bumf!'

'What do you mean, bumf – I know exactly where everything is kept – or did until you interfered – now go away and let me finish!'

'Not until you make me a promise you'll keep.' Sonal paused dramatically, for she well knew she was the apple of her father's eye.

'Certainly not! What promise?'

'That first thing tomorrow you go down to Computerama and get fixed up with a decent PC set-up and some suitable software – before you go down for the third time and all your past flashes before your eyes! I don't know how you've managed up till now, but with the new shop and the deliveries expanding, soon you won't need to stop for sleep – you won't have time!'

* * *

For several days Sonal's words echoed around Arun's brain like an advertising jingle that wouldn't go away. Eventually he brought the matter up with Lata. 'I think she's probably right. You should move with the times,' Lata responded. 'How can you even think of new outlets when you're drowning in the paper from just two!'

Outnumbered and out-argued, Arun was waiting the next morning outside the front door as they opened up Computerama for business!

■ **DISCUSSION TOPICS**

1 Is Sonal right to think that computerising the Patels' business would help? What factors do you think would affect the success or failure of installing a PC, printer and software packages?

2 What aspects of the family business would installing a computerised system most assist?

3 What other IT-based office equipment/systems would it be realistic for Arun to install to aid profitability and service?

4 Assuming that Arun's plans are successful and within two more years he has promoted his two nephews as branch managers of two more Minimax stores, how would this growth affect an existing computerised administration system in the Patel business? Should Arun take future expansion into account in planning to introduce computing applications? If so, how?

Case study activities

These activities develop NVQ competences in:

* *supplying information for a specific purpose;*
* *researching and retrieving information;*
* *presenting narrative, graphic and tabular information using an alphanumeric keyboard.*

■ *ACTIVITIES*

1 Arun asks his daughter to carry out a survey of current computer features and specifications in order to benefit from her advice and expertise. In pairs, undertake Sonal's project and then produce a suitable report using a PC with recommendations on your findings which Arun can follow and base his decision upon. You should note that the Patels' current annual turnover is £250,000 and that any purchases must lie within a realistic ceiling – whether acquired from profit, a bank loan or leased.

2 Next, explore your local market for best prices of the software application packages which you think Arun should install. Produce a schedule displaying your findings and justify your reasons for the 'best buys' you identify. Present your findings in a graphics/tabular form using appropriate software if available.

Activities to develop confidence and competence

The following activities develop NVQ competences in:

* *data processing, reprographics and printing;*
* *storing and supplying information;*
* *information processing using: word processing, spreadsheet and database software applications packages;*
* *telecommunications and data transmission using fax equipment.*

1 Using Email on a LAN and designing a database record

You work as assistant to Mrs Kay Peters, Personnel Manager for Millenium Computers Limited. In the company's head office are some 250 staff. Recently Mrs Peters has successfully negotiated with Middleton District Council a special reduced rate for membership for Millenium's head office employees of the town's well-equipped leisure centre.

The details of the special offer are:

Full Adult Membership (including advance booking rights: £20 per annum (amounting to a discount of 20%).

Social Membership (giving access to bars and evening recreational activities e.g. bridge, snooker, chess etc). £13 per annum (amounting to a discount of 15%).

Family Membership (including spouse and all children under 14 years of age) £34 per annum (amounting to a discount of 25%).

Middleton Leisure Centre is making this offer for six weeks from today. The Centres facilities include:

Swimming pool, water chute, conditioning suite, aerobics studio, main hall for badminton, circuit-training, indoor football, basketball etc, games rooms for card and board games, snooker/billiards room (5 tables), and two squash courts.

There is also a fully-licensed bar, a cafeteria and a crêche.

The Centre's professional staff mount a series of instructional and training sessions in a wide range of sports and activities each week.

■ ACTIVITIES

Draft an Email memo for Mrs Peters to send to Departmental Heads which will:

explain clearly and attractively the benefits of membership of the Middleton Leisure Centre;

ask heads to canvas interest and to supply a list of those staff likely to apply for which category of membership.

Millenium Computers are keen to promote a fitter and less stressed workforce and so a condition of obtaining the reduced cost membership is that staff have to register their applications with the Personnel Department.

Using appropriate database software, design a record which will contain the information you think Mrs Peters will want to collect and collate.

Using a spreadsheet

You have recently joined the Departmental Office of the Business Studies Department of Westlands College of Technology as an office assistant. Your Head of Department, Jack Foster, has a gruelling time during enrolment each year in keeping abreast of the fast-changing recruitment picture and in making information quickly available to the Vice Principal's office. Soon after your arrival, he decides to put your spreadsheet know-how to work with this brief:

'I'd like you to design me a spreadsheet file to do the following:

Firstly, to list each course we offer according to its mode of attendance under these headings:

  a full-time
  b part-time day
  c part-time evening
  d full-cost

(You may either use real course codes and titles, or invent simulated ones, and provide ten courses for each of **a**, **b** and **c**, and five for **d**.)

Your file must provide in vertical tables a total of enrolled students for each course and a section total for each mode of attendance, so that as the totals for individual courses rises or falls, so does the section total.

Also, I need to know the full-time equivalent totals for **a**, **b** and **c**. Another vertical column will be needed to convert actual enrolled totals into these 'FTE' equivalents according to the following ratios:

  each full-time student = 1
  each part-time day student = 0.4
  each evening class student = 0.2

Lastly, the spreadsheet must be able to tell me the overall FTE student total for categories **a**, **b** and **c**.'

Produce a spreadsheet file which will meet Mr Foster's needs.

Using a printer

As a means of promoting Middleton Leisure Centre's special offer, Mrs Peters has decided to post a set of A4 posters on corridor and departmental noticeboards. She therefore asks you to design a suitable A4 poster, using the most effective features of an available ink-jet or laser printer. You should then photocopy it five times, ensuring a high quality end-product. If possible, use five different colours of A4 copy paper to see which best suits your design and printing features.

Using a photocopier

By arrangement, check with your Departmental secretary to see what photocopying jobs you may carry out for the office and also submit as NVQ evidence.

Using a fax machine

The head of your department's Secretarial Services Section is in a jam! Tomorrow she is to be visited by the external verifier of an examining board who will review evidence for a Level 2 Administrative Business & Commercial Training Group (ABC) NVQ programme.

The Secretarial Head of Section has mislaid her copy of the ABC Level 1/2 Performance Standards booklet and urgently needs a copy of Unit 11 (Level 2) to go over this evening before the verifier's visit.

By arrangement, prepare a fax message to send to the Head of Secretarial Studies in a neighbouring College asking for a copy of the requested Unit 11 (Level 2) to be faxed back to you as a matter of urgency today.

Work experience attachment assignments

1 Find out how the LAN system in your organisation works. Arrange to make hard copies of its main operations menus, its Email messaging page layout and diary features etc.
2 By arrangement, devise and send an Email message to several LAN users which requires an answer. Make hard copies of your Email message and responses as evidence of your successful LAN operation.
3 Use the WP software employed in your organisation to produce a draft letter or memorandum required by your supervisor. Keep a hard copy to submit as evidence of your operation.
4 With permission, collect a series of specimen letters, memoranda, reports and minutes etc, which illustrate your organisation's preferred house style and layout.
5 By arrangement, interview selected staff to ascertain what kinds of task the organisation's spreadsheet software is used for. Make an oral report to your group upon your findings.
6 With authorisation, obtain hard copies of some non-confidential spreadsheet files. Go through them with the staff who created them, make your notes and then give a short presentation to your group on their design and use.
7 Ask your supervisor to arrange for you to collect three or four examples of database

records in use. Give a short presentation to your group on the fields set up for each record and the ways in which they are analysed.

8 Arrange to spend a morning with your organisation's DTP Unit. Find out what hardware and software are used and make step-by-step notes on the sequence employed to create a DTP'd document from word-processed and/or hand-written drafts. Try your hand at using a mouse to create text on a style sheet.

9 With permission, collect copies of a range of documents which have been produced in house with a desktop publishing system. For example, advertisements, bulletins, notices, forms, newsletters, brochures etc. Select what you consider to be especially good examples and share your findings with your group.

10 Arrange to spend a morning in your organisation's Reprographics Centre. Find out the range of features of the photocopying machine in use and, with permission, secure some non-confidential hard copies as specimens. Make notes of your findings about the operation of the equipment in the Centre. Under supervision, carry out several photocopying tasks and, when proficient, keep specimen copies of your photocopying work for evidence.

Also, find out in detail the costs of photocopying the documents commonly reproduced and how the organisation's photocopying needs are met cost-effectively. Keep a record of your findings to share with your group.

11 By arrangement, observe a series of fax transmissions and deliveries. When confident about using the organisation's fax equipment, arrange to send a fax which requires a response. Keep copies of both transmitted and received fax documents and covering transmission data sheets as evidence of your successful operation.

12 Find out how your organisation's fax documents are processed cost-effectively, and make notes of your findings. By arrangement, obtain a copy of the report issued by the fax transceiver, listing details of fax documents sent and their transmission costs etc.

Part 4

Business letters, memoranda and electronic mail

OVERVIEW

This Part explains in detail how letters are used to communicate various kinds of business message; it also examines the uses of memoranda and electronic mail as a means of exchanging information within organisations. You will learn the current conventions of letter and memoranda layout, as well as how to compose appropriate messages in response to differing business situations. In addition, you will learn how to create a tone and style to suit a specific context.

Within many organisations, the paper memorandum is fast giving way to its electronic counterpart – referred to often as Email. The creation and distribution of Email messages around local area networks (LANs) – a system of interlinked computers – is also explained and illustrated.

NVQ references

This Part covers the following BTEC First Diploma in Business and Finance and 'ABC/NWPSS' competences:

BTEC First Diploma:

Business Support Systems 1:
Competences: 5 and 6 Supplying information for a specific purpose and drafting routine business communications; 17 Maintaining business relationships with customers and colleagues.

ABC/NWPSS

Level 2:
Unit 2 Communicating information
Unit 8 Liaising with callers and colleagues
Unit 10 Creating and maintaining business relationships
Unit 11 Providing information to customers and clients
Level 3:
Unit 1 Communication systems
Unit 5 Preparing and producing documents
Unit 6 Processing correspondence

THE BUSINESS LETTER – A VITAL MEDIUM OF COMMUNICATIION

There is no longer any doubt that tremendous changes are being introduced into business and organisational life by information technology. Indeed, this Part examines the way in which electronic mail is being used to route messages around organisations in split seconds.

Nevertheless, the Post Office delivers in the UK each year many millions of business letters painstakingly produced on paper. Each letter is the result of a series of complex operations, from the making of fine quality bond paper, designing and printing upon it a multi-coloured company letterhead, composing and keying in its unique message, processing it for mailing and finally delivering it to its intended recipient by air, road or rail.

Given that faxed messages, telephone calls and electronic mail sent over wide area networks (WANs) are very much faster to deliver and can supply in the case of fax and Email a paper hard copy, why are so many millions of business letters still produced and delivered each year?

Paper-based business letters are often a preferred means of communication for the following reasons:

▶ Their fine quality paper and printed message appeal to the eye and so help the message to gain acceptance.

▶ Letters printed on notepaper provide a written record which remains intact over many years if carefully and systematically stored.

▶ Letters printed on paper such as contracts, tenders or agreements etc are legally acceptable documents. Legal uncertainties still surround messages produced, stored and distributed electronically.

▶ Despite the widespread use of computers in business, many people still find handling paper more familiar and comfortable – though this trend is changing fast as children enter primary schools equipped with computers.

Figure 4.1 illustrates some of the vital two-way links which letters create and maintain between an organisation and its external contacts.

Frequently occurring types of business letter

The following checklist illustrates the most frequently occurring types of business letter. With the help of relatives and friends, collect examples of as many types as possible in order to see how they are composed and laid out, and then display them in your base room.

Type of letter	Purpose
Sales	To persuade a consumer or account customer to purchase a described product or service.
Enquiry/ response	A paired exchange of letters; firms deal constantly with all kinds of enquiry – about their products, guarantees, technical details etc and answer them individually.
Complaint/ adjustment	Another paired exchange; many customer complaints are communicated by letter and need putting right; a letter of adjustment informs the customer of what has been done (if the complaint is deemed justified) to 'adjust' the complaint.

Fig. 4.1   The links formed by letters

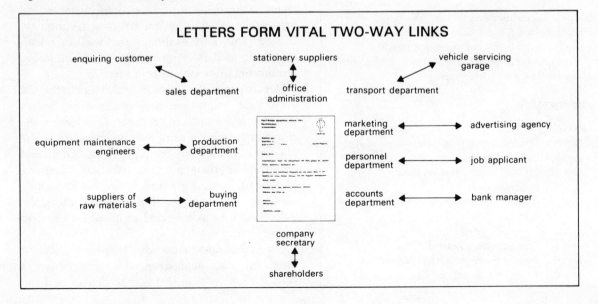

Collection	A company's accounts department sends letters of collection to those customers who have failed to settle their accounts within an agreed time limit; such letters confirm purchase details and request immediate payment.
Quotations estimates and tenders	Before undertaking to purchase expensive items, most organisations ask for a written breakdown of anticipated costs. If a firm tenders for a job or to supply equipment etc, the costs detailed in the tender are legally binding and cannot be changed.
Advertising and promoting	Many large firms send out regular mailshots to existing or potential customers to advertise their products or services; such a letter is often called 'unsolicited mail', because the customer did not 'solicit' or request it.
Disciplinary	Current industrial law requires that in cases of misconduct or breaking of regulations, employees must receive a final written warning; such a messge is usually delivered on company notepaper.
Covering	Written documents – technical specifications, schedules, forms, plans, etc are often sent through the post. As a courtesy these are usually accompanied by a written 'covering' letter to their recipient simply stating the nature of the enclosures and why they have been sent.

Fig. 4.2 Examples of organisations' logos

Open punctuation

Another established practice to be familiar with is that of open punctuation. It grew up from the savings which could be made by text processing staff if they omitted all commas and full stops in those entries *outside* the main body of the letter.

Thus the references, date, recipient's name and postal address, salutation, subscription, enclosure and copy abbreviations etc all remain unpunctuated (see the Pitman letter example of an open punctuation, fully-blocked letter on page 101).

Its counterpart, closed punctuation with a semi-blocked format is now very seldom seen.

HOW TO STRUCTURE A LETTER'S MESSAGE EFFECTIVELY

Helpful tips

▶ Decide beforehand what precise outcomes/actions are needed.

▶ Think about the recipient's personality and likely reactions and aim to win him/her to your side!

▶ Make out a rough checklist of the points you want to make and put them into an OPENING, DEVELOPMENT and CLOSING SEQUENCE.

▶ Check your letter (while in draft form) for evidence of the tone and style you seek to impart. ALWAYS AVOID: rudeness, sarcasm, talking down to people, wordy rambling, insincerity, hypocrisy.

▶ If your letter asks its recipient to undertake to do something for you, make sure you include an ACTION REQUEST in your final paragraph which also supplies a 'by when' date.

Fig. 4.3 How to structure a letter's message effectively

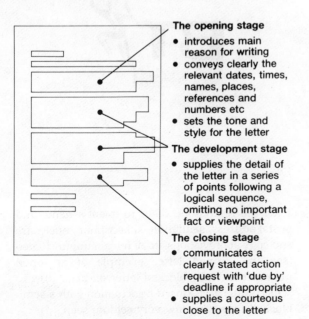

The opening stage
- introduces main reason for writing
- conveys clearly the relevant dates, times, names, places, references and numbers etc
- sets the tone and style for the letter

The development stage
- supplies the detail of the letter in a series of points following a logical sequence, omitting no important fact or viewpoint

The closing stage
- communicates a clearly stated action request with 'due by' deadline if appropriate
- supplies a courteous close to the letter

Format of the fully blocked letter

1 Company logo and trading name.
Five company addresses:
2 Postal, including postcode
3 Telephone number
4 Telex address
5 Cables address
6 Fax number and address
7 Prominently placed letter status indicator.
8 Your reference is that of the letter's recipient, John Green (JG) and of his assistant, Pat Dawson (PD).
9 Our reference is that of the letter's sender – here Ann Grant as the writer (AG) and Nicola Lawson, secretary (NL). The number 4 indicates this is the fourth letter written to John Green and is a helpful filing reference.
10 Date: expressed as day (number), month (word) and year (number) and *never* as 15/4/19—.
11 Recipient's full postal address: note town in capital letters and postcode on its own line (whenever practicable).
12 Salutation: Here the less formal 'Dear Mr . . . Yours sincerely' is used, as opposed to its formal counterpart 'Dear Sir . . . Yours faithfully'.
7–12 This letter's layout conforms to the conventions of blocked format and open punctuation; in blocked format all lines commence from the pre-set left-hand margin as all punctuation (outside the body of the letter) is omitted.
13 Subject heading prominently displayed in capitals with good space around it; subject headings should convey briefly the letter's theme or subject.
14 Body of the letter: note that points are made succinctly in brief paragraphs and that the chosen style is informal without becoming overfriendly or familiar.
15 Eye-catching enclosure symbol: note that *** and / are also sometimes employed.
16 Appropriate subscription for 'Dear Mr, Mrs, Ms or Miss, etc'.
17 Sufficient space allotted for writer's signature.
18 Typescript confirmation of writer's name and job title (Note: some female letter-writers include Mrs, Ms or Miss after their names).
19 Further confirmation of an enclosure included; see also 'encs', 'enclosure', etc.
20 All business letters must include the address where the company is registered and its registration number to comply with the Companies Acts and EC directives.

Fig. 4.4 Format of the fully blocked letter

1 Pitman Publishing

2 128 Long Acre
London WC2E 9AN

3 Telephone 071-379 7383

4 Telex 261367
Pitman G

5 Cables Ipandsons
London WC2

6 Fax 071-240 5771
Pitman Ldn

7 CONFIDENTIAL

8 Your ref   JG/PD

9 Our ref   AG/NL/4

10 15 April 199-

11 Mr J Green
Appletrees
Windmill Lane
Peppard Common
READING
Berks
RG24 3PC

12 Dear Mr Green

13 PROPOSED TEXTBOOK ON SECRETARIAL ADMINISTRATION

14 Following upon our telephone conversation of Tuesday last, I am
pleased to confirm that our Project Committee met yesterday, and
that your proposal was fully considered. As a result, Mrs Jean
Simpson, Publisher, Secretarial Studies Division, wishes me to
offer you a contract to publish your text early next year.

May I take this opportunity to offer my personal congratulations
with the sincere hope that your first textbook will prove a
resounding success. I should also like to assure you that your
manuscript will receive my careful attention in the coming
months, so please do not hesitate to let me know if I can help
in any way.

---15 I enclose a copy of our standard Agreement form for your
information and shall contact you shortly to arrange a convenient
date to finalise contract details.

16 Yours sincerely

17 *Ann Grant*

18 Ann Grant
Editor Secretarial Studies Division

19 enc

20 Pitman Publishing Division of Longman Group UK Limited Registered Office 5 Bentinck Street London W1M 5RN Registered number 872828 England

EXAMPLE OF A SALES ENQUIRY FOLLOW-UP LETTER

Speedy Stationery Services Limited

10 West Road
Middleton
Southshire MS9 45K
Tel: Middleton 478964

SSSL

Your ref   PGT/JR S 162

Our ref   KP/JT   FICL 24

12 July 199-

Mr P G Truman
Chief Buyer
Fidelity Insurance Co Ltd
24 New Street
TRENTON
Northshire   TR14 6NS

Dear Mr Truman

FREEFLOW CONTINUOUS COMPUTER STATIONERY

Thank you for your letter of 9 July 199- in which you enquired
about the availability of continuous computer stationery.

I am pleased to inform you that my company has recently secured
an exclusive agency for Freeflow Continuous Computer Stationery.

The paper used is of good quality and is not prone to irritating
breakage by tractor feed sprockets.

I have enclosed a brochure from Freeflow which will provide you
with more detail on the advantages of continuous stationery. Our
current price-list is also enclosed and in view of your valued
past custom, I am pleased to extend to you an additional discount
of 10% on orders placed before 1 August 199- for 12 or more
Freeflow 5 kilo packs.

Please let me know if I may provide you with any additional
information.

Yours sincerely

P Preston

P Preston (Mrs)
Sales Manager

encs

copy to: G Knight Sales Representative Northshire

SPECIMEN LETTER OF COMPLAINT

South London Garages Limited

121 WIMBLEDON ROAD LONDON SE1 5GT
HMF and Porsche Authorised Dealers
High Quality & Trusted Service!

Tel: 01-567-8901/4 Telex: 456901 Solondgar Fax: 01-345-6677

Our ref: BS/GJ/HMFUK.78   Your ref:

25 March 199-

For the urgent attention of:

Mr P Goodwright
UK Sales Director
Hessische Motor Fabriken (UK) Ltd
HMF House
110-112 Ipswich Road
PETERBOROUGH
Cambs   P16 9HK

Dear Mr Goodwright

NON-DELIVERY OF ORDER KX4592: FIVE HMF TURBO TOURERS MK II

On 12 January 199- my company placed a telexed order (5466 90-12-01 12.15)
with you for five HMF Turbo Tourer Mark II saloons, specifying three Moonlight
Silver and two Stardust White models. The telex included details of required
delivery dates arising from firm orders from long-standing, repeat-purchasing
customers.

Your telex reply (ref: 7856 90-12-01 2.46) confirmed our order and indicated
that there would be no problems in meeting the specified delivery dates - all
now gone by - nor in supplying the colours our customers requested.

I am therefore extremely concerned that the commitments which South London
Garages Limited has given to valued customers cannot be met because of your
inability to deliver the five HMF Mark IIs as promised.

At present my sales staff are under a great deal of pressure from the
customers involved, who are now threatening to cancel their orders worth a
total of £126,450:00.

My company simply cannot afford to lose such valuable business, and I am
therefore asking you to intervene in this matter personally so as to ensure
a satisfactory outcome for my customers as a matter of extreme urgency.

I look forward to hearing from you at your earliest opportunity.

Yours sincerely

Brian Smith

Brian Smith
Sales Manager

copy to Gordon Watson General Manager

PRODUCING CIRCULAR LETTERS AND MAILSHOTS

The introduction of word processing into offices – sales, accounts, purchasing etc – in the 1970s made the production of personalised circular letters possible. Simply, the word processing operator keys into the WP software the body of a single, all-purpose, standard letter. Spaces are left in its layout for the inclusion of items like:

▶ an individual's name, job title and address;
▶ an individualised salutation e.g. Dear Mr Jackson
▶ information relating to an individual or firm to be inserted in a subject heading e.g. Overdue Account No . . . . For £ . . . .
▶ repetitions of the recipient's name etc within the body of the letter e.g. 'a place at our Briefing Seminar has been reserved for you, Mr Roy Jackson, and we . . .'

Having set up the standard letter in the mailmerge operation of the WP software, the operator merely has to summon up the personalised information from previously keyed-in lists and 'merge' the two together. In this way it is possible to produce quickly hundreds of circular letters which have the appearance of having been written separately to each individual.

Figure 4.5 illustrates the area of a circular or 'form' letter which may be personalised by WP mailmerging:

Fig. 4.5 Mailmerge insertions
LOCATIONS OF MAILMERGE WP INSERTIONS

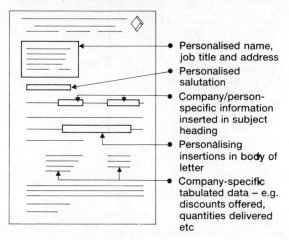

- Personalised name, job title and address
- Personalised salutation
- Company/person-specific information inserted in subject heading
- Personalising insertions in body of letter
- Company-specific tabulated data – e.g. discounts offered, quantities delivered etc

CREATING EFFECTIVE TONE AND STYLE IN BUSINESS LETTERS

The tone of a written document stems from a combination of factors. First there are the aims and objectives of the written message: whether to sell a product or to recover a bad debt. Then there are the needs and expectations of the receiver of the document and the relationship between writer and recipient, such as retailer and customer. Lastly, there is the reason for writing: trying to put right a customer's complaint, or to hasten the delivery of urgently needed spare parts. Tone, then, is the result of all these factors. It gives the impression which the reader of the message receives, and it comes from the choice of words which the writer makes to express his message, and the structure of the sentences which convey it to the reader.

Aims and objectives

Does the document seek to:

▶ transmit factual information?
▶ persuade a customer to buy?
▶ urge a debtor to pay up!
▶ motivate a sagging sales force?
▶ discipline a wayward member of staff?
▶ answer criticisms or complaints?
▶ analyse and solve a problem?

The relationship between writer and reader

Much depends on the existing relationship between writer and receiver:

▶ is the receiver above or below the writer in the organisation's hierarchy?
▶ is the recipient a customer?
▶ is the recipient a member of staff?
▶ does the recipient report to the writer?

Profile of the recipient(s)

▶ what characteristics of the recipient will influence the way the message is received?
▶ is there one recipient or many?

▶ is the recipient young or old, male or female?
▶ is he an expert or layman?
▶ what attitudes or views does he possess?
▶ is he likely to be sympathetic, hostile or indifferent?

The needs of the situation

The tone of the document must respond to the needs of the situation:

▶ may the writer adopt a familiar or friendly tone?
▶ must the message be written in formal language?
▶ is the situation one in which the writer is informing? Or persuading? Or both?
▶ does the writer need urgent action from the recipient?

Choosing the right words

Once the writer has considered all the above points, he may then set out to use words which will best create the right tone. Sometimes colloquial expressions – 'Don't push it too far' – may be perfectly in order; at other times a more formal wording is needed – 'Do not attempt to sell the product too aggressively'. Occasionally the tone will need to be formal – 'Unless payment is made within seven days, legal action will be taken'. It is *always important* to ensure that the most appropriate words – the best words – have been carefully chosen.

Choosing the right sentence structure

The effect of sentences upon tone – whether short and sharp or complex and long – is also important to consider.

The short sentence can be very effective:

Company profits rose by 35% last year.

Order *your* copy now!

But a succession of them can prove very dull and even irritating:

Thank you for your letter of 14 July. You enquired about holidays in the USA. There are several we recommend. The first is in New York. It is for 7 days. It includes 3 sight-seeing tours. It costs £650.00. The second is in Florida . . .

Alternatively, longer sentences may be needed to explain complicated ideas:

There are a number of selling points concerning the Simplex personal computer which the sales force should bring to the attention of customers. The first concerns the computer's display screen which features a high-definition VGA colour screen. Further, the screen displays the equivalent of the full depth of an A4 sheet so that the user can always see the whole of the page of the letter or report being created. The second selling point is that with 20 megabytes of memory on hand, the Simplex's response time is always instant and the irritation of slow responses to commands is eliminated totally! . . .

A frequent problem with the composition of long and complex sentences is that the writer loses the thread of what he is trying to convey:

Not having used your cordless, desktop dictating maching, though I *am* used to dictating machines, which my company has used for the past fifteen years, which I think allows me to consider myself as someone rather more experienced than a newcomer to dictating practices.

Here, the writer has become hopelessly lost, trying to make too many points within the scope of a single sentence; he has forgotten what he set out to convey at the beginning of the sentence.

In short, the writer must seek at all times to *control* the length and structure of his sentences so that a clear and appropriate tone is conveyed through them. He should vary the mix of longer and shorter sentences, so that the message is easily understood by the reader, and at the same time is made interesting because of its varied rhythms.

Checklist of tips on how to create effective tone and style

Choice of words

Take pains to select 'best fit' words – those which best suit the context of your letter. For example, when writing to a lay person, non-expert, avoid jargon and insider technical terms. In all business letters, avoid slang and over-familiar colloquial words such as 'fix it', 'busted', 'thrown a wobbly' etc. And above all, choose words which are short and simple rather than long and complex:

fire	*not* conflagration
ready-made	*not* prefabricated
home	*not* domicile
stretched	*not* elongated etc

Sentence structures

The normal word order in English looks like this:

Subject + Main Verb + Extension
Jane   finished   the report at 4.30 pm

But if every sentence we wrote followed precisely this structure, our readers would very soon become bored:

Jane finished the report at 4.30 pm. She took it to her manager. He read it carefully. He made several changes. Jane keyed these in. The manager was happy with the report.

To prevent prose paragraphs becoming boring, effective writers vary the length and structure of their sentences:

[1]*By 4.30 pm* Jane had finished the report. She took it in to her manager,[2]*who read it carefully* [3]*and made several changes.* Jane keyed these in [4]*and* the manager was happy with the report.

As the above example illustrates, some tricks of the trade are to introduce some information before the subject [1] and to link sentences together [2, 3, 4].

Short sentences for impact

Nevertheless, short sentences, deliberately constructed, have a distinct impact:

Sales last year increased by 75%.

Advertising pays.

By the same token, long and complex sentences quickly lose the reader:

Having taken particular pains to read the instructions, which were printed in very small – almost indecipherable – print, which caused her to remember her appointment next week at the opticians, because she didn't want to assemble it incorrectly, she couldn't understand why it didn't work.

As you can see, the writer has become quite lost in trying to cram too many ideas into a single sentence:

Guideline: Keep your sentences shorter rather than longer and when in doubt, opt for a full-stop and start a fresh sentence.

Connecting words and phrases

When writing in continuous prose, the effective writer interlinks his or her ideas with helpful connecting words or phrases which assist the reader in absorbing the information:

Although the work was difficult, he pressed on doggedly.

Remember also: Even though   Though

She passed the examination with distinction *because* she had studied long and hard.

Remember also: as   since   as a result of

Despite endless difficulties, they reached the summit.

Other useful connectors include:

and, but, if, whether, nevertheless, moreover, furthermore, when, whenever, etc.

Register

The term 'register' is used in the context of tone and style to mean a kind of scale of communication which may range from very informal to very formal:

Put 't' wood in't hole would you!

Close the door, please.

Or from the very simple to very complicated:

The fire burned the house down.

The inferno resulted in the entire residence being incinerated.

Using an appropriate register in business letters is very important because their recipients:

▶ don't like to be talked down to;
▶ feel uneasy if they do not follow complex technical language;
▶ dislike over-familiarity;
▶ undervalue information which is delivered in a 'chatty' trivialising way;

▶ switch off if forced to wade through labyrinths of long sentences and multi-syllabic words.

The profile of the recipient

In order to create effective tone and style in a given situation, it is essential to take into account the kind of person to whom a letter, memorandum or Email message is being sent. Whether the recipient is young or old, an expert or layman, potentially sympathetic or hostile to the communication will all combine to make a large impact on the way in which you put the message together. The following checklist provides you with some useful guidelines and pointers to those aspects of a recipient's profile or make-up to consider when constructing your message.

Age: Younger people may be more likely to be receptive to new ideas; as people get older they sometimes become set in their ways, views and beliefs and may therefore need particular persuasion in order to respond positively to the unfamiliar.

Background: People who have 'come up the hard way', or studied at 'the University Of Life' may be suspicious or antagonistic towards those with degrees and qualifications. Similarly, someone living in the heart of London is likely to have a completely different lifestyle from that of a lifelong resident of the Cotswolds.

Expertise: When two specialists talk together about their subject, the air is soon thick with technical jargon and complex 'insider' ideas which the layman listener finds quite baffling. Therefore, always remember that your recipient may not know your work specialism and may need to have ideas and explanations expressed simply but without the feeling of being talked down to.

Organisational position: Rightly or wrongly, people who have devoted many years of energy and effort in climbing the organisational ladder often possess a developed sense of their position – of their authority, status and the respect owed to them. It therefore pays to adopt a tone which is not 'forelock-touching' but neither over-familiar.

Personal prejudices: Whether we believe it or not, we all have sets of personal views and beliefs which are not entirely logical or rational – our likes and dislikes about people, behaviour or things. When composing any written message, it is therefore always helpful to keep in mind any personal views or prejudices you know your recipient possesses and to avoid or 'soft-pedal' around them accordingly.

LANS AND WANS: SENDING AND RECEIVING EMAILED MESSAGES

A LAN (Local Area Network) is an interconnected network of computer terminals contained within a local area, e.g. an office building, linked to a central computer processing unit, sometimes called a 'file server'. Special software in the central computer enables each user to call up an electronic memo page on the VDU and enter a message on it. The sender calls up preset recipients' electronic addresses on the screen and indicates those who are to receive the message. By depressing the 'send' key the message is routed to each named recipient in a fraction of a second. This process is called electronic mail or Email. The software enables the recipient to discard the message once read, file it for a given 'bring-forward' date or store it permanently. The arrival of each message is usually shown on the recipient's screen by an overriding flashing signal, e.g. 'NEW MAIL FOR YOU'. Many Email systems also inform the sender of the date and time when a recipient opened his or her 'mailbox' and first read the message. Answering an Email message follows similar procedures to sending, and WP, spreadsheet or graphics files may be 'enclosed' and routed with Email messages. While the LAN enables employees to intercommunicate within a single site, its Wide Area Network (WAN) counterpart links people electronically all over the world.

As you can readily imagine, this incredibly fast information system is revolutionising the ways in which people at work exchange messages, since Email can deal just as readily with number tables and graphics as it can with text. In addition, by use of a modem device, laptop computers can be linked into a LAN/WAN system so that the user can 'read' mail or dispatch a memo or letter from a location which may be remote from the user's normal office base. LAN/WAN systems can interconnect not only with printers, but also with fax, telex, intelligent photocopiers and computerised microfiche systems.

Guideline: Think carefully about the situation your letter is responding to and select your words, and sentence structures so as to create a register in harmony with the letter's purpose and recipient.

COMPOSING EFFECTIVE BUSINESS MEMORANDA

The simplest and best way to consider the business memorandum is as an internal letter sent to other people within the organisation in which you work. Except possibly as an informational copy sent, say, to a close associate like an advertising agency employee working on a commissioned project, memoranda are not sent to external organisations.

You will doubtless be pleased to know that most of what you have learned about composing letters is entirely applicable to memoranda! Guidelines about structure, tone and style apply just as much to internal co-workers as to external customers or connections.

However, the layout of the memorandum is different and needs to be mastered. Fortunately, it is quite straightforward. While no universally agreed layout exists, the diagram on page 109 illustrates the generally accepted format used in offices.

Memorandum layout

1, 2, 4, 6, 8 and 10: Typically, the layout of a memorandum has the labels MEMORANDUM, TO, FROM, REF (short for reference), DATE and SUBJECT set out as illustrated below in the model. These components are usually preprinted on memorandum pad sets.

1 Note that sometimes a company will add its name and logo across the top of the memorandum – perhaps as a means of reinforcing its corporate image within the organisation.

3 In memoranda, recipients may sometimes be referred to by their job title only – in this case, Sales Manager. It is also acceptable to use a name and job title: Jean Harris, Accounts Director. It is not customary, however, in memoranda for the titles Mr Mrs Ms or Miss to be used as they are in letters.

5 The sender's reference: in this example Norman Miller is the author of the memorandum and Rosemary Foster is his secretary. The memorandum has been produced in November and is the fifteenth written to the Sales Manager since the start of the month – hence the reference NM/RF/11/15. Note that various offices will have adopted different systems for organising referencing systems and that these have to be learned on the job.

6 and 7 See 3 above.

8 and 9 The format for setting out the date in a memorandum is exactly the same as that for the letter. And note that 22/11/9— is only ever used on handwritten sales receipts or informally handwritten notes.

10 and 11 The layout conventions for the subject heading of a memorandum are the same as those for a business letter. It should immediately convey the main theme of the message and assist filing and routing within an office.

12 The message of a memorandum is normally set out in fully blocked format nowadays, although you may still encounter some semi-blocked versions. To aid quick and easy absorption of the message, a memorandum's paragraphs are kept short and sweet. Notice that the author kills two birds with one stone, sending instructions to his District Managers by means of copies of the memo.

13 The convention for indicating the recipients of copies is the same as that for the letter – as is also that for indicating an enclosure.

14 Memoranda are normally produced on A5 or A4 bond stationery. The conventions used to label the continuation sheets of letters may also be used for long A4 memoranda. *Note:* good memorandum dictators tell their audio-typists at the outset of a memo dictation whether to use A5 or A4 paper.

MEMORANDUM [1]

TO [2]   Sales Manager [3]   [4] REF NM/RF/11/15 [5]
                                                          [8]
FROM [6] Regional Sales Manager North [7]   DATE 22 November 199- [9]

SUBJECT Special Discount on Mercier Beaujolais Villages [11]
[12]
Thank you for your memorandum of 19 November 199- in which you
confirm that an additional 5% discount may be offered to
established account customers purchasing ten or more cases of the
Chateau Mercier Beaujolais Villages.

At this time I have 145 cases in our Leeds warehouse and am
copying this memorandum to all District Managers directly asking
them to brief their sales representatives accordingly. I also
confirm that they will advise customers that the offer definitely
finishes at the end of this month.

[13] copies to: All District Managers

14

Guidelines for writing successful memoranda

Do:

– check your facts and figures carefully before starting. Nothing is more infuriating than to work to respond to a memorandum containing errors or omissions.

– take care to compose an eye-catching and accurate subject-heading. Remember that your memo may be competing with lots of other paper documents for your recipient's attention.

– structure your message simply: start with relevant background and updating information and then lead on to issues and options before finally stating your required action/follow-up needed *by a specific date*.

– think carefully beforehand to decide who should receive informational copies of your memoranda – people are quickly upset if they think they have been left out of the picture. By the same token make sure each recipient receives copies of any enclosures you include.

– check all your memoranda before dispatching them to ensure that no important parts of the message or action(s) needed have been omitted in error. Also at this time, proof-read carefully for typographical errors etc.

Don't:

– leap straight into the production of the memo. Make a checklist first of the points you wish to make and then put them into a logical running order.

– allow your memoranda to become too long and rambling.

– ever allow your memoranda to lapse into angry attacks, sarcasm or belittling of people etc. Always leave for several hours memo drafts composed while you were under stress. Once dispatched, unwise memos can never be retrieved unread! And remember that you may need a favour of a colleague tomorrow whom you antagonised or 'put down' today!

– forget to check your memoranda for appropriate and effective tone and style suited to the profile of your recipient(s).

– delay in sending memoranda – effective action generally needs to be taken promptly.

– fall into the trap of indulging in 'memo warfare'. If a problem arises between you and a colleague it is much better to sort it out face-to-face than to indulge in firing 'memo-missiles' at one another over several days or weeks.

ACTIVITIES AND ASSIGNMENTS Business letters, memoranda and electronic mail

---

■ *THE QUICK CHECK-IT-OUT QUIZ*

 1 Why is the use of the paper-based letter still so popular in business?
 2 List the main commonly occurring types of business letter and explain briefly the purpose of each.
 3 List the preprinted components of a business letterhead and explain what each communicates.
 4 Explain the difference between 'Our ref' and 'Your ref'.
 5 What would you put on a letter and its envelope to ensure that it is only opened and read by its named recipient?
 6 What is the purpose of a letter's postcode?
 7 What salutation would you use with 'Yours faithfully'?
 8 When would you employ 'Best wishes' or 'Kind regards'?
 9 What do these signs indicate in the left-hand margin of a letter: --- / ?
10 How should a secretary or assistant sign a letter dictated by an absent manager?
11 Describe briefly how to structure a letter's message effectively in paragraphs.
12 Explain the difference between open and closed punctuation.
13 What are the characteristics of a fully blocked letter layout?
14 How is the technique of mailmerging used in word processing circular letters?
15 What does the letter writer need to do in order to create effective tone and style in letters and memoranda?
16 Explain how to set out and construct a memorandum.
17 Outline briefly what changes IT is making in the creation, routing and filing of textual messages.

A case study

WEDNESDAY AFTERNOON AND THURSDAY MORNING

Wednesday afternoon

'Christine, I thought I told you never to type over mistakes! Look at this letter. It's perfectly dreadful! I certainly can't allow it to go out like that, can I?'

The voice of Miss Parkstone, office supervisor, carried across the typing pool, causing some of the girls to grin and exchange knowing smirks. Christine Dawson felt her cheeks burn as she blushed crimson.

'I'm sorry, Miss Parkstone – I was hurrying to catch the post.' Christine did not add that she was also hurrying to make sure that she left work on time. Her boyfriend, Derek, was picking her up at exactly 5.35 on the corner, and they were driving up to London on his bike to go to a pop concert.

'More haste, less speed,' remarked Miss Parkstone, stating the obvious. 'Though you're quite right, Mr Gulati does want the letter to go off tonight without fail.'

'But it's already 5.20,' replied Christine, 'and I . . .' Her voice trailed off as she decided not to finish her sentence.

'Well, I should have thought you had more pride in your work. Now, just buckle down to it, it shouldn't take you long. There's a good girl. I'll be in my office. And – no mistakes this time!' Miss Parkstone strode off.

The typing pool was full of bustle and chatter, as the girls put the cover on another day's work at Westwood and Meaker, Manufacturers of

Cooking Utensils and Enamelware.

'Don't do it for her! It's only 'cos she's got it in for you!' The suggestion came from Christine's friend Diana.

'Oh, she really made me fell small!' gasped Christine, whose nervousness was rapidly turning to anger as she saw the minute-hand of the office clock falling to the six. 'She's always so right and perfect! And anyway, the mistake was hardly noticeable!' But the heavy red ring of Miss Parkstone's biro around it clearly meant that another letter would have to be typed, since further efforts at camouflage would prove useless.

'Come on!' whispered Diana. 'Just leave it there! Grab your bag and slip out with the rest of us. She can't make you stay on! Serve her right!'

'All right,' decided Christine. 'Derek'll be waiting by now anyway.'

Thursday morning

'And when I returned, the letter was just where I'd left it, but there was no sign of Christine. I thought she'd popped out to the er . . . Anyway, at 5.45 there was still no sign of her – she'd obviously just left without saying anything. Really, it was most annoying. I was here myself until seven, finishing off Christine's letter – among other things. But I knew you wanted the letter to reach Harlow's by the week-end. I don't know how I shall carry on if my authority is continually being flouted by untrustworthy 17-year-olds!'

'Very well, Miss Parkstone,' sighed Mr Gulati, 'you'd better ask Christine to see me at ten o'clock . . .'

Case study activities

These activities develop NVQ competences and awareness in:

- *acting in accordance with rights and responsibilities of job role;*
- *contributing to achieving organisational goals and objectives;*
- *presenting a positive image of the organisation;*
- *working with and relating to others.*

In groups of three or four, discuss the following questions and set down agreed responses:

1 How perfect does a business letter have to be to be mailed to a customer?
2 Was Miss Parkstone exceeding her authority in pressuring Christine to stay on after office hours to reprocess the letter?
3 Placed in Christine's position, how would you have handled the situation – including Diana?
4 How do you think Mr Gulati should conduct his interview with Christine on Thursday morning?
5 To what extent should an office worker commit to working on after the end of the office day in order to finish an urgent job? Should management lay down guidelines,

including some form of reward, or is the whole matter best left to the individuals concerned?

■ *GROUP ACTIVITY*

Select trios (the people role-playing Mr Gulati and Miss Parkstone could be members of an adult group or teachers) to play Christine Dawson, Miss Parkstone and Mr Gulati.

First prepare your ground and then role-play the interview in Mr Gulati's office when the matter of the letter is discussed.

Arrange to audio or videotape the role-play sequences of each trio. (Each interview should last approximately 5–8 minutes)

Play back the recordings to the whole group and evaluate each interview for effective/ineffective handling of the situation.

■ *INDIVIDUAL ACTIVITIES*

These activities develop NVQ competences in communication in writing and receiving and responding to a variety of given information:

Memoranda

1 Compose a memorandum to be sent to all office staff outlining the circumstances in which staff may be requested to work up to an additional half-hour in cases of urgency at the end of a working day and the arrangements to be made to obtain an equivalent amount of 'time off in lieu' – staff are expected to make mutually acceptable arrangements with their supervisors.

Note: all after-hours working is to be undertaken on a voluntary basis.

2 Carry out your researches and then produce a memorandum from Miss Parkstone to all text processing staff on what erasing and correction techniques are acceptable in the production of letters and what are not. Include a paragraph explaining how finished letters are to be checked for acceptable standards of production.

Activities to develop competence and confidence

Letters

1 Sales enquiry letter

Your company, Delta Furnishing Limited, manufacturers of three-piece suites and armchairs etc is located at Delta House, Third Avenue, Middleton Industrial Estate, Middleton, Westshire MD4 6TG.

You work in the Sales Department as assistant to the Sales Manager. Each month, the Department sends out several hundred circular sales letters to customers about special offers. The name and address of each customer is held on a labels database. Thus, at will, up to 750 labels can be printed on continuous rolls of adhesive labels.

Recently the printer employed to do label print runs 'died of old age'. Now you need a replacement to print labels using a single column roll. Your manager, Mr Keith Simpson, doesn't want to spend a lot as his budget is tight, but he wants a reliable machine which can work with an Amstrad desktop PC using an MS-DOS operating system. The continuous roll labels you use are sprocket-driven, with perforations running down either edge of the backing paper.

Your customary suppliers are: Excel Office Equipment Limited, 22–24 Westwood Way, Middleton, Westshire, MD7 4RF.

Compose a suitable letter explaining what sort of labels printer you need and asking for sales literature and quotations on two or three makes.

2 Sales enquiry follow-up letter

First carry out your research locally and via office equipment magazines and then, as Miss Jane Foster, Sales Manager of Excel, produce a letter which responds suitably to the one you received as a result of a member of your class's efforts in Question 1 above.

3 Letter of complaint

Your company recently purchased a beverage dispensing machine from Semperflo Beverages Ltd of Highdown Industrial Estate, Birmingham BS3 4RA. Since its installation it has repeatedly broken down, and your company has no alternative means of providing for coffee-breaks etc.

Write a letter of complaint with a suitable letterhead employing the open punctuation, fully blocked format.

4 Letter of adjustment

As Sales Manager of Semperflo, you learned upon investigating the complaint outlined in Question 3 that the defect was caused by faulty installation by subcontractors whose services you no longer employ.

Write an appropriate letter of adjustment, with letterheading, to redress the complaint, providing recipient details as necessary, using the fully blocked format.

5 Final letter of collection

Account Customer: Fred The Butcher Limited
                     5–7 High Street
                     Hanlow
                     Wessex HW3 GF1

Branch Manager: Mr Jack Beresford

Account No. B16492

Goods Delivered and Dates:

Date:	Invoice No:	Description:	Cost:
3/3/9—	KJ49256	6 × blue/white striped aprons	£ 74.50
10/3/9—	KJ49421	16 laundered white smocks	£ 62.85
		March total:	£137.35
12/4/9—	KJ496537	12 packs greaseproof wrapping paper	£ 29.55
24/4/9—	KJ498679	16 laundered white smocks	£ 62.85
		April total:	£ 92.40
		Total due on 30 April 199—:	£229.75

Registered Head Office of Fred The Butcher Limited:
29 Shambles Lane, London EC4 5TH

You work as an accounts assistant at Food Services Limited, a company specialising in servicing the clothing and materials needs of a wide range of High Street food retailers. The Hanlow branch of Fred The Butchers Limited has failed to respond to three phone calls and two letters seeking to obtain payment for goods sold on account in March 199— to the branch totalling £137.75.

Your manager has asked you to draft a final letter to the appropriate person at the head office of Fred The Butcher in order to secure payment of the outstanding debt, as it is now June 14 199—. Note you ceased to supply the Hanlow branch with goods on April 30 199— because the March account had not been settled by the due date of 15 April 199—.

Produce an appropriate final letter of collection.

6 Job application letter

As you are studying at present, you find yourself in need of some extra cash to help pay your way. Yesterday the following advertisement appeared in the Sits Vac columns of the *Westerham Gazette*, your local newspaper:

WANTED!

**Man or Girl Friday to help on
Saturdays or Sundays!**

We urgently need energetic part-time office assistants to help process a rush of sales orders and maintain our effective office administration.

Ability to keyboard plus computer know-how an advantage. Good communication skills essential

Excellent hourly rates of pay plus productivity bonus.

Apply in writing to: Mrs Hazel Masters
Sales Manager
Gayglo Cosmetics Limited
PO Box 24
WESTERHAM
Surrey   WH2 8AK

Compose a suitable letter of application detailing your background and educational experience/qualifications etc. *Note:* you may include a curriculum vitae if you wish.

7 Advertising letter

You are the Secretary of your school/college's Student Association. A major project of the Association is to obtain funds to refurbish the Student Common Room with new chairs, tables, noticeboards and refreshment bar etc. At the last Committee Meeting, it was decided to mount a boot sale in three weeks' time on Saturday 21 May 199— from 10.00 am to 1.00 pm. Admission for car boot stall-holders was decided as £1.00 per car, but free for browsers and shoppers. Your Committee is going to run a Fast Food Bar selling snacks and drinks. Each person admitted will be given a free ticket for the Giant Raffle: first prize a case of claret, second prize two tickets to your local cinema, third prize a gift token worth £5.00 to spend at W H Smith Limited.

First, design a suitable letterhead for your Student Association. Then, on one side of A4 bond notepaper, produce a suitable letter to send to parents and friends of your school or college student body. Your aim is to make the boot sale appealing and to indicate clearly the 'what, where and when' details of the event. The letter is to be signed by the Chairperson of your Association, Miss Jean Richards.

■ *GROUP ACTIVITY*

Analysis of letter tone and style

In groups of three or four, study the pair of letters illustrated on pages 115 and 116 in which a complaint is made and remedied (or adjusted). Decide which particular words, phrases and sentence structures and use of register make the letters effective. Exchange your opinions then in a general class discussion.

6 Norfolk Gardens
Newtown
Midshire   NT4 6TG

23 March 199-

The Branch Manager
Domestilectrix Limited
5 High Street
Newtown
Midshire   NT2 3AJ

Dear Sir

On Thursday 21 March 199- I purchased a Johnson Glida electric iron from your branch, model number HT456341, receipt number 094 for £27.42. The iron immediately proved defective when I tried to use it later that day.

Before using the iron, I followed the instructions carefully about filling it with water and setting the temperature control correctly in order to iron my linen skirt.

However, as soon as I placed the iron on my skirt, it immediately scorched it, burning a hole in it and consequently ruining it. A replacement will cost at least £60.00. Apart from the damage to my skirt, I am now without an iron and so put to considerable inconvenience, since my job requires that I am smartly dressed at all times.

I should therefore be grateful if you would arrange for both the iron and the skirt to be inspected without delay and arrangements made to replace them as soon as possible.

Yours faithfully

Julie Dawson (Miss)

DOMESTILECTRIX LIMITED

5 High Street Newtown Midshire NT2 3AJ

Tel: Newtown 89764/6

Your ref
Our ref   TF/AD

24 March 199-

Miss J Dawson
6 Norfolk Gardens
NEWTOWN
Midshire   NT4 6TC

Dear Miss Dawson

JOHNSON GLIDA IRON COMPLAINT

I was extremely sorry to learn from your letter of 23 March 199-
of the trouble you have experienced with the Johnson Glida
electric iron you recently purchased from this branch.

I have made arrangements for our service engineer to contact you
as soon as possible, so that he may call to inspect the iron and
the damage done to your skirt.

Once the iron has been inspected and proved to be defective, he
will be pleased to supply and test a replacement for you, which
he will bring with him. Also, if you would kindly inform him of
the replacement cost of your skirt, I will make arrangements on
his return for a cheque to be sent to you for the full amount.

May I once again offer my sincere apologies for the inconvenience
which you have been caused and express the hope that the action
outlined above will prove to be to your satisfaction. The
Company values your custom and I hope this regrettable incident
will not prevent you from using my branch in the future.

Yours sincerely

T. Franklin

T Franklin
Branch Manager

Work experience attachment assignments

1 As a class, collect as many specimen business letterheads as possible printed on A4 notepaper. Display these in your base room and decide which features of logo design, use of colour, choice of font size and style etc have been most successfully combined to project the image of the organisation on the letterheads your class collected.

2 Through your workplace supervisor, make arrangements to see how a circular letter is mailmerged via word processing and obtain a specimen copy of the end product. Note which parts of the text are common to all dispatched letters and which parts personalised for each individual recipient.

3 Make arrangements to interview two or three senior secretaries and ask them for their tips and guidelines for producing effective letters.

4 Carry out similar interviews with two or three managers and find out what advice they can supply on techniques of letter composition.

5 On your return to your group, give a short presentation on your findings acquired for 3 and 4 above.

6 Arrange with your workplace supervisor to try out sending and receiving an Email message on the organisation's LAN or WAN system. Make notes of the process and take a hard copy of the message(s) you send and receive. Give a short presentation of the process to your group on return to your class.

7 Find out the circumstances in which paper memoranda are still employed in your workplace. Write a short account of your findings – with specimen memos if possible.

8 Research the ways in which letters are filed in your work place. Make notes of the system(s) employed and report back to your group.

9 If your organisation has a mailroom, make arrangements to spend some time there learning about the range of operations undertaken. Make notes and write a short account of your findings for display on your base room noticeboard.

Part 5

Why meetings are held in business and how they are administered

OVERVIEW

In Part 5 you will find out why meetings are used so frequently in business and public sector organisations. You will examine the purposes for which meetings are most suited, how they are conducted, who does what, and how their business and outcomes are recorded in particular formats as business documents. Having studied this Part carefully, you will be able to take part productively in a meeting and possess the skills to administer a meeting.

NVQ references
This Part covers the following BTEC First Diploma in Business And Finance and ABC/NWPSS competences:

BTEC First Diploma

Business Support Systems 1:
   Competences: 6 Drafting routine business communications, 17 Maintaining business relationships with other members of staff.

Administration:

   Competences: 7 Arranging meetings involving three or more people.

ABC/NWPSS

Level 2:
Unit 2   Communicating information
Unit 10 Creating and maintaining business relationships
Unit 19 Arranging travel and meetings
Unit 8   Servicing meetings: administering and taking notes

Level 3:
Unit 2   Communicating information
Unit 10 Creating and maintaining business relationships
Unit 19 Arranging travel and meetings
Unit 8   Servicing meetings: administering and taking notes

WHY MEETINGS ARE USED IN BUSINESS

A simple definition of a meeting is: 'The coming together of two or more people sharing a common aim or goal to exchange information and views or to reach decisions which they accept as binding upon them.'

This definition embraces three basic elements of an effective meeting:

SHARED GOALS

  1 Its participants must start from a common interest or shared position (even if disagreement follows). They must share an interest in reaching common goals or objectives. In other words, there must be some shared bond which links their interest in and contributions to the meeting.

MEANS OF MAKING DECISIONS

  2 Most meetings aim to reach a decision after a period of discussion on a given topic. Sometimes such a decision emerges as a 'sensed' majority view, usually called a 'consensus decision'. But sometimes, especially in formal meetings, votes

are called for in order to arrive at a decision.

MEANS OF
EXCHANGING
VIEWS AND
IDEAS

3 Sometimes, however, meetings are called in organisations just to enable participants to update each other on developments, to exchange ideas or views on a topic of common interest, or to receive information, instructions or briefings on, for example, new company policies or products.

The legal aspect

Another reason why meetings are called regularly in business or the public service is the legal requirement. Over the past one hundred years a number of Acts of Parliament – Companies Acts – have been introduced to protect various interested parties connected with companies – customers, suppliers, shareholders, creditors and so on. So company directors – the people with the responsibility for seeing that the firm is run on legal lines – are charged with ensuring that directors' meetings, annual meetings of shareholders, extraordinary meetings (to discuss an important development), creditors' meetings (to discuss how people owed money by the company may be paid off) etc are properly advertised in advance, conducted according to legal requirements and held within given deadlines. By the same token, meetings held in local or central government organisations must comply with similar legal requirements. County Council meetings, for example follow a set of rules called 'Standing Orders', and further rules exist for admitting the general public to certain types of meeting.

Thus the legal aspect requiring meetings to be held ensures:

1 that interested parties know what is going on and know when to attend a meeting;
2 that informatiion and views communicated in meetings are faithfully recorded and made available to those people (all directors, all shareholders, the local community etc) with a right to know;
3 that business is conducted according to company or public sector law, without 'convenient' omissions, shortcuts or concealments occurring.

The human aspect

Underpinning the calling of all meetings in organisations is undoubtedly the human aspect. Why, for instance, should a company go to the trouble, time and cost of bringing together, say, ten regional directors from all over the UK to a meeting in Birmingham to discuss a worrying decline in sales when each could be reached promptly by telephone or fax? Why should a District Council call a public meeting to discuss the building of a large new housing estate when it could simply go ahead on the basis of its given authority?

In the first example, the company's senior management team feels that the cost of bringing its regional directors together is justified because of the invaluable *face-to-face communication* which will take place. Direct person-to-person discussion often produces a 'chemistry' which leads to good decision-making and which prompts those participating to stick together and unite as a group in the face of a challenge.

In the second example, the District Councillors decide to involve and consult the people likely to be affected by the building of the housing estate. In this way, they are more likely to keep their electorate's goodwill and to 'take people with them', rather than alienating them or riding roughshod over them simply by using the powers they possess.

Thus two powerful reasons for meetings being used in both private and public sector organisations are as follows:

▶ Face-to-face, direct communication affects participants much more strongly than phone calls, faxes, letters, Email or memos.
▶ Open meetings involving the public or interested parties are seen as a valuable way of creating good public relations, retaining goodwill or influencing public opinion.

TYPES OF MEETING IN THE PRIVATE AND PUBLIC SECTORS

The following checklist illustrates the major types of meeting used in business and public organisations to help them reach their desired goals.

Private sector

Shareholders' meetings

These are usually called annually to receive and accept the annual report of the company's directors, to elect/re-elect them and vote on any changes to company procedures.

Creditors'/receiver's meetings

When a company becomes bankrupt or is liquidated (wound up after debts have been paid off) meetings have to be called to advise those to whom the company owes money; an official receiver is appointed to wind up a failed company's affairs and supervise who gets what of any money still left.

Extraordinary meetings

Sometimes (say when a company wishes to fight being taken over by another) extraordinary meetings of shareholders may be called by its directors to seek to hold their loyalty etc; or a meeting may be called to seek authority to undertake a new venture.

Internal company meetings

Companies frequently call meetings of its managers, supervisors, trade union representatives, specific work-force members etc in order to:

plan, consult, inform, brief, motivate, brainstorm, problem-solve etc.

Such meetings may be formal with written records being made, or quite informal – sometimes resulting from an unplanned meeting occurring.

Public sector

Public enquiries

The government sometimes sets up public enquiries (after disasters or accidents) to establish what went wrong and what may be done to avoid similar future occurrences. Such meetings are often presided over by judges.

Public meetings

Sometimes such public meetings are held when there is a controversy, say, over the route of a proposed motorway, and government inspectors are appointed to chair the proceedings.

County/District Council meetings

The elected councillors (or members as they are also called) conduct the business of the council through general meetings and committee meetings at regular intervals.

Parish council meetings

In a similar way, parish councillors hold regular meetings in village or community halls to consider the implications of very local matters, advising their district or county councillor.

Internal officers' meetings

Just as in business, the officers of local government and managers of the Civil Service hold regular meetings to progress the policies of their respective elected members.

Committee meetings and voluntary organisations

The British must be lovers of meetings, since it is the committee meeting which acts as the driving force in countless clubs, and associations up and down the country. Indeed, the committee meeting, whether in private, public or voluntary sector organisations, forms the backbone of the more formal type of meeting where written notices of forthcoming meetings are sent in advance to members, where agendas listing items for discussion are drawn up and circulated, and where minutes are produced which summarise the main points of debate and discussion and record precisely what action to be taken was agreed upon.

THE ROLES AND DUTIES OF THE OFFICERS OF A TYPICAL COMMITTEE

Committees are created in many types of organisation – company, council, club or association – to help achieve organisational goals through meeting to discuss topics of importance and to agree upon decisions to be carried out.

Over many years committees have developed and extended particular roles and duties for the members or officers who form them. These duties, along with other rules and procedures which all the organisation's members agree to accept and observe are set down in written form in a constitution or rule book. (In local government these rules are usually referred to as Standing Orders). The following section sets down the main responsibilities of each committee officer. Make sure you are fully familiar with each role, for you may be asked to serve on a committee – at school, college, work or social club – sooner than you think!

The chairman

Essentially the chairman's role is to coordinate the work of the committee, to act as its leader and to ensure that it carries out its business according to the constitution or established rules.

Between meetings the chairman works with the secretary to carry forward the work of the committee, making sure that decisions agreed to at the last meeting are in fact carried out. He or she also uses the time to consult with other members of the organisation and interested external contacts about matters of common interest.

Arising from work in progress and matters of fresh importance, the chairman and secretary work together to produce an agenda for the next meeting. Items for inclusion in this agenda may also be put forward by committee members. Some committees are run formally in this regard and require such items to be sent in writing (sometimes in a specific format – *see* below – to reach the secretary within a given deadline in advance of the meeting.)

During meetings the chairman has a number of important tasks to carry out. First, he must check whether the meeting is quorate. This means whether a sufficient number of the committee (usually two-thirds) are present. If they are, then 'a quorum' exists. If not, then the committee is 'inquorate'. In this case the meeting is called off and a fresh one called. Next, the chairman checks to see who is absent and who present. Names in both categories are recorded by the secretary.

The chairman then asks members to confirm whether the minutes of the last meeting are accurate and as such acceptable by the committee. At this

Fig. 5.1 Committee structure

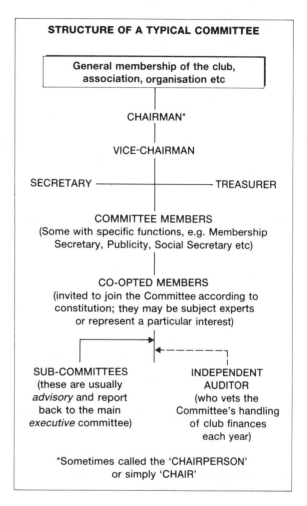

stage members may discuss any amendments arising from omissions or inaccuracies but are not empowered to reopen discussions or change decisions.

Following on, the chairman takes the committee through any matters arising from the last minutes. Here there may be some updating or reporting back by members to the committee on events or actions occurring since the last meeting.

The chairman then presides over each item of business – the actual 'meat' of the meeting which committee members have come to discuss. In some committees each item of business is voted upon after discussion, but in others, the chairman gauges 'the feeling of the meeting', in other words confirms to the committee the decision to which a majority has agreed by nodding of heads. If he gets this wrong, the committee will quickly signal their disagreement. Such an informal 'consensus' approach has the advantage of not openly dividing the committee. Where votes are taken, the chairman usually has a casting vote. This means he has two votes and uses the second only if the committee are deadlocked. Most chairmen prefer not to vote at all unless absolutely necessary. Such a preference helps them maintain a fair impartiality towards committee members.

During the process of discussion the chairman takes pains to ensure that:

▶ each member has an opportunity to contribute;
▶ no single member 'hogs the floor';
▶ tempers do not become frayed; no one is allowed to doze or day-dream;
▶ the rules are not ignored or abused by 'steamrollering' members;
▶ where guidance is needed or the authority of the constitution he is able to supply it fairly;
▶ accurate records are kept; to this end he may repeat some wording carefully, or summarise a complex argument.

Towards the end of the meeting the chairman will ask members if they have 'any other business' to bring forward. This item allows each member to draw to the committee's attention any matter of personal interest. Note, however, that the time allowed for discussion is usually brief. If the matter is considered important, it is usually included in the agenda of the next meeting.

Qualities of the chairman

As you can see, the role of a chairman, especially if the committee is a lively one, is very demanding. In particular, a chairman needs to possess these qualities:

patience ■ sense of fairness ■ relaxed authority ■ expert knowledge of the rules ■ interpersonal skills ■ quick-wittedness ■ ability to weigh arguments ■ ability to summarise ■ self-confidence and decisiveness ■ sense of humour

The role of the secretary

It falls to the secretary of a committee to carry out its administration effectively. So don't ever accept such a role unless you're prepared to work hard!

To compensate, however, the secretary is at the very centre of all that goes on. Chief among the secretary's tasks are:

▶ to issue notices and agendas to members for forthcoming meetings;
▶ to answer incoming letters and to write any requested by the committee;
▶ to draw up a chairman's agenda for the next meeting; this mirrors that sent to members, but also includes helpful background details and memory-joggers etc, which the secretary thinks will aid the chairman during the meeting;
▶ to collect from members any items for the agenda and to ensure their wording conforms to procedure;
▶ to make sure the meetings room is properly set up with stationery, pens, refreshments etc, and is well lit, ventilated and heated;
▶ to ensure spare copies of agendas, previous minutes and any papers to be tabled (put before the meeting) are to hand;
▶ to take down the minutes of the meeting in note form and later to produce an accurate set of minutes in the format used by the committee;
▶ to assist the chairman and offer support if needed during the meeting;
▶ to have available sets of previous minutes and constitution or rules for reference if asked.

In many ways the secretary acts as the committee's database of information as well as its memory – and sometimes as its conscience! The result of personally undertaking the bulk of the administration results in the secretary having the work of the committee at his or her fingertips. For this reason in many committees the role of secretary is regarded as a stepping-stone to that of chairman.

The role of the treasurer

The committee treasurer is responsible for maintaining accurate records of the financial transactions of the committee. This role requires the treasurer to:

▶ keep a record of cheques written and statements etc received from the club's bank;

▶ store safely (for an auditor to examine) any bills, invoices or statements received for purchases made;

▶ record any petty cash transactions.

▶ keep records of any monies owed to the committee by its debtors;

▶ and to record any monies the committee owes to its creditors.

During the course of the club's financial year the treasurer will be required to report to the committee upon its financial activities and, in particular to supply up-to-date balances of the club's income and expenditure. As a result of taking the club's financial pulse at regular intervals, the treasurer is usually in a position to either 'bless or damn' any project the committee wishes to undertake which involves its money:

> 'A good idea, chairman, but simply not on the cards financially, I'm afraid . . .'

Towards each year end, the treasurer will pass over the accumulated financial records to an auditor for vetting. The auditor may be a friendly accountant or bank manager who does the job for nothing, or may be an officially appointed firm of chartered accountants, where large sums of money are involved.

Reports to the Annual General Meeting

Both the chairman and the treasurer report back formally to assembled members at the club's Annual General Meeting. The chairman summarises the year's activities and outcomes, and the treasurer produces the audited accounts for the year and takes the meeting through them.

Other committee members

The vice-chairman

This role is undertaken by a senior committee member and chiefly requires an ability to substitute as chairman at short notice if the chairman is unable to attend.

Membership secretary

A role specifically given over to controlling applications for membership and collection of subscriptions.

Publicity secretary

A role which promotes the club by the issue of press releases, photographs and reports to the press, local TV or radio etc.

Social secretary

Responsible for putting on dances, parties, fêtes, children's events etc for the membership.

Minutes secretary

Some organisations have a member whose sole job it is to take down and produce the minutes of meetings.

Note: Other specific roles and duties may be created at will by the committee for any individual member to undertake.

SPECIALIST TERMS USED BY COMMITTEES

The following list includes some of the principal terms used in committee meetings. This list is by no means exhaustive, however, and you should use it as a basis for your own, more extensive check-list of important technical terms relating to meetings.

Ad hoc from Latin, meaning 'for the purpose of', as for example, when a sub-committee is set up to organise a works outing.

Adjourn to hold a meeting over until a later date.

Advisory providing advice or suggestion, not taking action.

Agenda a schedule of items drawn up for discussion at a meeting.

AGM Annual General Meeting; all members are usually eligible to attend.

Apologies excuses given in advance for inability to attend a meeting.

Articles of Association rules required by Company Law which govern a company's activities.

Bye-laws rules regulating an organisation's activities.

Chairman leader or person given authority to conduct a meeting.

Chairman's Agenda based upon the committee agenda, but containing explanatory notes.

Collective responsibility a convention by which all committee members agree to abide by a majority decision.

Committee a group of people usually elected or appointed who meet to conduct agreed business and report to a senior body.

Consensus agreement by general consent, no formal vote being taken.

Constitution set of rules governing activities of voluntary bodies.

Convene to call a meeting.

Executive having the power to act upon taken decisions.

Extraordinary meeting a meeting called for all members to discuss a serious issue affecting all is called an Extraordinary General Meeting; otherwise a non-routine meeting called for a specific purpose.

Ex officio given powers or rights by reason of office. For example a trades union convener may be an ex officio member of a works council.

Honorary post a duty performed without payment – Honorary Secretary.

Information, point of the drawing of attention in a meeting to a relevant item of fact.

Lobbying a practice of seeking members' support before a meeting.

Minutes the written record of a meeting; resolution minutes record only decisions reached, while narrative minutes provide a record of the decision-making process.

Motion the name given to a 'proposal' when it is being discussed at a meeting.

Mover one who speaks on behalf of a motion.

Nem. con. from Latin, literally, 'no one speaking against'.

Opposer one who speaks against a motion.

Order, point of the drawing of attention to a breach of rules or procedures.

Other business either items left over from a previous meeting, or items discussed after the main business of a meeting.

Proposal the name given to a submitted item for discussion (usually written) before a meeting takes place.

Proxy literally, 'on behalf of another person' – 'a proxy vote'.

Resolution the name given to a 'motion' which has been passed or carried; used after the decision has been reached.

Secretary committee official responsible for the internal and external administration of a committee.

Secret ballot a system of voting in secret.

Sine die from Latin, literally, 'without a day', that is to say indefinitely, e.g. 'adjourned sine die'.

Standing committee a committee which has an indefinite term of office.

Seconder one who supports the 'proposer' of a motion or proposal by 'seconding' it.

Treasurer committee official responsible for its financial records and transactions.

Unanimous all being in favour.

Vote, casting when two sides are deadlocked a chairman may record a second or 'casting vote' to ensure a decision is made.

HOW TO PRODUCE THE DOCUMENTS USED IN MEETINGS

Each document used to administer meetings has a very specific job to do. As a result, its format and structure are unique and need to be learned – particularly as the people who take part in meetings expect such documents to possess a distinct and recognisable appearance and to communicate information according to sets of established rules.

Fortunately, there are only a few documents to master:

The notice

Simply a means of conveying the day, date, time and location of a forthcoming meeting, with sometimes an invitation to participants to suggest items for inclusion in the agenda.

The agenda (for participants)

Essentially a checklist, prepared in a careful sequence of items of business, plus standard inputs to link successive meetings together.

The Chairman's Agenda

Basically the same agenda as that produced for participants, but with added confidential notes for the chairman of background detail, reminders, suggestions etc which the secretary hopes will help the chairman to run the meeting successfully.

Motions and proposals

In some formal meetings items of business (sometimes put forward by committee members) are set out in a wording which invites the response of 'yes' or 'no' – so that a vote may be taken; the 'That . . . be . . .' construction is normally employed:

That club subscriptions be increased to £15.00 annually with effect from 1 January 199—.

Such items have to be proposed and seconded by named members. Prior to the meeting they tend to be called 'proposals'; during the meeting the chairman may refer to 'the motion before us' and, if agreed upon, after the meeting the proposal is termed 'a resolution'.

Minutes

The decisions reached by a committee or group in a meeting are usually recorded by the secretary in a kind of summary referred to as the minutes of the meeting.

There are three main ways of producing such minutes:

Narrative minutes

So called because they 'narrate' or tell the story of the meeting by briefly summarising who said what during the discussion preceding the making of the decision about a given item of business. Such minutes are written in the third person – 'The Treasurer reported . . .', 'Mrs Jones asked whether . . .' and use a construction called reported speech (*see* page 133).

The plus side of narrative minutes is that they provide an excellent insight into the various opinions and views which led to a particular decision being made; the minus side is that narrative minutes are time-consuming to produce and seldom manage to please everyone reported upon!

Resolution minutes

This being so, some committees – particularly those in the form of boards of company directors – prefer minutes which only record the outcomes reached, using a standardised sentence format:

It was resolved that **the new colour copier be launched at the next Business Equipment Exhibition in Birmingham on 3 April 199—.**

The advantage here is that none of the arguments or disagreements which may have preceded the decision are recorded – so the image of the board remains undented. The disadvantage is that no one ever knows whose judgements in the long term are sound and whose are not. For this reason, some managing directors opt for narrative minutes.

Action minutes

This form of minutes normally follows that for narrative minutes with an added feature of a right-hand column headed '**Action By:**' Thus whenever an action is agreed upon, a named member of the committee or meeting group is chosen (by the chairman) to carry it out:

	ACTION BY:
It was decided to write to the manager of the Dog & Duck to book the skittle alley for the 5th February 199— from 7.30 pm	Jean White Social Sec.

Action minutes work very well in a company or keen voluntary committee since there is no doubt subsequently about who was supposed to take action on what. In some voluntary organisations, however, participating members may feel they are being driven along too hard, and 'wooed too little', and stop attending meetings as a result.

Other documents

Naturally, different types of meeting may from time to time circulate all kinds of documents at meetings – maps, plans, photographs, reports and letters etc.

A common practice – especially when time has run out and prevented a prior circulation – is to 'table' a document at the meeting, i.e. put it on the table at each member's place. In this instance most committee procedures permit the document to be received and read and sometimes to be discussed, but not to become the source of any decision, simply because some might feel it was sprung on them without any opportunity for prior reflection or discussion.

Letters to and from the committee, termed collectively correspondence, are the most common form of other document handled by committees. They may either be photocopied and circulated to members or simply read out by the chairman or secretary in whole or part. Some committees include a standard item of business called 'Correspondence' in their agendas.

Set out below are specimens of each of the documents referred to in the above section, together with guidelines on how to produce them in accordance with current conventions. Take care to study each specimen thoroughly, for whether you become a committee member or its secretary, an informed knowledge of the rules governing the production of meetings documents will help you carry out your role more expertly and confidently.

NOTICES USED TO CALL MEETINGS

1 The preprinted postcard

To save time and effort, many voluntary clubs use preprinted postcards to call meetings. The Honorary Secretary needs only to enter the day, time and location, plus the latest date by which agenda items must be received.

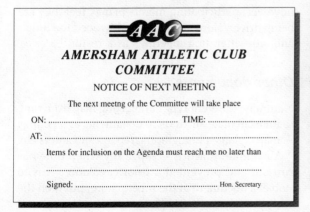

2 The individually typed letter (A4 or A5)

Where the participants enjoy a high status, such as company directors, county councillors or college governors etc, each may receive an individually typed letter of invitation – or if the letter is photocopied, it will be 'topped and tailed' by the MD in his handwriting: 'Dear Sir Geoffrey . . . Yours sincerely'.

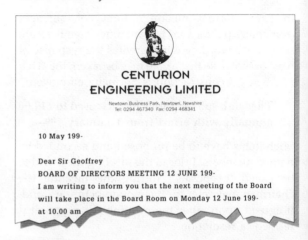

3 The circulated memorandum or Email notice

In many organisations, the electronically mailed memo – sent simultaneously to specified staff's PC terminals – is used informally to call meetings. *Note:* Many LAN systems have electronic diary software able to scan each participant's diary and select the first date and time available to all!

SPECIMEN MEETINGS AGENDA FOR PARTICIPANTS

A4 or A5 bond stationery with either pre-printed or emboldened typescript title of committee.

The day, date, time and location of the next meeting is set out clearly as the first entry to act as a follow-up reminder of the previously dispatched notice.
[Note: to save expense, some secretaries combine the notice and agenda in a single mailed document as shown here.]

(1,2,3) Items 1, 2 and 3 traditionally occur in the order shown. The secretary notes those present and gives the apologies of those unable to attend (previously notified to the secretary). Once the minutes of the last meeting are approved, the Chairman signs and dates them and the secretary files them in sequence.

(4) Some committees which regularly receive correspondence position the item immediately before the main business of the meeting.

(5) A formal proposal. Note the construction of the wording and the identification of proposer and seconder.

(5-8) Items 5-8 represent the main business of the meeting. Note: effective secretaries write each agenda item in such a way that the matter to be discussed is perfectly clear to members; in this way they know what to expect and prepare for. Thus '7 Jean Saunder's Report' would prove a poor agenda item title.

(9) Members are given a (restricted and brief) opportunity to bring up any item of personal interest.

(10) Members consult diaries to decide upon a convenient date for the next meeting.
Note that as a courtesy all recipients of an agenda are informed as to its total circulation.

AJAX ENGINEERING COMPANY LIMITED

STAFF SOCIAL CLUB COMMITTEE

The next meeting of the Social Club Committee will take place on Tuesday 21 February 199- at 5.00 pm in the Training Suite.

AGENDA

1   Apologies for absence

2   Minutes of the meeting of 19 January 199-

3   Matters arising from the minutes

4   Correspondence: Letter from the Managing Director confirming the £10,000 donation towards refurbishing the Social Club.

5   Proposal:

       That retiring members of company staff and their spouses be given free life membership of the Social Club.

            Proposer: Pamela Everett
            Seconder: Jack Carter

6   Repairs needed to Sports Ground Clubhouse after recent storm damage.

7   Report on progress of the Annual Theatre Visit from Jean Saunders, Chairman, Working Party.

8   Updating on Social Club funds: Angela Roberts, Club Treasurer.
     Financial report to be tabled.

9   Any other business.

10   Date of next meeting.

Circulation: Chairman, Secretary, Treasurer, Committee Members.

Information Copies: Managing Director, Personnel Director.

Document format

Note the consecutive number of items (some agendas and minutes roll these forward in a single progression, i.e. 1–151, etc over a series of meetings). Also, entries are commonly now set as sentences. Initial capitals Like: *Apologies For Absence* are falling out of use. Note also the spacing between entries for easy reading and use of emboldening for the heading.

SPECIMEN EXTRACT OF CHAIRMAN'S AGENDA

A4 or A5 headed notepaper used, or emboldened typescript employed for title.

Day, date, time and location set out clearly as a reminder to Chairman.

CHAIRMAN'S NOTES
Note that some 6-8 cm should be allocated to a vertical column of space into which the Chairman's own handwritten notes may be entered.

SPACE BELOW EACH AGENDA ITEM FOR SECRETARY'S NOTES
A Chairman's Agenda is set out with the secretary's confidential and supportive notes shown clearly beneath each agenda item.

TONE OF SECRETARY'S NOTES
Generally the tone of the secretary's notes is informal without becoming colloquial or over-familiar.

AJAX ENGINEERING COMPANY LIMITED

STAFF SOCIAL CLUB COMMITTEE

CHAIRMAN'S AGENDA

For the Committee Meeting to take place on Tuesday 21 February 199- in the Training Suite at 5.00 pm

CHAIRMAN'S NOTES

1   Apologies for absence.

Susan Barnes' husband rang to say that she is progressing well after her car accident - he hopes she'll be out of hospital by middle of March, depending on tests, etc.

(Remember: Send 'Get Well' card)

Derek Lawson wrote to say he will be away on a Training Course in Leeds.

2   Minutes of the last meeting.

3   Matters arising from the minutes.

You will remember that Susan Barnes was involved with discussions with Personnel Dept regarding the creche; I understand she was due to report back that the creche installation proposal was accepted in principle - good for recruitment, etc.

Report back for Susan Barnes

4   Correspondence

Only letter this month is from MD. This is the largest donation I can remember the Club receiving.

Don't forget ask Secreta... to write 'Than... you' letter ... MD

Guidelines on information to include in a Chairman's Agenda

Committee chairmen appreciate agendas which 'flag up' previous decisions acting as precedents, reminders of any previous heated or hurt feelings over a topic which has resurfaced, 'real' explanations of situations which have to be handled delicately or diplomatically at the meeting, plus any other useful pointers on how a member may react; last-minute updates or information relevant to an item; hints on how to handle a particular item or member: 'Joe likes a pat on the back each year for organising the theatre outing' etc.

Document format

Note the blank space (a vertical right-hand column) left for the chairman's own personal notes and reminders. Note also the space between each agenda item for the secretary's guidance notes and prompts.

SPECIMEN EXTRACT OF NARRATIVE MINUTES

Commonly produced on A4 bond paper either with preprinted heading or emboldened typescript for major title.

The first entry confirms the day, date, location, time and type of meeting to which the minutes refer.

It is customary to list (first in sequence of status: Chairman, Vice-chairman, Secretary, Treasurer, then in alphabetical order the names and titles of those present.

(1) The names of those who have tendered apologies for absence from the meeting are listed (Note: this is an essential courtesy all committee members should observe.)

(2) Note that procedure for item 2 'Minutes of the last meeting' permits members to propose amendments only in terms of accuracy or omission. Note the customary way of reporting the signing of these minutes.

(3) The 'Matters arising from the minutes' item usually provides opportunities for the committee to be updated and informed of developments since the previous meeting concerning items discussed.

(4) Note the structure of reported speech used to convey the meeting's response to the MD's letter.

AJAX ENGINEERING COMPANY LIMITED

STAFF SOCIAL CLUB COMMITTEE

Minutes of the Committee Meeting held on Tuesday 21 February 199- in the Company's Training Suite

The Meeting commenced at 5.00 pm

MINUTES

Present: Shirley Johnson, Chairman, Paul West, Secretary, Angela Roberts, Treasurer, Tariq Aziz, Jack Carter, Pamela Everett, Christopher Knight, Jean Saunders, Winston Richards.

1   **Apologies for absence.**

Apologies for absence were received from Susan Barnes and Derek Lawson.

2   **Minutes of the meeting of 19 January 199-.**

Winston Richards drew the meeting's attention to Item 5: Visit to Mary Rose Exhibition. He affirmed that he had said that criticism of the planning of the visit had been 'ungracious', and not, as minuted, 'ungrateful'. The Chairman approved this amendment of the minutes which she then signed as a true record of the meeting of 19 January 199-.

3   **Matters arising from the minutes.**

Item 4: Installation of Creche.

The Chairman reported on Susan Barnes' behalf on the developments concerning the installation of a creche at the Company's South Road site, which had been accepted in principle by the board of directors as a means of aiding recruitment of both office and shop floor personnel.

4   **Correspondence: letter from Managing Director confirming £10,000 donation to Social Club.**

The Chairman read the Managing Director's letter to the Committee, who were extremely pleased to learn the extent of the company's generous donation. All agreed that the sum would form an excellent basis for the fund-raising series of events being planned to finance the renovation of the Social Club. Angela Roberts agreed to draft a letter of thanks for the Chairman's signature.

(5) The way of minuting a proposal is to set it out in full (as in the agenda format) and then to report on how it was received, using reported speech. The outcome of a proposal must always be included, e.g. 'The committee agreed unanimously to support Miss Everett's motion'.

5   Proposal:

That retiring members of company staff and their spouses be given free life membership of the Social Club.

> Proposer: Pamela Everett
> Seconder: Jack Carter

In proposing her motion, Pamela Everett emphasised the increasing funds upon which the Social Club could rely and that it could well afford to provide life membership gratis to retired company staff. She added that many had given lifetimes of service to both the Company and the Club.

(9) Note the brevity of the reports upon member's 'other business'.

9   Any other business

Christopher Knight asked whether there had been any progress in getting the fruit machine repaired, as its income was very useful. The Secretary reported that Ace Games Limited had gone out of business and efforts were being made to reallocate a service contract.

The Secretary reported that the bar extension licence had been granted for the forthcoming Forties Fancy Dress Dance.

(10) The date, time and location are clearly shown as an early reminder. Note the use of the word 'scheduled', used because future events may require a change of date, etc.

It is customary to provide spaces for the Chairman to sign and date the minutes at the subsequent meeting of the committee.

10   Date of next meeting

The next meeting was scheduled to take place on Tuesday 22 March 199- at 5.00 pm in the Training Suite.

Signed: Chairman
Date:

SPECIMEN ANNUAL GENERAL MEETING AGENDA

Annual General Meeting agendas are sent to all club/associaton/organisation members.

A4 or A5 bond stationery employed, depending on the number of agenda items. Note: if in doubt, use A4 and space generously.

Name of organisation prominently displayed either on printed headed note-paper or in emboldened upper-case typescript.

Description of meeting centred in emboldened upper-case typescript. Date, time and location of the meeting are clearly displayed.

AGENDA ITEMS 1-7

(1) The customary opportunity to report on tendered apologies from those unable to attend.

(2) Note: the meeting referred to here is not the last committee meeting but the *AGM held 12 months previously.*

(3) There may be updates on one or two items discussed at the last AGM.

(4) The Chairman delivers a summary report to the meeting of the major events, activities and developments, etc. of the year just ended.

(5) The Treasurer provides a balance sheet/financial report of the organisation's activities over the year. Usually a set of audited accounts is distributed to members - either in advance, or at the meeting.

(6) In accordance with the organisation's 'standing orders', constitution or articles of association, several (by rotation) or all the officers are either re-elected or new, incoming officers voted into post.

(7) Any number of additional business items may be added. This example shows that of a presentation to the outgoing chairman.

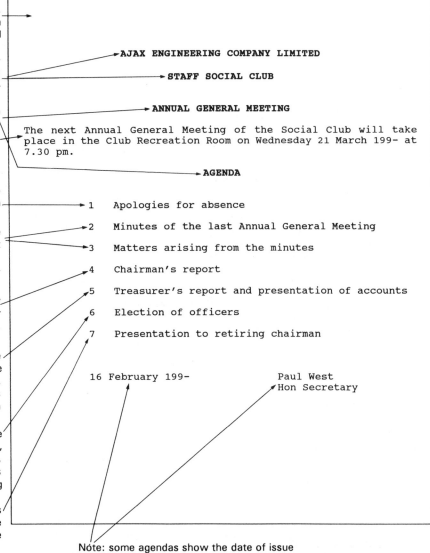

AJAX ENGINEERING COMPANY LIMITED

STAFF SOCIAL CLUB

ANNUAL GENERAL MEETING

The next Annual General Meeting of the Social Club will take place in the Club Recreation Room on Wednesday 21 March 199- at 7.30 pm.

AGENDA

1   Apologies for absence

2   Minutes of the last Annual General Meeting

3   Matters arising from the minutes

4   Chairman's report

5   Treasurer's report and presentation of accounts

6   Election of officers

7   Presentation to retiring chairman

16 February 199-   Paul West
                                         Hon Secretary

Note: some agendas show the date of issue and the originator of the agenda.

SPECIMEN AGENDA OF AN EXTRAORDINARY GENERAL MEETING

AGENDA ITEMS

Note the omission of 'Minutes of the last meeting' and 'Matters arising from the minutes'. This is because there are none - EGMs are specially called 'one-off' meetings.

(2) Proposal
While no fixed rules apply to the wording of agendas, where matters of grave importance are concerned, and to give officers a powerful vote of confidence, the main (and perhaps only) item of business is expressed as a formal proposal and a vote formally taken.

(3) Any other business
This item is sometimes omitted from EGM agendas to avoid further, protracted discussion on the main business item.

BULSBERRY CRICKET CLUB

EXTRAORDINARY GENERAL MEETING

An Extraordinary Meeting of the Bulsberry Cricket Club has been called for Friday 12 April 199- at 7.30 pm in the Clubhouse.

AGENDA

1   Apologies for absence

2   Proposal:

That the Club takes all legal action available to it to resist the placing of a compulsory purchase order on the Club's sports field, arising from the M32 extension route now being put forward by the Ministry of Transport.

Proposer: Richard Knight
Chairman

Seconder: Kim Barton
Vice Chairman

3   Any other business

3 April 1991

David West
Hon Secretary

ANNUAL AND EXTRAORDINARY GENERAL MEETINGS IN BUSINESS

It is worth noting that both the AGM and EGM of sports and social clubs have their counterparts in business. Here shareholders have a similar role to club members, except that they have on occasion far more power. They may, for example, vote to oust a managing director at a company's AGM if it is felt that he or she has failed the company badly. By the same token, an Extraordinary Meeting of Shareholders may be called if a company is threatened, for instance, with a hostile take-over by another, and the board wishes to make its case to its shareholders for resisting an offer to buy their shares at what is considered too low a price.

HOW TO WRITE MINUTES IN REPORTED SPEECH

Earlier in this Part the term 'reported speech' was referred to as the accepted means of composing the minutes of a meeting.

The term simply means that what was said at the meeting has been reported upon by the secretary by setting down a summarised account of it.

The main features of reported speech

Once you have fully familiarised yourself with the main features of reported speech, writing minutes becomes much simpler because of the straightforward rules you can apply:

1 All first and second persons singular or plural become third person

Person		
	Singular	Plural
1st	I	we
2nd	you	you
3rd	he, she	they

Thus if someone actually says in a meeting to a female member committee member:

. . . 'I hope that you will change your mind!'

in reported speech this would become:

. . . He hoped that she would change her mind.

Note: 'I' has become 'he' and 'you' has become 'she'.

Clarity factor In changing first and second persons singular or plural to third persons, the minutes secretary may quickly confuse a reader who was not at the meeting. And so it may be necessary for the minutes secretary to insert a title or name for 'he' or 'she' etc to make quite clear who said what to whom:

The Chairman hoped that Miss Jenkins would change her mind.

or:

Miss Jenkins considered that both the proposer and the seconder of the motion before the meeting had entirely missed the point . . .

2 The tenses of the verbs used by speakers 'go one further back'

You may already have noticed in the above example that 'I hope' – present simple tense – has become in reported speech 'he hoped' – past simple tense.

Similarly, Miss Jenkins actually said at the meeting

'I consider that both the proposer and seconder have entirely missed the point . . .'

and the perfect simple tense of the direct speech 'have missed' is pushed one further back in reported speech to become 'had missed' in the past perfect tense.

The basic reason for changing tenses of the verb in this way is the result of the passage of time. During the meeting the speakers are talking 'now', in the present. But the secretary reports sometime later and the 'now' of the meeting becomes the 'then' of the past.

The following table shows you how the main tenses of the verb change from direct speech (that shown between the inverted commas '   ') and its reported version (no inverted commas used):

Direct speech	Reported speech
I go	He said he . . . went
I am going	he was going
I went	he had gone, he went
I was going	he had been going
I have gone	he had gone
I have been going	he had been going
I had gone	he had gone
I shall go	he would go
I shall be going	he would be going
I shall have gone	he would have gone

Note: When the future tense is used in direct speech (I shall) this becomes a conditional tense in reported speech: (he said that he would). The reason for this is that the conditional tense conveys the intention to do something which lies in the future at the time of speaking:

'I shall go to Bristol tomorrow.'

He said he would go to Bristol the following day.

But in writing the minutes, the secretary has no way of confirming whether 'he' did or didn't go!

3 The distancing effect

As the secretary is composing the minutes at a later point in time and in a place remote from the Committee Room, a number of key words are changed to reflect this, as the examples below illustrate:

this becomes **that**

these becomes **those**

now becomes **then**

here becomes **there**

today becomes **on that day**

tomorrow becomes **on the following day**

Example

Direct speech

'I think **this** proposal deserves the close attention of everyone **here** today. I shall be speaking to the staff **tomorrow** and shall convey to them these suggestions on which you have all agreed.'

Reported speech

He thought **that** proposal deserved the close attention of everyone **there that day**. He would be speaking to the staff **on the following day** and would convey to them **those** suggestions upon which all present had agreed.

Questions in reported speech

In direct speech, questions are formed by changing the word order of a statement [Anyone can assure me] and adding a question-mark at the end of the sentence. Also, 'questioning' words like 'asked' or 'enquired' are used to show a question is being asked:

'Can anyone assure me that enough tickets will be sold to cover the cost of this expensive band?' asked the Treasurer.

In reported speech such questions are turned back into statements and the question-mark omitted:

The Treasurer asked whether anyone could assure her that enough tickets would be sold to cover the cost of that expensive band.

Note here also the use of 'whether' in reported speech: asked whether . . . wondered whether . . . enquired whether . . . etc.

TAKING PART IN MEETINGS: THE ORAL ASPECT

The following guidelines will help you develop the skills and expertise needed to take part successfully in meetings by using oral communication effectively.

Before the meeting

▶ Scan your copy of the agenda to decide which items are most important to you and therefore which outcomes you wish to influence.

▶ Carry out your homework on these items by retrieving any documents from your files which relate, noting down facts and figures and making photocopies of key documents to refer to at the meeting if need be.

▶ Consider carefully what your key arguments will be on each item and make a checklist of them for easy reference.

▶ Rehearse the key points you wish to put across on any item:

'I don't think we should hold another disco until this Committee *is absolutely convinced* that it can *rely* on the Social Activities Sub Committee. If people at this table had not *rallied round*, Jackie Williams would have been *left to do it all on her own!*

In this way you will ensure your points make a real impact at the meeting.

▶ Make sure you can put names and official titles to all the faces of those who will be present. It doesn't help at all to have to refer to:

'My – er – colleague sitting opposite . . .'

▶ Anticipate what the main views and arguments are likely to be of those who will oppose your own. Take the trouble beforehand to set these down and to jot against each your own counter-argument.

During the meeting

▶ Decide carefully where to sit. Senior committee members usually sit at the head of the table, and it is often useful to take a seat near to them. At all events find a place from which you can easily see and be seen.

▶ Check out carefully who is arriving. If important matters are at issue, you can be sure that supporters and opposers will arrive in force! Weigh up the number of those present likely to support or oppose particular items.

▶ Listen for clues from opening statements on 'which way the wind is blowing':

'Item Six, ladies and gentlemen. The proposal that the Club should undertake a publicity drive to recruit new members so as to increase its funds. *A sensitive issue,* but the Treasurer's report to the last meeting *gave cause for serious concern.'*

The sections in italics clearly reveal to the alert listener which view the chairman takes of the matter!

▶ Listen also for the coded remarks people make – often a very British way of implying something indirectly rather than coming out with it:

'I'm rather worried about . . .	= 'I'm dead against . . .'
'Miss Smith is, I fear misinformed about . . .'	= 'Miss Smith is totally wrong about . . .'
'Mr Jones appears to be inadvertently misleading the Committee when he asserts . . .'	= 'I think Mr Jones is telling fibs! . . .'

While the above examples take a rather light-hearted view of coded messages, they do make the important point that:

People don't always say what they really think or mean at meetings!

So always be alert for hidden agendas and indirect messages.

▶ Choose carefully your moment to intervene in the discussion of an agenda item. It often pays to let others first reveal their own positions and arguments. Then you can stress your own points while demonstrating the flaws in the ones you oppose.

▶ Use every opportunity to reinforce the points being made by participants with whom you agree:

'John's absolutely right there!'

And if you can squeeze a telling remark in quickly – seize the moment:

'John's absolutely right there! And if we add a modest joining fee for all new members of, say, £10.00, an extra fifty members would clear the Club overdraft!'

▶ Despite provocations, frustrations and irritations, *never lose your temper in a meeting!* Although a diplomatic chairman may smooth things over, angry words spoken in haste often result in the creation of long-term hostility.

▶ In the same way, avoid at all costs being the cause of someone losing face at the meeting. No one likes to be shown up in front of others. And in meetings, as in the whole of organisational life, it's better to make allies than enemies! By the same token, do not allow yourself to become flustered or upset.

▶ Always avoid the temptation to carry on a private conversation with a neighbour during the meeting. It distracts others and is a high-profile form of bad manners!

▶ Take care to deal with others in a courteous fashion at all times. While they may not always show it, people appreciate good manners and politeness:

'I think we shall have to agree to disagree on that point.'

'If you don't mind my interrupting, Chairman . . .'

'While I respect Jane's position on this, nevertheless . . .'

▶ Lastly and most importantly, *keep what you say short and sharp*! No one listens to people who blather on. Indeed what good points they may have to make simply drown in a sea of waffle!

After the meeting

▶ You are almost certainly representing a group of colleagues when you attend a meeting and so don't forget to report back to them quickly on the meeting's major outcomes. And avoid the desire to act as an information hoarder.

▶ Sometimes business items at a meeting are confidential. Despite close friendships etc, you are honour-bound to respect such confidentialities and not release them into the organisational grapevine.

▶ Remember too, that virtually all meetings take

place beneath the umbrella of collective responsibility. This means that even though you personally were against a particular view that won the day, you are obliged to support it afterwards. So this kind of remark is definitely out:

> 'Of course, Bill, Angela and I were totally against the whole thing! It'll never work, mark my words . . .'

Summary

Prepare – Research – Practise – Anticipate – Position Yourself – Listen – Interpret – Choose Your Moment – Keep It Calm, Courteous And Short – Report Back Promptly – Respect Confidences – Support Decisions.

ACTIVITIES AND ASSIGNMENTS Meetings

■ *THE QUICK CHECK-IT-OUT QUIZ*

1 Why are meetings so frequently held in organisations?
2 List three different kinds of meeting held by limited companies; and another three held in public sector organisations.
3 Explain the meaning of the following: collective responsibility, consensus decision-making, executive, advisory.
4 Explain briefly the roles and functions of the principal officers of a committee.
5 Explain the difference between an AGM and an EGM.
6 What do these specialist terms mean: ad hoc, ex officio, nem con, proxy, sine die?
7 Explain the difference in contents of a members' agenda and a chairman's agenda.
8 Explain how a formal proposal is set out.
9 What is the difference between narrative and resolution minutes?
10 What is special about the layout of action minutes?
11 List the sequence of items of a committee agenda.
12 What are the main features of reported speech?
13 What principal NVC signals would you expect to see during a meeting?
14 What steps can a member take to communicate effectively in a meeting?
15 What are the duties of a committee member directly after a meeting has taken place?

Case study

RIGHT! LET'S MAKE A START

The monthly committee meeting of Newtown Social Club. Present: Ron Dixon, chairman; Sally Pierce, secretary; Jack Slade; Eileen Johnston; John Turner; Peter Smith; Pauline Osgood.

CHAIRMAN: Right! Let's make a start then! Jack, if you're ready . . .? Oh, you haven't got an agenda . . . No, I know, we were a bit late getting them out. Sally, have you got a spare? Oh, well perhaps you could share with Pauline? Good. Right. Apologies for absence. Fred Kemp can't make it. His wife's mother's come down with a nasty bout of 'flu in Leeds, and he's had to drive her up there, though, as he said, the car's not really up to it . . .

SALLY PIERCE (secretary): (breaking in) I think everyone's received a copy of the minutes Ron.

CHAIRMAN: Ah, right. Anyone see anything amiss?

EILEEN JOHNSTON: Well, it would be nice to see my name spelled right, if only once!

SALLY PIERCE: Oh, sorry! My fault again!

CHAIRMAN: Well, if you're all happy with the minutes, I take it I can sign them as a true record . . .

JACK SLADE: No, hang on Mr Chairman, I'd like to go back on the discussion we had on the annual coach trip to London next month. As I said, *I* think we should include a stop at Kew Gardens . . . very educational *and* the admission's very reasonable.

PETER SMITH: Mr Chairman! Surely we're not going all through that again! I thought we'd made the arrangements at the last meeting . . .

CHAIRMAN: Yes, well Jack, I think we'll have to stick to what we decided. Perhaps next year . . . Now, Matters Arising . . .

JOHN TURNER: I looked into the possibility of our booking the St Mark's church hall for the jumble sale next month but they're already booked for the 25th, so I spoke to Peter who said he would check with St Paul's with the vicar.

PETER SMITH: Oh, er, well, I've been pretty busy at the office lately . . . I'll get on to it straight after the meeting. (whispering to John) Thanks a lot, mate!

JOHN TURNER: (whispered reply) Sorry! I assumed you'd already found out!

CHAIRMAN: Item Number Three, resignation of Mr Harris, bar steward. I'm sorry to have to report that Charlie's resigned and that we won't have a bar open next week unless we find a replacement as a matter of urgency . . .

PAULINE OSGOOD: I didn't know Charlie'd resigned!

JACK SLADE: Yes, walked out in a huff I heard. Fed up with the way some members treated him!

PAULINE OSGOOD: Well, I'm not surprised. Take that Mrs Hitchcock for example. Always pushing in at the bar with her 'My good man . . .'

SALLY PIERCE: Why don't we approach Mr Rowbotham? He's retired now but still pretty active. He might be glad of the job.

JACK SLADE: What, George Rowbotham! You must be joking! I remember when he used to help out at the Dog and Duck. Hundreds of 'em laid out on the grass, dying of thirst!

SALLY PIERCE: All right! *You* think of someone, then!

JACK SLADE: Now there's no need to get hoighty toighty with me, Miss Pierce. Just trying to make a constructive remark, that's all!

CHAIRMAN: Well, perhaps we'd better move on to Item Four, Renewal of the Curtains in the Club Room . . .

Case study activities

These activities develop NVQ competences in:

- *composing and formatting an appropriate business document: narrative minutes;*
- *summarising information for a given purpose;*
- *working effectively with others in a group task.*

1 In groups of three to five, consider the case study carefully and make a checklist of what in the group's view are the main shortcomings of the way the meeting of the Newtown Social Club is held.

2 Compose a set of minutes in narrative form for that part of the meeting covered by the case study extract. Compare your version with those produced by the other members of your group and decide which is best and why.

Activities to develop competence and confidence

These activities develop NVQ competences in:

- *formatting and composing specified business documents;*
- *selecting required information;*
- *using English in a specific business context;*
- *summarising information for a stated purpose.*

1 Composing the notice of a meeting

Situation

You are Lesley Davies, Secretary of the Vulcan Engineering Limited Offices Services Quality Circle – a group which meets monthly to discuss how to improve the ways in which office support staff work.

Today, you take this call from Chris Andrews, the Circle's chairperson:

CHRIS: Hello, is that you, Lesley? Oh, I'm glad I've caught you! Look, I'm in an absolute tearing hurry, but had to ring you about the next meeting of the Circle. I've had to change the arrangements we agreed as I'm being sent on a course next week.

YOU: Oh that's OK – lucky you!

CHRIS: Could you get out a quick memo to call a Circle meeting for next Wednesday at 1.00 pm – Oh and make sure they know we've had to change the venue! The Training Suite's booked, so I've managed to bag the old Interview Room on the Second Floor. Room 203 I believe . . . Must dash – Oh and add a note to say 'Agenda follows' and I'll give you a ring at home tonight! Bye!

Using a suitable memorandum or Email format, compose a notice to call the meeting as requested by Chris Andrews.

2 Producing a committee members' meeting agenda

'Ah, Jim, come on in. I've been trying to sort out the items for inclusion in the agenda for the next committee meeting. I saw that written proposal from Jack Burton about changing the date for the Christmas Dance from Saturday 14th December to the 21st. Jack reckons there'll be more of a Christmas spirit nearer the day. You'd better put his proposal into the appropriate format. The seconder is Mrs Bignall. Then there's the complaints about the club-room bar prices. We must deal with that. Oh, and while I remember, I believe you said we've had a number of letters from fixture secretaries asking for dates for next summer's first team cricket fixtures. We ought to settle that one. As you know, I couldn't persuade Ken Palmer not to resign as Hon. Treasurer. You've had four nominations? Yes, well, it's most unfortunate but we can't afford to let the situation drag on. I'll ask Ken meanwhile to act as a caretaker. I think that's about it. Could you draft a committee members' agenda? You'd better give some thought to the running order. I'd help out but I'm late for a section meeting. Thanks a lot!'

As Honorary Secretary of the Lifelong Insurance Co. Ltd Sports & Social Club, Ashburnley Crescent, Richmond, Surrey SU16 4TJ, draft the agenda asked for. The meeting is on Thursday 18 September 199– at 8.00 pm in the Clubhouse Committee Room.

3 Composing narrative minutes

The following piece of dialogue is the transcript of an item of business at a meeting entitled:

5 Christmas Dance Arrangements

Assume you are the secretary at the meeting and set out the passage in reported speech as for a set of minutes you are producing:

CHAIRMAN: Right, I think we should proceed to Item No 5, Christmas Dance Arrangements. Jim, would you like to bring us up to date?

JIM BARNES (secretary): Well, as the committee requested, I wrote to the Kingston Disco organisers last week asking if they could play for us on the 22 December, but as yet I haven't heard from them. The room over the White Lion is definitely booked but we shall have to make arrangements for the bar pretty soon. Tickets should be ready for sale by next Wednesday 22 November.

MRS BLACK: Mr Chairman, could I ask that the tickets are distributed more promptly this year to departmental representatives. Last year we hardly had time to sell them and many staff were approached only a day or two beforehand.

CHAIRMAN: That's a fair point. Jim, could you please see to that. What about publicity, John?

MR JOHN WHITE: No problems. The posters are ready to be put up and I've arranged for a small handout to be put in staff payroll envelopes next week.

Going back to the music side, though, I'm rather worried that we haven't got a group booked yet. I happen to know that the Brian Benner Quintet and Disco are free on the 22nd. Why don't we approach them?

CHAIRMAN: The music is a key item, and I think John's suggestion should be taken up since Kingston Disco haven't replied. Would you contact The Brian Benner Quintet as a matter of urgency, Jim, and let me know the outcome as soon as possible – I take it that we're all agreed on that? Right, well, I think we can now proceed to Item No 6 . . .

4 Producing a resolution minute

This is how the Managing Director confirmed a decision taken under item six of the Board Of Directors' Meeting of Apex Office Equipment Limited:

'Well, the vote is eight to three that we proceed with our plan to extend our product range by purchasing Buildex Limited and thus their range of plastic stacking filing trays. I think this is a sensible decision because we shall be able to increase our profits by cutting out the middle-man'.

Reread the section of this Part on producing resolution minutes and then set out the above item as it would appear in a set of resolution minutes.

5 Composing a formal proposal to include in an agenda

The following conversation took place between Jo White, Honorary Secretary of the Middleton Branch of the Association of Administrative & Clerical Staff (AACS) (a national trade union with some 1.5 million members spread across a wide range of office-based occupations) and Terry Simpson, the Branch's Honorary Treasurer:

> TERRY: I think Head Office has gone way over the top with their proposal to insist on a Committee Member having to resign if he or she misses two consecutive Branch Committee Meetings!
>
> JO: You're right – I can remember missing three last year all because of a series of mishaps – once when I was ill, then because the meeting got changed at the last minute . . .
>
> TERRY: Well are you prepared to second me if I propose that the Committee should put something down on paper to send up to the National Executive to the effect that we don't think it's right – especially when members are giving up their spare time.
>
> JO: By all means, but we'll have to think out carefully how to word it. You string the words together and I'll jot them down . . .

In pairs, consider carefully what form of words would best communicate the feelings of the Hon. Secretary and Hon. Treasurer and then produce a formal written proposal and set it out as for a meeting agenda.

■ INTEGRATED ASSIGNMENT

The following integrated assignment develops NVQ competences in:

- *receiving and responding to given information;*
- *participating in oral and non-verbal communication;*
- *adopting behaviour and language suitable for a particular context;*
- *working with others in a group task;*
- *composing and formatting appropriate business documents.*

6 Integrated assignment: simulating a meeting

In groups of seven to ten, carry out the following activity:

Elect a Chairperson.
Elect a Secretary to take notes.
Consider the following scenario *individually* before the simulation starts and make notes of your own ideas and suggestions.

If possible, set up a video or audio tape-recorder to record the meeting simulation.

Scenario

Part of the curriculum at your school or college is to encourage an awareness of the needs of others in society who may be in need of help or support. At this time, your Head Of Department has asked for a detailed set of proposals from selected classes on acquiring a sum of money – from some sort of event or activity which the class would mount – to be given to a worthy cause. The Head is also open to suggestions as to what charity should be selected.

Your class has decided to take up the challenge and a meeting has been called of a Charity Event Working Party to produce the plans and proposals asked for by the Head.

Your group are now assembled to hold a first meeting so as to 'get the show on the road'!

■ *ACTIVITIES*

1 Hold a meeting for approximately 20–30 minutes to consider ideas and suggestions for a suitable event.
2 Take a decision on which event to select and plan for.
3 Decide when to meet next and what items to put on the agenda for the next meeting.
4 After the close of the meeting, consider constructively together how well the meeting went; did members respect the chairperson's authority? Who interrupted/'slept'/ always seemed negative etc? How well were decisions made? In retrospect, how could the group have contributed to making a better meeting?
5 If you were elected Secretary, produce a set of minutes for the meeting.
6 If your group was able to record the meeting, produce a set of minutes of the meeting from the recording made.
7 Produce an agenda for the next meeting of the group.
8 Produce a set of written proposals to send to your Head Of Department outlining what event your group has selected and why.

Note: You may decide to move from simulation to reality with your charity event ideas. If so, develop your proposals in a series of meetings which result in a successful event taking place.

Work experience attachment assignments

1 With the help of your work place supervisor, collect non-confidential examples of notices, agendas, written proposals and minutes of meetings held in the organisation. Display these in your base room as examples of current practice.
2 Arrange to interview two or three managers and ask them:

   What they see as the techniques required to draw up an effective meeting agenda.

   Make notes of your findings and draw up a checklist for display in your base room.
3 Interview two or three secretaries or assistants who regularly take the minutes of meetings. Ask them to detail what tips and guidelines they can give on how they take effective minutes.
   Make notes of your findings and produce a factsheet for your group.
4 Arrange to talk to several managers who chair and/or take part in meetings regularly. Find out from them what skills they can identify which enable them to take part effectively in meetings and to chair them.
   Make your notes and give your group an oral briefing of your findings.

5 If possible, arrange to sit in on a meeting in your workplace as an observer and watch how the various participants behave and react etc. Watch for NVC signals and how the participants indicate their support or resistance to ideas and views. Compare your observations with the pointers supplied in this text.

Afterwards, discuss with the meeting's chairperson how he or she thought the meeting went.

Part **6**

Summaries and reports

OVERVIEW

Part Six examines the use in organisations of techniques of summarising and oral and written reporting. The skills needed to produce a summary are explained, and how summaries are employed in a wide range of situations. Step-by-step guidelines on report-writing are provided so as to enable you to construct and present different kinds of report suited to various circumstances. A series of models and examples are also included to help you gain a clear understanding of what the end product should look like.

The ability to acquire information, organise it succinctly and present it so that it is quickly and easily understood is one of the most important competences you will need when working in an organisation. So study this Part patiently and practise the activities and assignments carefully. If you remember the step-by-step techniques described you will quickly master the skills of summarising and reporting.

WHY SUMMARISING SKILLS ARE SO IMPORTANT IN ORGANISATIONS

All types of organisation – whether a manufacturing company or a local government department – rely on information which is accurate and easy to absorb and understand. The following checklist illustrates some of the typical situations in which summarising skills are used to make the process of exchanging information prompt and easy to act upon:

Situation	Summarising medium
Sales representative phones in to his district office to explain to the manager the nature of a customer's complaint and what has to be done to put it right.	Phone call from representative to manager outlining main points and emphasising action to be taken urgently.
The Works Manager has received a number of reports from supervisors about a growing tendency among staff to ignore or short-circuit safety regulations.	Notices are posted on all Works notice boards summarising the regulations in force for HASAW and requesting full commitment and vigilance.
The Office Manager is unable to attend the monthly meeting of Departmental Heads, so asks his Deputy to attend in his stead.	On the Manager's return, the Deputy supplies a brief oral report, summarising the main points of the meeting.
A customer writes in to a wholesaler to ask for details about a brand new product, say, a personal CD player, which has just come on to the market.	The wholesaler composes a letter to summarise the main features of the new product and to emphasise its attractions.
Staff turnover in a particular hotel – part of a national chain – has significantly risen over the past two months. The situation is worrying and the personnel manager needs to know what is going on.	The personnel manager sends her assistant to the hotel to investigate and to compose a written report setting out findings and recommendations to put the matter right.

The above checklist provides only a brief indication of the myriad of summarising situations – requiring both oral and written skills – which occur daily in business and public service. Given that summarising skills are so generally and frequently used, what are their major features, and how are they applied?

The following guidelines supply a step-by-step approach to gaining summarising techniques you can employ in a wide range of situations at work.

THE TEN-STEP PLAN FOR PRODUCING A SUMMARY FROM TEXTUAL SOURCE MATERIAL

Follow this step-by-step plan carefully and you will produce summaries which are not only faithful to the original, but which also make sense to their readers!

STEP ONE
Check to make sure you fully understand your brief – *what is it exactly you have been asked to produce in summary form?* Establish clearly in your own mind whether there is an imposed word limit (of say 300 words for a press release), or whether you are to use your own judgement in producing a summary of original material to about a third of its length.

STEP TWO
Devise a working title for your summary – you can always modify it at the final drafting stage. Such a title should reflect accurately what the summary is about and what its main points should concentrate upon e.g.

> **How To Use Company Stationery Cost-Effectively**

or,

> **What To Do In Cases Of Emergency**

STEP THREE
Gather together all source documents – manuals, memos, letters, reports, photocopied articles etc relevant to the summary you wish to produce.

Read through each carefully, say, three times to:

a catch the general drift of the meaning of the document's content;

b identify any difficult words or phrases to check out in the dictionary, as well as any key technical terms;

c obtain a clear understanding of how the piece is structured – e.g. how the main points appear to be sequenced and where examples and illustrations have been placed.

STEP FOUR

Make notes – *in your own words and in an abbreviated form* – of the points which, according to your devised title are most relevant and essential. The point of writing them in your own words is that first, you will set them down more briefly, and that second, you will be better able to link such points together in a continuous paragraph.

However, there will almost certainly be some phrases or terms of the original which you will need to use. For example, it takes several words of our own to convey what is meant by specialist words such as:

    recession wow and flutter contagious

Set out your notes in double spacing and with plenty of space between each one, so that you can later add a point or amend your wording etc.

STEP FIVE

When you have selected your main points, go back to the original and double check the following:

a You have not omitted a main point.

b Your wording clearly conveys the gist of the point – *even though, for the moment you have set it down in a form of note-taking abbreviation.*

c You have not included points which are repetitions or restatements of other points or which are examples or illustrations which can be omitted without losing some essential meaning. (Note: sometimes examples are important and do need to be included).

d Make a final check that the points you have chosen are all relevant to the title you devised.

STEP SIX

Decide upon the most appropriate format in which to present your summary. In so doing consider:

Who is the summary for?

What is the nature of its content – would it be easily read as continuous prose, or better set out in a schematic layout?

Do any graphic or visual items need to be included?

STEP SEVEN

According to the layout decided upon, produce a first rough draft *using double spacing*. Seek to communicate the sense of the ideas of the original, rather than trying to produce a 'scissors and paste' cut-down version of sentences or phrases from the original – it is very difficult if you do this to link points together successfully.

When connecting your points together as a sequence of related ideas, remember to use 'cementing' words or phrases like: *Next, As a result, Moreover, This being so,* etc which help the reader to move from one point to the next.

STEP EIGHT

If you are subject to a limit on the number of words, *seek to produce a first draft which has about 10% more words than you are allowed.* It is much easier to prune out 30 words from 300 than to cast around for some additional points to expand in a draft of 240 words where 270 is the limit.

STEP NINE

Read through your first draft carefully. Check it against your list of abbreviated points to ensure that you have not overlooked any. Look for spelling or punctuation errors or omissions (especially apostrophes and full stops). Most of all check that your sequence of sentences makes sense as a connected piece of writing. The most common fault committed when summarising is to produce a series of points which appear to have no connection with each other!

This is your last chance to change your wording, polish it or add or omit a point, so take pains and proof-read carefully.

STEP TEN

Produce your final version using appropriate office equipment. Do any final transcription checks at this stage. Add items such as circulation details, details of sources etc.

The acid test

The acid test of all summaries is that they should be read by recipients as if originals in themselves. No one should need to read the original first to make sense of the summary, nor to feel that some material has somehow been left out.

SUMMARISING: WORKED EXAMPLES

Consider the following sentence:

> Although the journey from work was not particularly long, the train was crowded with commuters and other travellers and when the office manager eventually arrived home, he felt tired and drained.

This sentence contains some 31 words, the key ones are:

> journey from work, not long, train crowded, office manager arrived home, tired, drained

There are 13 *key* words. Other words like 'particularly', 'commuters and other travellers', and 'eventually' all help to make the sentence more interesting and to make its meaning more precise and detailed. However, if we were required to reproduce the key ideas of the sentence, we could write:

> The office manager's journey from work was short, but his train was crowded and he arrived home feeling tired.

This shortened version contains 19 words, but a more polished and refined version is possible:

> Travelling on a crowded train, the manager's short journey home from work left him exhausted.

Though the omission of the word 'office', and the substitution of 'exhausted' for 'drained and tired' may change the meaning of the original sentence somewhat, its sense remains the same, and its meaning has been broadly conveyed in less than half the words of the original.

When considering the summary of a collection of sentences in a paragraph, it will be necessary to identify the *key points* of the paragraph in much the same way as the key words of the sentence were located:

> The new young office assistant glanced nervously around the busy, open-plan office, and stood at the door, not certain where she should go. Almost at once, a smartly-dressed man wearing gold-rimmed glasses rose from his desk and walked over to her, with a welcoming smile on his face.
> 'Good morning,' he said, 'I'm Peter Harris, senior clerk, and you must be our new assistant. Miss,

Jenkins, isn't it? Do come with me, and I'll show you to your desk.'
> 'Oh, thank you, Mr Harris. I was wondering where I should go,' answered Penny gratefully. She was escorted to a pleasant position near a window, and on her desk someone had thoughtfully placed a small vase of fresh flowers.
>
> 117 words

Making notes

The paragraph contains six key ideas, which may be expressed briefly in note form:

1 Penny Jenkins – new assistant – stops at office door
2 Not sure where to go
3 Peter Harris (senior clerk) rises – greets her warmly
4 Escorts PJ to desk
5 Desk pleasantly located by window
6 Fresh flowers on desk – put there thoughtfully by someone

The rough notes contain some 39 words.

If we assume that the original paragraph is to be summarised in about a third of the length of the original, then the rough notes are probably too generously written, since it usually takes as many words again to transform notes back into complete sentences. Since the target length of a summarised version is to be 40 words, it may be necessary to reduce the notes further, before attempting a first rough draft.

It may be necessary to re-phrase ideas like 'not sure where to go' and 'put there thoughtfully by someone' so that they are expressed more economically. Similarly, 'by the window' may be left out.

Notice that the rather lengthy wording of the direct speech exchange between Peter Harris and Penny Jenkins has been expressed much more simply by 'greets her warmly' and 'escorts PJ to desk'.

When summarising a passage, it is generally better to put over the *sense* of the original, than to try to use either the same words or sentence structures. Of course, it is necessary sometimes to make use of specialist words, where a great deal of meaning may be contained within a single word.

Writing a rough draft

A first rough draft of the summary may emerge as follows:

> Penny Jenkins, the new assistant, entered the office
>
> hesitantly, unsure of where to go. Immediately
>
> Peter Harris, the senior clerk, greeted her warmly
>
> and escorted her to her desk, which was pleasantly
>
> located. On her desk someone had thoughtfully
>
> placed a vase of fresh flowers.
>
> > 45 words

A little careful pruning is needed to shorten the rough draft by some five words. Notice that the rough draft has been set out on alternate lines, so that any alterations may be made clearly:

> Penny Jenkins, the new assistant, entered the office *hesitated at*
>
> *the office entrance* hesitantly. Immediately Peter Harris, the senior
>
> clerk, greeted her warmly and escorted her to her *,and on which*
>
> desk, which was pleasantly located/ On her desk
>
> someone had thoughtfully placed a vase of fresh
>
> flowers.

The final version

The final version of the summary appears, then, as follows:

> Penny Jenkins, the new assistant, hesitated at the office entrance. Immediately, Peter Harris, senior clerk, greeted her warmly and escorted her to her desk, which was pleasantly located, and on which someone had thoughtfully placed a vase of fresh flowers.
>
> > 40 words

If the original paragraph had been part of a longer story or article, then it would need a title. A suitable one might be:

> Penny's First Day at Work

If you compare the summarised version with its original, you will notice that certain parts have been omitted, since they were not considered absolutely essential. Ideas like 'busy, open-plan' have been left out as have the references to Peter Harris's smartness and glasses. Ideas like 'with a welcoming smile on his face' have been conveyed much more briefly by 'greeted her warmly'.

HOW TO PRODUCE EFFECTIVE REPORTS

Making an oral report

Providing one's supervisor or manager with an oral report of an incident, set of events, meeting or discussion with clients occurs so frequently in organisations that the report is given almost without realising it, following prompts like:

> 'Oh, by the way, Jean, how did Mr Johnson like your design for the new chocolate bar packaging?'
>
> 'Look, I'm late for a meeting with the Works Manager, tell me briefly how the meeting went with the Shop Stewards . . .'
>
> 'What did you find out, Bill, when you looked into last month's sales representatives' expenses?'

The requesting and supplying of needed information forms an almost continuous dialogue between managers and their staff, since managers cannot manage effectively without having their fingers on the pulse of their areas of authority all the time.

Oral reports are needed in a range of everyday situations

▶ To explain to a superior why a customer has become upset.
▶ To relay to an absent manager the details of an unexpected visit by one of the firm's directors.
▶ To provide the main details of a meeting attended as a representative of the department.
▶ To convey to the boss the problems of getting work completed on time because of machine failure.
▶ To pass on quickly the main points of an important telephone conversation to the manager and/or colleagues.

and so on to cope with an endless stream of events which go to make up a day's work!

Asking for what amounts to an oral report is easy. Providing one which contains all the relevant facts delivered clearly and coherently is much more difficult and amounts to another communication skill to be mastered. The following checklist provides a helpful set of tips and guidelines:

Step-by-step checklist for giving oral reports

1 If you think you are likely to be asked to provide an oral report at a later stage, *make sure you listen actively and attentively to what is being communicated.*
2 If at all possible, *take notes of the main points you are receiving.* No one can be expected to carry names, dates, numbers etc in his head and accurately relay them after subsequent periods of interruption or concentration on other business.
3 Before delivering your oral report, *think carefully about a logical sequence* into which to structure your points. For example:

> Background   Main Topics   Actions Decided
> Introduction   Development   Summary etc

4 Dont feel at all shy about *referring to your notes as you speak* to check out a name or exact quantity etc.
5 As you are speaking, *keep an eye on your receiver* to check whether he or she is taking in what you are saying. *Make regular pauses at the end of delivering main points* in case your receiver needs to clarify a point or ask a follow-up question.
6 At the end of your report, *repeat what you consider the most important point or action needed:*

> 'So it became clear on speaking to Sandersons that, unless we can guarantee delivery by this Saturday, they'll definitely cancel the order!'

7 All the time you are speaking, listen to yourself and *take pains to avoid irritating speech mannerisms* such as 'umming or erring', repeating phrases like 'sort of', 'you know', 'know what I mean?' etc.
By the same token, *take your time and do not gabble.* Many people change into a fast gear when they are nervous or excited; but always remember that listeners take much more in if the pace is steady and the message is delivered clearly.
8 Whenever possible – and depending upon the importance of the oral report – *make a brief written summary, perhaps in memorandum form, to confirm your spoken report.* Such a memorandum may begin:

> Further to our conversation of this morning, I am writing to confirm the following: . . .

Example of an orally delivered report

Alan Spicer, giving an oral report of a departmental managers' meeting he attended in place of his boss, Mr Jones, sales manager.

'As you requested, Mr Jones, I sat in on yesterday's meeting for you, which Mr Jackson (deputy managing director) chaired. Only the production manager couldn't attend.

'Matters were very much routine until Item 5 on the agenda – ''Proposal to form a Training Department.'' Mr Jackson set out the background which you know about. One important development has taken place, though, that affects us directly. It seems that the budget won't stretch to building a new training centre, so we're likely to be asked to give up our storage rooms on the ground floor. However, the main point was that all the departmental heads are in favour – Miss West submitted a summary of production's views. Mr Jackson asked the personnel manager to submit a detailed scheme for discussion at the next meeting. Heads were asked to submit suggestions to Mr Jackson by next Wednesday.

'There wasn't anything else particularly important, except that the introduction of the staff holiday rota arrangements were given the go-ahead.

'Under Any Other Business, Mrs Davidson complained about the poor response to the forthcoming Social Club Dance, so I've asked Julie to do her best to sell some more tickets.

'I think that was about it. Is there anything you'd like me to follow up?'

Clear beginning At the outset, Alan confirms those present and who chaired the meeting.

Development of essential and relevant points in the middle Aware of the scope of Mr Jones' interest, Alan skips over some early items of no relevance to the sales department – his report selects the particularly relevant points.

Confirmation of action Mr Jones must take himself He anticipates those areas in which his boss must make a response and provides the key details and deadlines.

Descent to more minor points Alan also confirms that action may now be taken on the rota system.

Confirmation of conclusion and request for further instructions arising from the meeting Nearing the end of his report, which has gone through the same sequence as the meeting's business items, Alan relays details of action he has taken on his own initiative. He closes by asking if there is anything further he should do arising from the meeting.

As the example above illustrates, Alan displays the care and attention which he devoted to his role of substitute at the meeting.

He follows the order of the items discussed at the meeting and dispenses with those parts which he does not think sufficiently important – so he is having to use his judgement as he goes along, selecting only the main and relevant points as he sees them in the context of Mr Jones' and the sales department's needs and interests. Alan also structures his oral report to proceed from the most important to the least important – he realises that Mr Jones is a busy man and has no time for trivia. In addition, he is particularly careful to ensure that Mr Jones is made aware of action which is shortly expected of him, particularly since the instructions come from a representative of top management, Mr Jackson. Lastly, Alan checks that no further action is expected from him, so that he may dispose of the meeting, as it were, in his mental checklist of 'matters outstanding', and move on to his next job.

Logic not magic!

There is nothing magical about the ability to deliver effective oral reports. The secret is to listen alertly as a participator in all office business, to make careful notes, to develop a clear memory, and to practise delivering information in a fluent, organised and logical sequence.

HOW TO PRODUCE WRITTEN REPORTS

Producing an effective written report is a demanding task. It is demanding because a series of activities needs to be undertaken conscientiously if the written end-product is to do its job successfully.

Though the production of a written report takes time and effort, the skills needed are straightforward and may be readily mastered with patience and practice.

From the outset, it helps to know when, where and why written reports are used in organisations and also to be aware of the different kinds of written report that are employed in different situations.

Why do organisations need written reports?

Managers working in both business and public sector organisations request the production of written reports for a variety of reasons, the most common of which are set out below:

Reasons for requesting written reports

1 To provide a written record of an investigation or of an event such as an accident or machine breakdown.
2 To supply busy managers with the main aspects of a problem which needs solving.
3 To offer recommendations for solving a problem or improving an unsatisfactory situation.
4 To enable a group of people, say, a board of directors or a working party or committee, to digest information which has been carefully structured and attractively presented; having absorbed the data, the group may then discuss it and decide upon actions in the light of that information.
5 To keep managers and senior executives informed about what are often complex matters in a summarised medium which is easy to read and take in. For this reason the words 'For Information Only' are often set against a manager's name on a report's circulation list.

Business matters requiring the production of a written report tend to be important and are given a high priority. Otherwise the energy and effort put into producing them would not be justified. For this reason, written report writers take pains, not only with the quality of the content of such reports, but also with their presentation, using nowadays techniques of desktop publishing to supply visual appeal.

Standardised and investigatory reports

Basically, there are two different types of written report. For routine situations occurring frequently or at regular intervals, preprinted forms tend to be used to save time and to ensure that required data is not omitted in error. In situations which cannot be anticipated, or which are quite clearly 'one-off', where, for instance, a problem has arisen which needs investigating and then resolving, then an investigatory report is composed. Several differing structures, much like picture frames in which to 'hang' the unique features of such a report, are available to the report writer. Examples of such structures appear on pages 159 and 161 in this Part.

Standardised reports

The most frequently used report in business is the standardised report. This type of written report is used to record and transmit information on a host of topics required at regular intervals. Examples of this include: the salesman's weekly report, in which he accounts for his customer calls, orders taken, expenses incurred and so on; the safety inspection report required daily, weekly or monthly in factories or workshops which checks machinery or equipment; and the progress report which a clerk of works on a building site may be required to submit to his architect to show that work schedules are being maintained. Since such reports are used regularly, they are usually made on carefully designed, preprinted forms, on which the essential information is simply and economically entered in boxes or where an appropriate option is selected and identified:

```
GUILLOTINE MACHINE No. 3

Date of last inspection: 24/6/19—

Safety status of machine:
   Excellent ☐  Satisfactory ☐

                          Withdrawn from
   Service within seven days ☐   use on inspection ☐
```

Though such reports are quick and simple to compile, and though the design of the form prevents required information from being omitted, they tend not to cater for the complex answer, and are quite unsuitable for dealing with investigations into 'one-off' problems.

The investigatory report

Problems in organisations have a way of coming into view like the tip of an iceberg – small indications of something being wrong are picked up at first, and then a subsequent investigation reveals a much larger bulk of the problem which had not been entirely recognised or perceived. Good managers and their staff therefore keep constantly alert for any signs of difficulty or trouble, and once they have picked up the vibrations of a problem – say two consecutive months of declining turnover in a retail store, or evidence of a falling off in staff morale, an individual member of staff or a working party is briefed to investigate the matter in depth and to report back. Such a report often includes recommendations on what corrective course of action to take.

Since no two problems are exactly the same, the format for this type of report must be flexible. Also, since the subject matter of the report will differ in each case, the writer must use his discretion in devising a suitable order or sequence in which to present it.

There are, however, some important principles, both of format and structure which need to be learned. Once these have been mastered, you will be able to cope with writing an investigatory report clearly and coherently, and to display your information in ways which help the reader to understand and digest it readily.

The five stages of report writing

In order to produce an effective written report, its writer must conscientiously follow the five steps set out below, which describe the processes of gathering the relevant information, organising it suitably and producing a first and then final draft.

Stage 1: Clarifying the report's terms of reference

At the very outset it is essential for the report writer to be crystal clear on the precise instructions the report's commissioner (i.e. the manager requesting the report) has laid down. For example, does the report require the presentation of the findings of an investigation only, or have recommendations for its solution also been requested?

Painstaking managers tend to set out their instructions, called the report's *terms of reference*, in a memorandum requesting the report. Such a

Fig. 6.1   *Examples of bought-in standardised forms for daily use and regular event reporting*

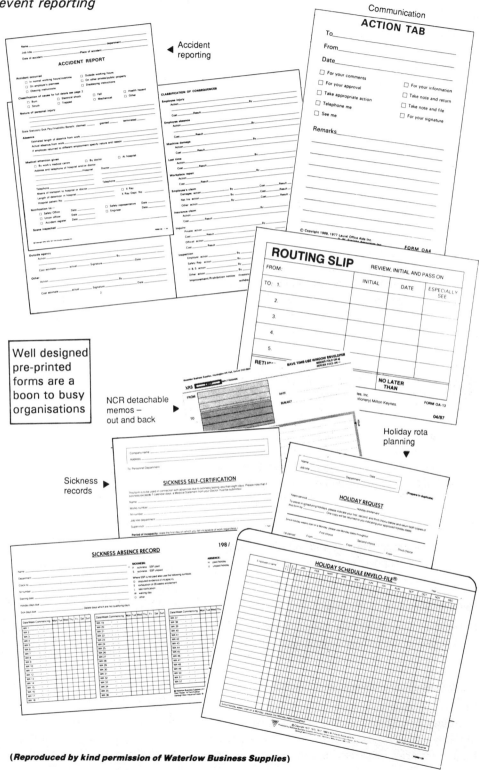

(*Reproduced by kind permission of Waterlow Business Supplies*)

memorandum will also state the deadline for the submission of the report and the staff who should receive a copy. Also, it will make clear whether the investigations should be undertaken confidentially.

Sometimes, however, the report's terms of reference may only be communicated orally in course of conversation:

> 'Frances, we're receiving indications that all is not well with our procedure for handling telephoned customer enquiries. I'd like you to look into the matter and report back, so I may brief the MD.'

Such an orally transmitted request conveys only a vague notion of the reason for requesting the report, no indication of a submission date, and no confirmation as to whether recommendations for resolving the problem are needed.

The report writer must therefore obtain such clarifications right at the start and, ideally, confirm them in writing to the commissioning manager. While this procedure may seem over-zealous, it will certainly prevent a great deal of time and energy being wasted if the terms of reference for the report are misunderstood at the very outset.

Stage 2: Researching the relevant information

This stage is vital. Too many reports get written which are under-researched and which make assertions which cannot be justified from the assembled facts. The following checklist illustrates the typical avenues of research which report-writers follow:

Desk research

Checking out facts, figures and details in company files, earlier reports and relevant letters and memoranda etc.

Reference books in libraries

Relevant regulations, biographies, British Standards, EC directives, legal requirements etc are readily available in reference libraries.

Trade/specialist journals and magazines

Details of state-of-the-art equipment, software, techniques and practices are provided weekly and monthly in the hundreds of specialist trade journals held in libraries or subscribed to by organisations

e.g. *Which Computer, Nursing Times, Business Equipment Digest.*

Interviews with key people

Asking sets of prepared questions and exploring a situation with key managers, staff or customers is often the fastest means of uncovering underlying problems or difficulties.

Observing work/operations in action

Actions speak much louder than words, and unobtrusive observation of, say, sales assistants in action, or factory operatives at work may throw light upon a problem in a very clear way.

Assembling relevant documents

It often helps to assemble relevant adverts, photographs, graphics etc, and to analyse them carefully as part of the research process.

■ *'NOTE IT DOWN BEFORE YOU FORGET IT!'*
Needless to say, it pays to note down important data as it is unearthed! For this purpose pocket notebooks are handy. Also, some report writers make a habit of carrying with them pocket dictation equipment or postcard-sized lined card on which to jot down information and sources etc. The advantage of the loose cards approach is that they may be assembled later into related groups as the foundations for eventual report sections.

Stage 3: Organising the gathered information

The approach of the report's deadline will signal when enough time has been spent gathering in the raw data.

The next stage is, then, to organise it into groupings which will correspond to sections of the report's findings. To accomplish this requires some thought as to a logical and readily understandable sequence into which to structure main findings.

The examples on pages 159 and 161 will help you to gain an appreciation of how to structure your findings. And the following checklist illustrates often-used approaches:

▶ Start with the most urgent and important findings and end with the least important.
▶ Use a chronological approach beginning with

what happened first and progressing until the last (and most recent event).

▶ If appropriate, use a geographical structure, say, for parts of the country or regional sites, or the rooms/space in a building etc.

▶ Start with the current state of affairs and detail progressively what caused the event under investigation to take place, dealing with factors such as the people involved, the equipment, accommodation, processes and procedures and so on.

Stage 4: Composing a first draft

Use the techniques of presentation and conventions of layout explained in this Part to help you compose your first draft.

On completion, check your draft carefully for any important facts omitted or under-emphasised. Proof-read your draft carefully for WP errors and omissions. If possible, ask a colleague to read your draft and to vet it for the sense it makes, any lapses into bias and so on.

Stage 5: Submitting the final draft

When satisfied with the quality of both your content and your presentation, submit your report to its named recipients. Take care to include a circulation list and display prominently the report's CONFIDENTIAL status if appropriate.

Destroy any preliminary drafts which could confuse. Keep your original data filed safely – you may be asked to produce it to verify a point in your report.

Revise your grasp of the facts you discovered in case you are interviewed about them.

Systems for structuring and referencing reports

A particularly helpful feature of written reports is the dividing of their main sections and points into parts which are given an individual reference. In this way, a very specific item may be referred to as follows:

3.1.2 *Provision Of A Fax Transceiver*

All staff interviewed considered that their work would become more efficient with the installation of a Group 4 fax transceiver.

The reference 3.1.2 given to this part of the report indicates that it is situated in the third main section, and is the second point set down in the first subheading of the third main section, which concerns itself solely with the advantages of installing a fax.

The system for referencing reports illustrated above is called the decimal point referencing system. The following chart illustrates how it works:

Structure of short formal report

1.0 TERMS OF REFERENCE

2.0 PROCEDURE

3.0 FINDINGS
    3.1 First main section
    3.2 Second main section
    3.3 Third main section
        3.3.1 Sub-section
            3.3.1.1 Sub-point etc

4.0 CONCLUSIONS

5.0 RECOMMENDATIONS
    5.1 First recommendation
    5.2 Second recommendation etc

In the decimal point system, each major section is given a successive base number: 1.0, 2.0, 3.0 etc. The main points or subheadings of these major sections are correspondingly numbered in sequence after the decimal point: 3.1, 3.2, 3.3 etc. In detailed and lengthy reports a further subdivision is sometimes needed. In this case, it is simply a matter of adding another decimal point:

3.1.1, 3.1.2, 3.1.3, 3.1.4 etc.

It is worth noting that a mix of alphabet letters, Arabic and Roman numbers is sometimes used in just the same way in reports:

C 1 (i), C 1 (ii) or III 2 i, III 2 ii etc.

This mixed approach is thought to lack the elegance and simplicity of the decimal point system and is falling into disuse.

TECHNIQUES OF REPORT PRESENTATION

Today, the report writer can call upon a wide selection of printing facilities which are available from current word processing and desktop publishing software and ink-jet or laser printers. The following chart illustrates just a few of the visual aids to presentation which you can employ to make your reports more appealing.

REPORT ON THE USE OF

This print size is obtained by inserting a print command to extend character width.

THE EUROPEAN COMMUNITY AFTER 1992

This effect was obtained by emboldening and double spacing Courier font capital letters.

3.0   FINDINGS

This section heading is obtained by emboldening capital letters.

3.1 The Advantages of Flexible Working Hours

This effect may be obtained by using initial capital letters and the underscoring facility of the WP software in use.

The use of *colour photocopying* is particularly helpful in advertising agency work.

Words and phrases may be set at will in italics so as to emphasise them by using the appropriate WP print command.

20 JUNE 199-

This effect is obtained by using the double strike WP print command.

Types of written report

Essentially there are two kinds of investigatory report:

    a The short, informal report
    b The short, formal report

A short, informal report tends to be 1–3 A4 pages in length, and its more formal counterpart 5–20 plus.

The short, informal report layout tends to be used for reports which remain within a department or work unit and which deal with items which have a limited importance and lifespan. Longer, formal reports tend to involve all of an organisation, to be considered by senior management and to involve agencies and contacts outside of as well as inside the organisation.

The short, informal report

At the outset it is important to accept that there is no single layout or construction which is 'right' for this kind of report. Like most organisational documents, however, such a report does need to have:

A beginning, a middle and an end.

And so a number of ways of entitling the beginning, middle and end have been devised:

Beginning	*Middle*	*End*
INTRODUCTION	INFORMATION	CONCLUSIONS
or BACKGROUND	or FINDINGS	or ACTION REQUIRED
or SITUATION	or ANALYSIS	or RESOLUTION

For the rest of this section the main headings of INTRODUCTION, INFORMATION and CONCLUSIONS will be used to explain the structure and layout of the short, informal report.

'Topping and tailing' the report

Before considering the content of the report, it is important to check the kind of information which 'tops and tails' it:

TOP: At the top of the report you will need to set out:

▶ The name and job title of the person who has requested the report.
▶ Your name and job title as the report's author.
▶ The report's title.
▶ The date of the report (when it was completed and distributed; note some reports omit a day. and just indicate July 199—).
▶ A unique reference for the report; this may be set down as for a letter reference, or may include a WP file name.

As you have probably already worked out, for reports intended for internal circulation only, the A4 memorandum layout provides an ideal 'top' for a short, informal report (*see* Fig. 6.2).

Note: If the report's content is sensitive or for a restricted circulation, then it may need to be given a CONFIDENTIAL status.

TAIL: The 'tail' of the report will generally include:

▶ A list of personnel who have been sent a copy of the report:

Circulation: Managing Director (for information)
Office Administration Manager
Personnel Manager
Security Supervisor

▶ An enclosure reference (if any papers are attached).
▶ (In some organisations) A space for a signature and date. Note if the memorandum format is used, it is sometimes the practice for the author to initial it at its foot.

Fig. 6.2 *Memorandum 'top' for a short informal report*

MEMORANDUM

CONFIDENTIAL

TO: Office Administration Manager   **REF:** ofreorg.1

FROM: Support Services Supervisor   **DATE:** 2 May 199-

SUBJECT: PROPOSED REORGANISATION OF SUPPORT SERVICES
OFFICE

The report's introduction

While every investigatory report deals with a unique situation, there are, nevertheless, a number of items which the Introduction normally deals with:

▶ The reason the report has been requested – in other words its terms of reference.

▶ The background or context of the report; a brief survey of who, what, where, how and why, providing names, dates, locations.

▶ A survey or explanation of the main aspects of the problem or situation that was investigated.

The report's information

This middle section of the report sets out in a logical order the main findings which resulted from the investigations the report required.

The information will have been sifted and prioritised, so that only significant data is communicated. It will also be set down in a style which is impartial and factual.

It is good practice in this part of the report to deal with a single, unified item at a time. In other words, to divide into separate paragraphs each main topic:

The Advantages Of An Open Office Plan Approach

The main advantages of reorganising the Support Services Office in an open plan design are:

communication would improve,

space would be saved,

equipment costs would be reduced through multiple access to printers etc,

overall costs would be lower.

The Disadvantages Of An Open Office Plan Approach

The principal disadvantages would be . . .

Note that some informal reports are structured by means of continuous prose paragraphs with headings, while others – like that illustrated above – set out points in spaced and indented phrases. Thus, the report writer decides which approach best serves his or her purpose. Also, in short, informal reports detailed number referencing is seldom considered necessary.

The report's conclusions

In short, formal reports, the Conclusions section acts only as a summary of a much longer Findings section. Any proposals the report puts forward to set matters to rights are provided in its Recommendations section.

In a short, informal report, however, both summary conclusions and recommendations are included in a single conclusions section, since they are unlikely to be either complicated or lengthy.

The short, formal report

The structure of this report is divided into four or five sections (depending on whether recommendations have been asked for in the 'Terms of Reference'). The report is set down schematically as the following diagram broadly illustrates:

```
1.0 TERMS OF REFERENCE
2.0 PROCEDURE
3.0 FINDINGS
    3.1 Main Section Heading
    3.2 Main Section Heading
    3.3 Main Section Heading
        3.3.1 Section 3 Sub-Heading
            3.3.1.1 Sub-point of 3.3.1
            3.3.1.2 Sub-point of 3.3.1
4.0 CONCLUSIONS
5.0 RECOMMENDATIONS
    5.1 First main recommendation
    5.2 Second main recommendation etc.
```

The principal features of the schematically organised report to remember are that each section or point has a code for reference:

1.0, 2.0 or 3.3.1.2, etc

Also, headings are either in upper case, initial capitals underscored or initial capitals only, depending on whether they introduce a major section or a subheading. Lastly, as points become more detailed, they are progressively indented.

1.0 Terms of reference

In this first section of the report, the author details the scope of the report, or its 'parameters', within which he may investigate. Sometimes the report's commissioner asks for recommendations; at other times they are made by the recipient(s) of the report.

2.0 Procedure

Having outlined the report's scope, the writer identifies the means he or she adopted to collect its data:

- by scrutinising documents;
- by interviewing personnel;
- by visiting branches;
- by observation;
- by examination, analysis etc.

3.0 Findings

Here the detailed information which has been collected is sifted for relative importance and relevance and classified under appropriate headings, usually in descending order of importance, where the most important comes first.

4.0 Conclusions

In this section a résumé or synopsis of the principal findings is written, and is particularly helpful to those who may not wish to read the entire report.

5.0 Recommendations

Having classified the detailed information of the report and summarised its main conclusions, the writer's last duty, if required, is to identify the means by which a problem may be solved or a deficiency remedied, so that decisions may be made or advice acted upon.

STYLE AND TONE IN REPORT WRITING

1 Prefer an impersonal style

Though it is quite acceptable to use 'I' constructions in more informal reports, the intrusion of personality is best avoided:

Personal: I spoke to the foreman who said that . . .
Impersonal: Discussions with the foreman revealed that . . .

To convey a neutral and impersonal style, the use of the passive voice of the verb is particularly helpful:

Active: *I examined* company sales statistics . . .

Passive: Company sales statistics *were examined* carefully . . . ('by me' is omitted)

The use of third person 'it' constructions is also helpful:

It became evident . . . It would be necessary to . . . It is suggested that . . .

Third person noun constructions similarly convey a neutral, objective style:

The introduction of work study is likely to improve productivity.

2 Avoid familiar, colloquial language

The inclusion of familiar expressions and constructions will tend to prevent the report from being taken seriously:

He reckoned the training scheme was *pretty useless*. The new process has caused *a load of* problems.

3 Use conjunctions and linking phrases to show the connection between ideas

Some connecting words and phrases have the effect of reinforcing what has just been written:

Moreover, Furthermore, Indeed, In addition,

while others temper, qualify or balance a previous statement:

However, Nevertheless, On the other hand, Even so, It should be remembered, however, Although, Even though, etc.

Particularly useful are those sets of joining words which introduce statements to prove, justify or substantiate an assertion with a fact:

because, as, since, with the result that

Output is certain to fall *because* essential parts are in short supply.

4 Choose words and expressions which convey a precise meaning

The following examples illustrate words which

convey a precise and objective meaning:

analysed . . . rather than looked into

inspected . . . rather than looked over

alternative solution . . . rather than another way of solving the problem

cross-section of staff . . . rather than some staff at all levels

surveyed customers' views . . . rather than customers' views were checked out

5   Avoid longwindedness and multi-syllabic words

Prefer the short and simple word to the long and abstruse:

Not: Management submitted the sales turnover figures to a rigorous analysis and perceived an unacceptable level of error.

But: Management analysed the sales figures and found them to be wrong.

6   Wherever possible let facts and figures speak for themselves:

Absenteeism has risen by 17.4% in the first three months of this year.

Over 90% of those interviewed, some 54 staff, agreed that . . .

Sales turnover last month was £19,560, a decrease of 6.4% on July's figure.

7   Avoid making assertions which you cannot justify with fact:

It is clear that at least a third of departmental staff prefer the old system.

– Who says so? Can you prove it?

8   Remember that reports tend to be submitted to senior staff – so do not bully them!

Not: The bonus scheme must be introduced immediately or else staff will look for other jobs.

But: The board is requested to introduce the new bonus scheme as a matter of urgency in order to retain valuable staff.

> ■ *GOLDEN RULES*
> Keep it clear. Keep it factual. Develop the argument in logical steps and support opinion with fact as much as possible. Keep it short! Everyone has more than enough to read these days.

MODEL OF A SHORT INFORMAL REPORT

Reference heads section

The report is clearly headed with the appropriate information for dispatch and filing.

Note the use of the CONFIDENTIAL classification resulting from the nature of the report's information, since some staff are clearly open to criticism.

A report's title [1] should always indicate briefly yet clearly what it is about.

Introduction section

This section [2] establishes concisely: What? Who? When? Why?

Note that from the outset it is clear that the report will include recommendations for action [3]

Information section

The INFORMATION section [4] could be made up simply of continuous prose paragraphs, but the inclusion of sub-headings [5] helps to break down the information into more easily digested sections, which emphasise the particular areas of investigation Christine Fellows thought important.

Note that the first sub-section identifies and defines the range of stationery to be investigated. In so doing, an effort has been made to break down the range into logical groupings.

Much of the report's information relies on Christine's observations and discussions with staff [6] and, in the report, takes the form of assertions.

CONFIDENTIAL

FOR: Mrs K Pearson, Office Manager

FROM: Christine Fellows, Personal Assistant

Ref: CF/AB

12 August 199–

REPORT ON THE PREVENTION OF WASTEFUL USE OF STATIONERY AND REPROGRAPHIC
SERVICES ①

1.0   INTRODUCTION ②

On Tuesday 28 July, you asked me to investigate the current wasteful use
of stationery in the department and <u>to suggest ways</u> in which it might be ③
used more economically in future. My report was to be submitted to you
by Friday 14 August 199–.

2.0   INFORMATION ④

2.1   <u>Stationery Use Investigated</u> ⑤

The range of departmental stationery investigated comprised: headed
letter and memoranda notepaper, fanfold, tractor–fed printer paper,
cut–sheet printer and photocopying paper, fax paper and the range of
envelopes in use.

2.2   <u>Stationery Associated with Correspondence/Internal Mail</u>

The suspected increase in wasteful practices was confirmed upon   ⑥
investigation. <u>I spoke to executive staff</u> who confirmed that, despite
our extensive use of WP drafting, a significant proportion of
ostensible final copies were being returned because of errors still
present.

<u>Observation and discussion</u> with secretarial staff confirmed that
clerical and executive staff in particular are using printed
stationery and unused envelopes on occasion as message pads.

Regarding envelopes, white ones are being used where manilla would
serve, and much non–confidential internal mail is being sent in
sealed envelopes. No member of staff appears to be re–using envelopes.
Also, despite the introduction of the LAN, staff are still distributing
paper–based memoranda and attached copy files when multiple distribution
could be achieved through the network with commensurate cost–saving on
photocopying.

2.3   <u>Photocopying Practices</u>

The departmental copier is in need of servicing and staff are wasting
extensive amounts of copy paper as a result of a fault which creases
the paper.

Furthermore, departmental staff continue to use our three single–   ⑦
sheet copiers for batch copying instead of the much cheaper depart–
mental and company systems copiers, despite regular requests not to
do so.

2.4 <u>Increase in Stationery Costs</u>

I analysed the cost of departmental stationery, comparing this year's second quarter with the first, and this year's consumption to date against last year's.

The stationery bill for the second quarter of this <u>year is 29% higher</u> than for the first quarter (Jan–March £1110.22, April–June £1432.18).

Allowing for increases in price, the department's stationery bill for this year to date against an equivalent period last year <u>is some 18%</u> (8) higher – £4202.25 compared with £3561.23 last year. This increase does not appear to be justified by an equivalent increase in the output of the department. <u>Moreover, the rate of increase is rising</u>. (9)

3.0 CONCLUSIONS (10)

The investigations I have made <u>do justify the concern</u> expressed about excessive waste of office stationery and reprographic services and its impact on departmental running costs.

The increase in careless use of stationery is <u>not confined to one section</u> (11) but is to be found, in different forms throughout the department. If action is not taken immediately <u>the department is unlikely to keep within</u> (11) <u>its administration budget</u>.

I should therefore like to recommend the following measures for your consideration: (12)

3.1 <u>A meeting with senior secretarial staff</u> should be called to discuss the gravity of the problem and to obtain their cooperation in improving both managerial and secretarial performance. A refresher course could be mounted by the training department.

3.2 <u>Control of stationery issue</u> should be tightened; sections should be (12) required to account quarterly for stationery if this proves practicable in principle.

3.3 Consideration should be given to centralising <u>all</u> reprographics work carried out in the department so as to ensure that cost-effective approaches are optimised.

3.4 <u>Departmental policy on LAN Emailing</u> procedures and <u>message routing</u> (12) should be revised and all staff notified.

[Note: the underscorings in the report are only there to draw your attention to the circled points 1—12 explained in the commentary below; they form no part of the report's layout]

Mrs Pearson would need to rely on Christine's judgement – it is important, therefore, that in reports [7], investigators are just and fair, and as far as possible, support their assertions [8] by quoting facts, figures or clearly evident practices.

This reassures the report's reader that the report is based on fact, rather than opinion or purely personal views.

To this end, Christine has taken the trouble to examine the department's spending on stationery over the past 18 months. Her factual financial evidence is hard to ignore, and has the effect of emphasising the need for urgent action. [9]

Conclusions section

In the short informal report, the CONCLUSIONS section [10] provides a summary of the main factors [11] which arise from the INFORMATION section, and also relays to the reader any suggestions or recommendations [12] which may have been asked for.

MODEL OF A SHORT FORMAL REPORT

CONFIDENTIAL

FOR: P J Kirkbride, Managing Director   REF: HTD/SC/FWH 4

FROM: H T Dickens, Chairman, Flexible Working   DATE: 14 February 19--
       Hours Working Party

REPORT ON THE PROPOSAL TO INTRODUCE A FLEXIBLE WORKING HOURS SYSTEM IN HEAD OFFICE

1.0   TERMS OF REFERENCE

       On 7 January 19-- the managing director instructed a specially set up
       working party to investigate the practicality of introducing a system
       of flexible working hours in all head office departments, and to make
       appropriate recommendations. The report was to be submitted to him by
       21 February 19-- for the consideration of the Board of Directors.

2.0   PROCEDURE

       In order to obtain relevant information and opinion, the following
       procedures were adopted by the working party to acquire the information
       in the report:

       2.1   Current office administration literature was reviewed.
              (Appendix 1 Bibliography refers.)
       2.2   A number of companies were visited which have adopted flexible
              working hours systems and the views of a wide range of staff
              were canvassed.
       2.3   Current departmental working loads and practices were observed
              and evaluated.
       2.4   Soundings of likely staff responses were obtained from departmental
              managers and senior staff.
       2.5   The cost of introducing a flexible working hours system was
              considered.

3.0   FINDINGS

       3.1   Principles of the Flexible Working Hours System

              The essence of a flexible working hours system consists of
              establishing two distinct bands of working hours within a weekly
              or monthly cycle and of ensuring that staff work an agreed total
              of hours in the cycle.

              3.1.1 Core Time Band

                    During this period (say 10 15 am to 3 45 pm) all staff are
                    present at work, allowing for lunch-time arrangements.

              3.1.2 Flexi-time Band

                    Periods at the beginning and end of the day (say 7 45 am to
                    10 15 am and 3 45 pm to 6 15 pm) are worked at the discretion
                    of individual staff members in whole or part, allowing for
                    essential departmental staff manning requirements.

              3.1.3 Credit/Debit Hour Banking

                    According to previously agreed limits and procedures, staff
                    may take time off if a credit of hours has built up, or make
                    time up, having created a debit to be made good. Most
                    companies require that the agreed weekly hours total (in the
                    case of head office staff $37\frac{1}{2}$ hours per week) is reached but
                    not exceeded, though some firms adopt a more flexible approach,
                    which permits some time to be credited/debited in a longer cycle.

              3.1.4 Recording Hours Worked

                    In all systems, it is essential that logs or time-sheet
                    records are kept and agreed by employee and supervisor
                    for pay and staff administration reasons.

3.2   Discussions with Departmental Managers

Most departmental managers were in favour of introducing a flexible
working hours system, anticipating an improvement in both productivity
and staff morale. The sales manager saw advantages in his office
being open longer during the day to deal with customer calls and
visits. Reservations were expressed by both the office administration
and accounts managers arising from the likelihood of increased
workloads to administer the system.

3.3   Sounding of Staff Opinion

Discreet enquiries were made via senior staff regarding the likely
response of staff at more junior levels.

3.3.1 Summary of Favourable Responses

Secretarial staff in particular would welcome the means of
tailoring their work and attendance to fit in with their
principals' presences and absences. Many staff would enjoy
working when they felt at their personal 'peaks'. Over 35% of
female staff are mothers with children of school age, and would
probably welcome the opportunity to fit their work around
family responsibilites and according to seasonal daylight hours.
Weekday shopping opportunities would be improved and travelling
in peak rush-hour times avoided.

3.3.2 Summary of Unfavourable Responses

Few staff at junior levels intimated an unfavourable response
but more senior staff were concerned about key personnel not
being available when needed for consultation etc. Older staff
seemed less enthusiastic and any introduction of flexible
working hours would need to be carefully planned and full
consultation carried out.

3.4   Cost of Introducing a Flexible Working Hours System

The increase in costs of heating, lighting and administration of
the system would be offset to some degree by a decline in overtime worked and the cost of employing temporary staff to cover
for staff absences, which may be expected to reduce. (Appendix 3
provides a detailed estimate of the cost of introducing and
running a flexible working hours system.)

4.0   CONCLUSIONS

In the working party's view, the advantages of introducing a flexible
working hours system outweigh the disadvantages. Head office service to
both customers and field sales staff would improve; staff morale and
productivity are also likely to rise. Administrative costs do not appear
unacceptable and senior staff have the necessary expertise to make the
system work. Of necessity, the working party's view was broad rather
than detailed and the introduction of any flexible working hours system
should allow for the particular needs and problems of individual head
office departments to be taken into account as far as possible.

5.0   RECOMMENDATIONS

As a result of its investigations, the working party recommends that the
Board of Directors gives active consideration to the following:

5.1   That the introduction of a flexible working hours system be
      accepted in principle by the Board and staff consultations
      begun as soon as possible with a view to establishing a time-
      table for implementing the change.

5.2   That all departmental managers be requested to provide a detailed
      appraisal of their needs in moving over to a flexible working
      hours system and of any problems they anticipate.

5.3   That a training programme be devised by personnel and training
      departments to familiarise staff with new working procedures
      and practices.

5.4   That a code of practice be compiled for inclusion in the
      company handbook.

5.5   That arrangements be made to inform both field sales staff and
      customers at the appropriate time of the advantages to them
      of the introduction in head office of flexible working hours.

ACTIVITIES AND ASSIGNMENTS *Summaries and reports*

■ *THE QUICK CHECK-IT-OUT QUIZ*

1 Make a list of different communications media which may be used to convey information in a summarised form.

2 Outline briefly the ten main steps in producing a summary from written source documents.

3 What is the difference between a précis, a summary and an abstract?

4 What is a précis of correspondence?

5 Explain briefly the steps you would take to provide a clear and effective oral report.

6 For what purposes are written reports used in organisations?

7 What is the difference between a standardised and an investigatory report?

8 Make a list of situations in which a standardised report might be used in an organisation.

9 Where would you locate information needed for a written report?

10 What features of a WP software package and ink-jet or laser printer would prove useful in the presentation of a written report?

11 Explain the system you would use to reference a short formal report.

12 Explain the main differences between a short informal and a short formal report.

13 Outline briefly your guidelines for creating an effective report-writing style.

Activities to develop competence and confidence

The following activities develop NVQ competences in:

- *Selecting required information from a set of interrelated data.*
- *Summarising information for a stated purpose.*
- *Interpreting data presented in a visual form.*
- *Presenting information in a manner and format that are clear, easily assimilated and appropriate for intended use.*
- *Composing and using English in a range of business/administrative documents and contexts.*

■ *SUMMARISING: SKILL BUILDING EXERCISES*

1 Summarise the following:

a Jack read the letter's message with great care.

in 5 words

b The manager asked if he could be given a summarised version of the article, which was about word processing.

in about 11 words

c Janet opened her morning's post and quickly came upon a letter from a customer who was complaining about the delay which had occurred in delivering to her office a floppy disk storage unit which she had ordered.

in about 25 words

d 'It's all right for you!' said Peter irritatedly to Penny. 'You don't have to see the customers yourself when mistakes have been made in calculating the amount due on their monthly statements!'

in about 18 words

e Write a summary of the following article in not more than 130 words.

Though many of us receive business letters as a matter of routine, the production of a letter which is both attractive and effective combines the skill of a surprising number of people, some of whom will never meet!'

First, a paper needs to be manufactured which will feel appropriately crisp and smooth to the touch. It will also need to take both the printer's inks and the imprint of the electronic typewriter or computer printer without smudging or running.

Next, a graphic designer will need to produce a trade name, postal address, logo and possibly fax and telegraphic addresses in a suitable letterhead, which conveys an image to the receiver of the activities of the letter writing organisation.

At this stage, the notepaper is ready for the attentions of the letter's author and its typist or text processor. The person who 'writes' the letter may, in fact, never put pen to paper, but may dictate the message, either with the help of a dictating machine, or to a secretary who uses shorthand. The author will need to consider who is to receive the letter, the nature of its contents, and the right tone to adopt. The message must be carefully constructed and clearly expressed. At this point, the message may be transcribed – typed or word processed – on to the notepaper. The typist must take every care to ensure that no errors in transcription occur, and that the conventions of letter layout are followed.

Lastly, there are the carriers of the letter to consider – the office messengers, mailroom staff and postal service employees. Without their care, the letter may never reach its destination.

The production of a letter, then, is never routine – it is the result of a complex operation in which the creative and technical skills of literally dozens of people are combined!

300 words

■ SUMMARISING ACTIVITY
2 How to operate an imprest petty cash system

Virtually all departments in private and public sector organisations need to have direct access to modest sums of cash at regular intervals. The reasons are many and varied: to maintain a hospitality provision of coffee and biscuits, to make an emergency purchase of stationery between the regular supplier's visits, to pay for a junior member of staff's bus fare when delivering an urgent package across town and so on.

To meet such needs, the accounts department of the organisation provides a 'petty cash book' to each department which acts as an extension of the main cash book. The procedure for using the petty cash book is as follows:

1 The petty cash book is started up with an injection of cash from the firm's cashier. The amount decided upon varies according to the needs of the department which have been established over the year. The example below illustrates an initial injection or 'float' of cash of £50.00. The petty cash controller enters this amount in the 'Received' column and provides the cash book folio or page reference and date. The £50.00 thus provided is called an imprest, which means an amount of money forming part of an ongoing series of allocations.

2 As the petty cash controller meets individual requests for cash – whether to buy stamps, pay for fares or replenish milk, tea or coffee, etc – a voucher, numbered in sequence, is issued and signed for by the recipient of the cash so as to provide a written record. The controller then enters the description of the purchase and the number of the issued voucher (or receipt which is given a number) into the 'paid'

columns (see the example below). Additionally, the amount is entered into one of a set of analysis columns so that the various headings of outgoings may be brought together for the organisation as a whole in its accounts ledgers.

Fig. 6.3 Example of a petty cash book

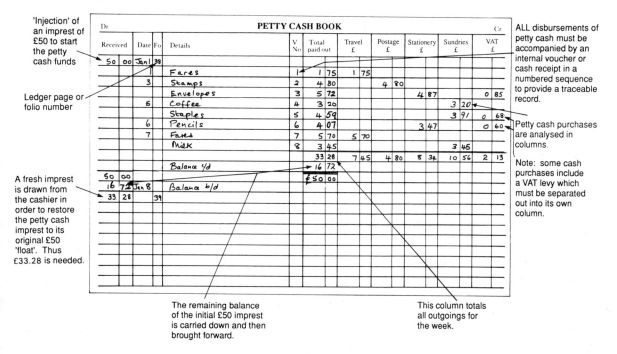

'Injection' of an imprest of £50 to start the petty cash funds

Ledger page or folio number

A fresh imprest is drawn from the cashier in order to restore the petty cash imprest to its original £50 'float'. Thus £33.28 is needed.

ALL disbursements of petty cash must be accompanied by an internal voucher or cash receipt in a numbered sequence to provide a traceable record.

Petty cash purchases are analysed in columns.

Note: some cash purchases include a VAT levy which must be separated out into its own column.

The remaining balance of the initial £50 imprest is carried down and then brought forward.

This column totals all outgoings for the week.

Fig. 6.4 Example of a petty cash voucher

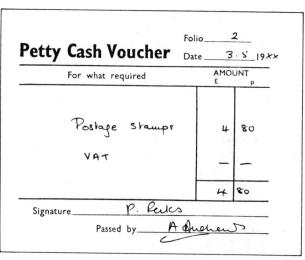

Such vouchers will be issued when staff request cash from the imprest system in order to make small purchases. The recipient of the cash signs for it and the request is authorised by the petty cashier.

This transaction is recorded in the petty cash book.

Note: Retailer's receipts are also retained and used as petty cash vouchers in the same way.

3 At the end of the petty cash accounting period – or as the petty cash imprest needs topping up – the various purchases are totalled and a balance is carried down representing what is still unspent from the original imprest.

4 The petty cash controller then obtains a further imprest, being the amount of cash needed to restore the imprest to its original sum. In the example, the second imprest needed amounts to £33.28, which transaction is also recorded in the firm's cash book, or in its computer system.

In this way a petty cash controller or responsible secretary is able to maintain a supply of small sums of cash for appropriate departmental needs for the duration of the financial year. As cash is involved, it is particularly important that due care be taken in maintaining the petty cash book and in issuing vouchers or obtaining receipts, so as to ensure that columns balance and that no sum of cash disappears from till or cash box which cannot be accounted for.

The imprest system and spreadsheet software

The recording of petty cash transactions is ideally suited to the computing and storing applications offered by even the most modest of spreadsheet packages.

The initial left-hand columns may be set up to record cash received, while the columns further to the right of the screen may be set up to detail amounts paid, voucher numbers and analysis columns in just the same arrangement as a petty cash book offers.

Additionally, the spreadsheet's ability to store numerical formulae used in repeated calculations enables the user to obtain running totals very simply and quickly. The process of carrying down and bringing forward is promptly keyed in and hard copies are available on demand, while the imprest may be speedily Emailed to the cashier for checking, along with a request for a top up!

Extract from *IT In The Office* Fry's Newsletter, 3 June 199—.

■ *SUMMARISING ACTIVITY SCENARIO*

You work as Assistant to Mrs Sheila Peters, Training Manager of Fry's Frozen Foods Limited. Currently your Department is undertaking a major project to produce a series of Training Manuals for specified company personnel. At present you are working on the one intended for secretarial support staff and clerical assistants. The major aim of the manuals is to aid new entrants to Fry's so that they quickly pick up the company's procedures for carrying out regularly occurring tasks.

Mrs Peters has been combing entries and articles from previous manuals on file and has also collected some examples of forms currently in use. Earlier today she gave you this following brief:

'I'd like you to put together a summary in about 280 words which explains simply how to operate an imprest petty cash system. Assume you are writing for a new employee who is unfamiliar with the procedures. Use the documents I've assembled to work from. Unfortunately there's no room in the manual entry to include an entire petty cash book example, but you could use some of the entries on the specimen as explanations. I leave it up to you.'

From the documents supplied, produce the summary in a format which you think best suits Mrs Peters' instructions and its intended use.

3 Making an oral report
The following activities develop NVQ competences in:

- *Summarising information for a stated purpose.*
- *Adopting behaviour and language suitable for a particular work context; using body language to support messages being transmitted.*
- *Working with others in a group task.*

In pairs, first carry out your research, and then give an oral report in not more than ten minutes to your group on one of the following:

How your work experience attachment organisation presents written reports produced for senior staff.

The kinds of activity your school/college reports upon through the use of standardised report forms.

The impact which techniques of desktop publishing are making on the design and layout of reports.

Arrange to sit in as an observer on a meeting of either your Student Association Committee, local parish council meeting, or a committee meeting of a club you belong to. With permission, take notes of the main items of business discussed and report back orally to members of your group. The report should take no more than 3–5 minutes.

Find out what services are available to your group locally to help them find either a first full-time post, or to assist them in returning to full or part-time work. Organise your findings and then deliver to your group an oral report of about 5–8 minutes.

4 Producing a short informal report
The following report-writing activities develop NVQ competences in:

- *Selecting appropriate English to convey information in writing.*
- *Using suitable business and administrative document formats.*
- *Collating and presenting data for a defined purpose/researching and retrieving information.*
- *Composing business documents/preparing and producing documents.*
- *Working with others in a group.*

a Your Student Association Committee has decided to carry out a 'root and branch review' of the activities which it puts on for your student body. Some activities are poorly attended and lately there have been a number of 'gripes and whinges' about the lack of any decent sports or social events.

In groups of three or four, devise a short questionnaire aimed at finding out what sorts of activity a sample of your student body would support. Then carry out a joint survey. Also, interview a number of students from different age groups and departments about the kinds of activity they would like to see mounted and make notes of your findings.

When you have obtained your data, copy it to each member of the group, and then, individually, produce a short informal report, with recommendations for submission to the Chairman and Committee of your Student Association.

Your report should not exceed three typescript pages of A4.

b Your supervisor in your work experience attachment organisation, Mr David Jones, is employed in the Personnel Department. The organisation is finding it increasingly difficult to recruit staff with the potential to proceed to posts of managerial responsibility. When interviewed, a number of applicants for posts in various departments said they would not want the stress of a management post. Others thought they would not enjoy being separated from workmates by having to give them orders. Yet others thought the demands of management would interfere with their leisure interests.

In order to assist the company in finding out more about your age group's attitudes to becoming a manager in an organisation, you have been asked to carry out some research among your classmates to find out what aspects of a management post would be most and least attractive to them, what particular reasons they may have for not wishing to accept management training or development and what organisations could do to make management careers more attractive to people like your classmates.

Produce a suitably short, informal report on not more than three sides of A4. Include your recommendatiions for action in your report.

c Your head of department wishes to purchase a laptop computer, so that he can work from home and plug into your computer network with a modem. He also wants to be able to use the latest releases of Wordperfect and Lotus 123, so sufficient memory is needed. And he's also fussy about the quality of display on the screen. Lastly, your manager is, of course, looking for value for money.

Find out what is currently on the market which would best meet the specification, and compose a short informal report with your recommendations.

■ AN INTEGRATED CASE STUDY

This case study involves researching and writing a short, formal report, producing a summary and giving an oral presentation. It is designed for working groups of three or four.

The case study develops the NVQ competences listed in this section for summarising and report-writing and also for oral reporting and working as a member of a group.

NVQs – A LIGHT HIDDEN UNDER A BUSHEL?

In the late 1980s the government of the day set up a council to review the delivery of post-16 vocational qualifications under the chairmanship of Sir Oscar De Ville. His brief was to explore ways and means of simplifying the 'jungle of vocational education and training qualifications' and to provide a means of ensuring that there was an equivalence at given levels of award between the qualifications offered by respected examining boards such as the Royal Society Of Arts Examining Board, the London Chamber Of Commerce & Industry Examining Board and the Business and Technology Education Council.

The results of the council's initial work led to the setting up of the National Council For Vocational Qualifications (NCVQ). It devised five steps or levels of NVQ award, where Level I provided a basic 'entry to work' standard, and

Level V provided a post-degree and professional/senior managerial level of award.

The NVQ Levels I–V awards broke new ground by establishing sets of competences for assessment both in educational institutions and 'on-the-job'. Moreover, the sets of competences considered appropriate to each NVQ Level were devised by various Industry Lead Bodies (ILBs) so as to relate closely to particular industries. For example, two such bodies, the Administrative Business & Commercial Training Group and the National Working Party on Secretarial Standards drew up the competences for Levels I and II, and Level III respectively in the areas of business administration and secretarial work.

Once such sets of competences were agreed upon, then the national examining boards working in that sector of industry or commerce were able to design examinations which incorporated the appropriate competences – at Level I, II or III etc.

Instead of students having to take 'sudden death' final examinations on a given day, NVQ courses enabled students to learn new skills, to practise them and then to be assessed for competence in them at times through the course *when they were ready*.

The outcomes of this far-reaching shift to imparting work-related skills on a proven 'can-do' basis are important both to the student and his or her current or future employer. The NVQ range of awards in vocational education and training will provide the means of a rapid and all-embracing improvement in the nation's workforce. They will aid not only teenagers entering the world of work for the first time, but also mature returners to work, whether mothers formerly engaged full-time in bringing up young children, or adults embarking upon a career change.

Case study activities

1 While the work of NCVQ has much to recommend it, unfortunately too few students, employees and employers in your locality are sufficiently aware of how different the NVQ system is from more traditional course examining and assessing practices. Therefore your Head of Department has asked you to work together in groups of three or four to find out what NVQ awards are being offered in your institution and locality and to produce a short, formal report with recommendations on how the NVQ series of awards – Levels I–III only – could be more effectively publicised to local parents, pupils, students, employers, employees and teachers.

2 Part of the process of publicising NVQs is for interested parties – teachers, careers officers, Training and Enterprise Council officials (TECs) and local councillors etc – to be sent a summary which sets out simply and clearly what NVQs are for and how they are delivered.

In pairs, design a suitable summary in not more than two sides of A4 printed text.

3 When your group has finished its report in **1** above, use the information acquired to provide the input for an oral presentation on NVQs and their importance to commerce and industry. With the assistance of your teacher, arrange to give your presentation to another class of students who will benefit from your new-found knowledge and insights.

Work experience attachment assignments

1 With the help of your attachment supervisor, arrange to interview several managers and ask them about the jobs they carry out which involve summarising skills. If possible, collect specimen documents which have involved such skills for display in

your base room and write a brief commentary for each on the reasons for their production.

2 Arrange to interview managers in different departments in order to find out what kind of oral reporting activities they are regularly involved in. Ask them what tips they can supply on delivering effective oral reports. Note them down and share them with your group.

3 With permission, arrange to collect a series of standardised forms which your attachment organisation uses for routine and regular reporting – e.g. of accidents or for reporting defective equipment etc. Display these for your group's information on your base room noticeboards.

4 Seek your supervisor's help to collect a number of non-confidential written reports. Check out the ways in which they are laid out and structured and compare them with the guidelines you have received from this Part. Discuss with the staff who have produced the reports which have been made available to you what aspects they consider important in producing effective reports. Make notes of your findings and give your group a short oral report. With permission, display the reports you have collected in your base room.

5 Arrange to interview two or three senior secretaries and/or personal assistants who are involved regularly in text-processing reports. Ask them about those features of WP and graphics software and of computer printers which they find most useful in producing reports. Make a checklist and report back orally to your group.

Part 7

Oral and non-verbal communication, including telephoning, reception and interview skills

OVERVIEW

Part Seven examines the skills which are needed in face-to-face and telephone communication. Many work roles, especially those in the retailing and service industries, involve employees in oral and non-verbal communication for as much as 70 to 80 per cent of their day. Shop assistants and telephone switchboard operators are constantly involved in spoken word interactions with customers and co-workers. Yet the oral skills of communication are in many ways undervalued – perhaps because we all believe we don't need to improve them!

This Part explains how you can improve your use of the spoken word at work. It examines the techniques of clear and attractive speaking, the role of non-verbal communication in face-to-face situations, oral communication within a group, how to use the telephone effectively, the oral aspects of reception work and how to take part in interviews.

An ancient but wise Chinese proverb is: 'Open your mouth that I may know you!' By studying this Part conscientiously and being prepared to accept some constructive criticism along the way, you will ensure that colleagues and customers alike get to know you as a fluent and successful oral communicator.

NVQ references

This Part covers the following BTEC First Diploma in Business and Finance and 'ABC/NWPSS' competences:

BTEC First Diploma

Business Support Systems 1:
   Competences: 3, 4 and 5 Processing incoming and outgoing business telephone calls, receiving and relaying oral and written messages, supplying information for a specific purpose; 16, 17 liaising with callers and colleagues

Business Support Systems 2:
   Competences: 2, 3 and 6 Creating and maintaining professional relationships with customers and clients, responding to customers' needs for information, and supplying information for a specific purpose

Administration:
   Competences: 1, 2 and 3 Processing incoming and outgoing telephone-calls, transmitting and transcribing messages and processing messages electronically;

   4 and 5 Receiving and directing visitors and maintaining the reception area

ABC/NWPSS

Level 2:
   Unit 8   Liaising with callers and colleagues
   Unit 10 Creating and maintaining business relationships
   Unit 14 Telecommunications and data transmission
   Unit 15 Reception
Level 3:
   Unit 1   Communication systems
   Unit 3   Reception

ACCENT AND PRONUNCIATION IN SPEECH

When George Bernard Shaw wrote his play *Pygmalion* about the cockney flower seller to whom Professor Higgins gave elocution lessons so as to pass her off as an aristocrat among aristocrats, he was making a wry comment about people who judge others by externals while missing their real qualities. In this case, Eliza was accepted in high society merely because her street-seller accent had been replaced by one in harmony with that of the gentry.

While regional accents all over the UK are widely accepted today for the richness and variety they bring to the English language, it is nevertheless essential for the Glaswegian, Geordie, Cockney or Cornishman to ensure that what they say to customers, colleagues or visitors is readily understood. Local dialect words like snicket, Old Bill, canny, skint etc are best restricted to use among local friends who are totally familiar with them.

This policy has been adopted for many years by the BBC and ITC. No matter where their weather forecasters, disc-jockeys or news presenters hail from, or what the lilt, ring or burr of their accents, *every word they say is pronounced clearly*! Their training and experience ensures that they do not use dialect words that only a minority in a national audience may understand. Nor do they indulge in speech habits which are the result of laziness. Nor do they indulge in what they think is a 'posh' accent, which to the listener sounds 'put on' and artificial.

So, given that regional accents – quite rightly – are a source of pride and indeed a birthright, what steps should the effective oral communicator take to ensure that he or she is always readily understood? The following checklist of Do's and Don'ts summarises some major points about accent and pronunciation to keep in mind:

Delivery and intonation

We naturally employ rhythms in our speech, saying some words or syllables quickly and others more slowly. In this way we are able to emphasise key words. What do you think, for example, would be the likely emphasised words in the following?

When engaged in spoken word communication

Do:

▶ Make time to pronounce clearly each syllable of a word or phrase: po-lice, not plice, law-and-order, not loranorda, half-an-inch, not arfninch etc.

▶ Sound your consonants clearly: bottle, not bo'all, Nothing, not nuffin, isn't, not ent, get off, not gedoff etc.

▶ Pause at the end of each sense group of words; if you run your words together, whether because of excitement or habit, you will make them much more difficult to understand – especially over the telephone.

▶ Sound the vowels of words clearly, without clipping or distorting them: wheel (with a long e and distinct l, and not wee-yaw; nice, (i as in eye) and not, noice or naice etc.

▶ Sound your consonants clearly – especially d, t, h, and p.

Don't:

▶ Leave the beginnings and endings off words or phrases: hot, not 'ot, hit, not 'it, it's OK, not s'ok, dripping not drippin', pudding, not puddn etc.

▶ Mumble or let your voice drop away towards the endings of your sentences.

▶ Speak in a flat monotone – place an emphasis on the words you wish to stress:

'I'm *extremely sorry* to have to telephone you at this late hour, but Mr Johnson is *most concerned* about the trouble you experienced this morning and wants me to *apologise most sincerely* for the inconvenience you were put to.'

This will help your receiver to pick up the key words and make your spoken words much more interesting.

'I'm not interested in any excuses, if it happens again, you're fired!'
'Sorry to butt in on you like this, could you possibly lend me your CD player?'
'If you want my opinion, the whole thing's a complete waste of time!'

Also, the way we make our voice rise and fall helps the words we say to get attention and to stress the most important ones:

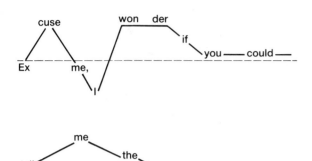

Imagine what a dull and dismal world it would be, if everyone went around, like robots, saying every word at an even pitch and emphasis:

> Ex-cuse-me-I-won-der-if-you-could-tell-me-the-time?

It is very important when speaking to use the techniques of delivery and intonation to help your listener(s) to follow the important parts of your speech. To make what you say more lively and interesting, use changes of pace and pitch and pauses.

Speech mannerisms

Whether we realise it or not, we all possess a number of favourite expressions which we over-use in conversation. These mannerisms, which some people use with irritating frequency, include:

> you know
> you see
> er
> um
> andah
> I mean to say
> if you see what I mean

Very often the speaker is quite unaware that such irritating speech mannerisms are occurring after almost every phrase. Be careful. Think what you are saying!

Don't become a cliché collector!

The other type of mannerism which creeps into speech is the over-use of stale, tired and quite colourless expressions – clichés as they are called. The following words and phrases belong to this washed-out, worn-out category:

> really great; at this moment in time; very nice; not too bad; fair, thing; get/got; fantastic; rough; wicked; it's all happening!; all right; a lot; situation; don't mind if I do; if you like; there you go!

How much would the following conversation tell you, for example, about the business studies course?

A How are you getting on in keyboarding?

B All right.

A So am I.

B Do you still have to look at the keys?

A Yeah!

B Yeah, so do I! Miss Jones don't like it though.

A No, she don't half go on if she catches you.

B Yeah! Here, what do you make of the new IT teacher?

A Yeah! he don't half talk funny.

It is unlikely that the two young students who might have had such a conversation learned anything beyond: they are both progressing quite well at keyboarding but are still experiencing some difficulty with touch typing; the IT teacher has, apparently, a peculiar accent.

It is only too easy to fall into the trap of becoming a 'cliché collector'. But the effect of trotting out endless, empty clichés is that you appear to have nothing really worth saying – and of course that isn't the case!

As we have already discovered, using the spoken word effectively involves accent, pronunciation, delivery, intonation, the avoidance of irritating speech mannerisms and over-use of clichés. The following checklist summarises ten golden rules for effective speaking.

Ten golden rules of speaking

Remember the following Golden Rules of Speaking and you will capture and keep your listeners' attention:
1 *Think* before you speak!
2 Speak clearly and attractively
3 Choose the *best* words – not just the first words that spring to mind
4 Avoid ugly and lazy pronunciation
5 Don't slur or distort words
6 Use variations in pitch and rhythm to achieve emphasis and interest
7 Avoid irritating speech mannerisms
8 Don't rely on clichés
9 Make sure your listener(s) are following what you say
10 Know when to stop to allow others to have their say!

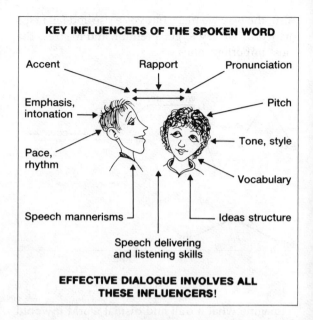

KEY INFLUENCERS OF THE SPOKEN WORD

Accent · Rapport · Pronunciation · Emphasis, intonation · Pitch · Pace, rhythm · Tone, style · Vocabulary · Speech mannerisms · Ideas structure · Speech delivering and listening skills

EFFECTIVE DIALOGUE INVOLVES ALL THESE INFLUENCERS!

Check your oral toolkit!

Before your next 'speaking engagement', check out your oral toolkit against the list below, and make sure your 'tools' are oiled, sharp and ready to use!

Accent: Be proud of your origins, but make quite sure your spoken word is intelligible to someone who comes from the other end of the country!

Pronunciation: Ensure your pronunciation of words is a help and not a hindrance to your listeners.

Pitch and emphasis: Make what you have to say interesting and appealing by stressing key words and varying the rise and fall of your sentences in natural rhythms.

Vocabulary: Take the trouble to select words which either accurately or persuasively convey your message; avoid stale, empty and over-used expressions as well as slang or colloquialisms in formal situations.

Structure and content: Practise thinking on your feet – your brain works at an amazing rate, so think ahead about what you should say next and what to leave until the end for emphasis.

Tone and style: Always monitor what you are saying to make sure that you are creating a style and tone suited to your recipient(s) and the situation.

Mannerisms: Make eye-contact from time-to-time and supply appropriate NVC signals; avoid irritating speech mannerisms; pause if you need to collect your thoughts.

Rapport: Your listeners will better hear and take in what you have to say if you take the time and trouble to build a friendly and mutually respectful relationship with them – by always considering *their* needs and viewpoints etc.

And always remember: a good wordsmith always keeps the tools of his trade in good repair, ready for instant use!

NON-VERBAL COMMUNICATION AND THE SPOKEN WORD

The term 'non-verbal' literally means 'not words', or outside of the spoken word. NVC, then, is the label given to body language signals which support or emphasise the spoken word such as:

Gesture; Posture; Movement; Proximity/ Physical contact; Facial expression

At the outset, it is important to realise that many of the NVC signals we send to others are unconsciously produced. We do not tend to think just beforehand:

I am now going to frown and fold my arms because I totally disagree with what is being said.

nor:

> I think I'll just sit here looking at my shoes and twisting my handkerchief because I want people to know that I'm feeling pretty nervous right now!

Indeed, some communication experts point to the value of NVC signals as messages precisely because many (but not all) are hard to fake and their senders are unaware that they are transmitting them. The following section examines different kinds of commonly occurring NVC communication and how the sensitive communicator can interpret them and so aid the oral communication exchange.

Facial expression

From earliest times man has used his facial muscles to produce expressions which:

▶ **show hostility and warn off:**
eyes unblinking, eyelids narrowed, forehead frowning and lips tight;

▶ **friendly greeting:**
eyes wide open, lips apart and ends raised in a smile;

▶ **fear:**
colour drained from face, pupils dilated and mouth dropped open; breathing in gasps.

By the time we are adult, we have become very expert in 'reading other people's expressions and responding accordingly. Facial expressions convey:

> hatred, hostility, anger, fear, nervousness, shyness, sadness, weariness, tenderness, love, pity, sarcasm, disbelief, happiness, contentment, boredom, displeasure.

In view of the extent of the moods and feelings which the human face is capable of expressing, it pays to make a study of facial expression:

either as **A confirmation and reinforcement of what is said.**

or as **An indication of what is being thought** *but not said.*

In other words, facial expressions may give away thoughts which are quite different from the words being spoken!

'So what went wrong? . . .'

'Good morning, may I help you?'

'Here's the crucial point'

'Search me'

'Hi, Joe, what'll it be?'

Non-verbal communication either reinforces the spoken word or acts in place of it.

Gesture

Like facial expression, gesture may be used either to reinforce what is being said, or – usually unconsciously – to contradict what is being said. It also signals a response to what someone else may be saying.

We use our hands a great deal to make gestures, though Anglo-Saxon descendants are almost immobile in this respect when compared with their Latinate European counterparts! Fingers can jab downwards to stress a point, form steeples in a praying position to signal a willingness to listen without commitment, or form fists to show hostility or resentment. Similarly, shoulders shrug to convey 'search me', heads nod or shake in agreement or disagreement and arms stretch out to signal 'what can you do?' or, 'don't blame me' etc. Fingers may be laced and held behind the head to indicate a relaxed attitude or arms may be folded across the chest as a sign of defensiveness.

Posture

The word posture is used to describe the ways in which we hold our bodies in different circumstances. Sometimes we slump, slouch and sprawl, and sometimes we stand erect or hunch up. A person's posture in NVC terms often signals how he or she is feeling overall in a given situation.

For example, a candidate at a job interview is likely to sit tidily in a chair (so as not to appear over-familiar by lounging in it) and to lean forward when asked a question so as to show interest and alertness. The same person at home, watching a soccer match from the sofa is likely to be sprawled back, arms along the back of the sofa and legs stretched out or resting on the coffee table!

As a rule of thumb, the more confident and relaxed we feel, the more we tend to let our bodies stretch out. The more nervous or anxious we are, the more likely we are to hunch our limbs together – and in extreme cases, assume the foetal or 'unborn child in the womb' position.

Movement, proximity and physical contact

As part of an NVC research programme, a scientist once carried out an experiment to discover how people react to the closeness of others. In this case, he kept moving his chair nearer to the person to whom he was talking. As he did so, the other edged his away. This action and response eventually took them to the other side of a 40-foot wide room! At no time did the 'target' realise what was happening!

This experiment reveals the importance that human beings attach to their personal space. It also throws light on the conditions and relationships which affect proximity or nearness. Lovers tend to fuse together on a bench, while group leaders like managing directors or senior politicians demand a certain area of space around them. Usually, the nearer we allow others to approach us (dentists and doctors excluded!) the closer our relationship tends to be with them. Moreover, in some cultures, bodily contact is avoided save for very close personal relationships.

The ways in which we move also signal our responses or reactions to situations. People feeling confident tend to move in slower, surer ways, while people feeling ill-at-ease tend to make quick, short and jerky movements. Indeed we can all tell the difference between someone striding towards us, chin jutted out and eyes in slits, and someone sauntering towards us with hands in pockets!

Another NVC movement giveaway is when people fiddle with keys, pens or paper at meetings. Such 'playing' may indicate boredom, a total lack of interest in the proceedings, frustration or impatience. Doodling conveys similar signals.

Paralinguistics

This aspect of NVC has been left until last to examine, since it sounds like a cross between a tropical disease and the study of an ancient foreign tongue!

What the term paralinguistics stands for, however, is a fascinating area of NVC – the sounds and noises we make which are not actual words or phrases, but which nevertheless communicate very distinct messages:

> 'Ahem' says the discreet chambermaid clearing her throat and in so doing announcing her presence to the honeymoon couple in their suite.

> 'Ooops' cries the tailor when making too long a cut into his material.

> 'Tut-tut' responds the gossip on hearing a piece of news requiring sympathy.

Other paralinguistic signals include sighs of relief, whistles of surprise, sucking on teeth and tongue-clicking to indicate thinking over or reflecting on something.

Summary

All NVC signals form part of face-to-face communication, whether or not we realise we are sending them. It is therefore important for the effective oral communicator to spend some time studying NVC in action, so as to interpret such signals correctly and respond to them appropriately.

Also, as a sender of the spoken word, it pays to give more conscious attention to NVC. A friendly smile helps to disarm an irate customer; walking confidently into an interview room creates a good impression; shaking hands warmly shows openness and goodwill etc.

■ *NVC HEALTH WARNING*

It is commonplace for student doctors to acquire in turn the diseases and complaints they study. Be on your guard against reading too much into NVC signals – the colleague who walked past you in the corridor without returning your smile may have had his mind on other things than the intention of deliberately snubbing you!

TAKING AND PASSING ON ORAL MESSAGES

A busy department runs on a hectic network of oral communication. Incoming messages arrive via international/national telephone systems, in-house public address systems (in factories or warehouses), callers dropping in, overnight messages recorded on answerphones, audio-dictation tapes posted in by busy sales reps, video recordings, internal telephone extension links and so on.

By the same token, departments employ a wide range of telecommunications equipment, including confravision and telephone conference hook-ups, to send outgoing oral messages to colleagues and clients, whether on the next floor or a continent away. Indeed, we may think of multi-storey office blocks as veritable Towers of Babel, such is the volume of two-way oral communication carried in and out on radio waves and telephone lines!

As a result of this endless spoken word traffic, and the fact that executives and support staff are frequently away from their desks or bases, it is often necessary for colleagues to take oral messages on behalf of absent personnel.

While taking and relaying messages is straightforward – provided that a series of simple steps is followed – far too many passed-on messages cause confusion and wasted time and effort because careless errors have been allowed to creep in. Wrong days and times, a final digit missed off a phone number, a misspelled customer's name or location, wrong quantities written down for a

phoned-in order and so on all cause irritation and delay.

Taking and passing on oral messages is therefore an extremely important activity, and one not to be undervalued because the message is for a colleague rather than for oneself.

How to take and relay oral messages efficiently

The following checklist supplies a series of easy steps as guidelines for you – both as a message giver and receiver:

As a message giver

Make sure you

1 Pass your message to someone whose identity you have established – you may need to go back to him or her later on the telephone or by letter.
2 State clearly who the message is for. Give his or her name and job title to avoid mistaken identity – there may be several Smiths, Clarks or Joneses in the firm.
3 Impress on the message taker – if appropriate – that your message is urgent and supply a deadline by which an answer is required.
4 Express the details of your message clearly, *slowly* and put your main points in a logical order. Remember that the message taker may be taking notes of what you are saying.
5 Repeat or spell any difficult names, addresses, numbers etc.
6 Make sure the message taker has fully grasped all the essential points of your message before you leave. Obtain feedback to make sure that this is so.
7 Remember to say where the person for whom your message is intended may reach you later in the day or week.
8 Do not forget to thank the message taker for his time and trouble.

As a message receiver

Make sure you

1 Find out: who the caller is; the organisation he or she represents; for whom his or her message is intended.

2 Check and make a note of the time and date of the call. Sometimes this information is very important.

3 Obtain the precise details of the message. Make a special note of names, dates, telephone numbers, quantities etc.

4 Stop the message giver whenever you fail to take in part of the message. Ask for the part you missed to be repeated. Ask for spellings whenever you are unsure of names, places, etc.

5 At the end of the message repeat its essential details back to the message giver. This will give him an opportunity to check that you have not missed anything out or misunderstood any part of the message.

6 Unless the message is very short and simple, be sure to *write it down*, first in rough notes and in a fair copy immediately the caller has departed. Do not allow the caller to leave until you are sure you have taken the message correctly!

7 Take *immediate action* to pass the message on to its intended recipient. It is easy to forget when you are busy.

As a message relayer

Make sure you

1 Don't delay in passing on your message – it may be urgent as far as its intended recipient is concerned.

2 Always check your rough notes and fair copy on the message pad carefully for errors or omissions *while the message is fresh in your mind.*

3 Never simply place the message sheet on a colleague's desk – it may blow away or become buried under a batch of papers likewise deposited. Make a point of telling the recipient that a message is awaiting him or her.

4 If possible support your written message with an oral confirmation – you can quickly explain a lot and so give the recipient a better notion of the message's urgency, subtle points or key action needed etc.

EXAMPLE OF A COMPLETED MESSAGE USING A PREPRINTED MESSAGE PAD

Priority status.

URGENT YES ✓ NO

Essential information in case message is wrongly delivered.

Message for *Jack Foster, Accounts Dept*

Time *11.15* Date *22.5.19--*

Sometimes the dates and times of receipt of message are very important. Also provides note of time elapsed since message arrived.

When you were out

M s *Sandra Jones, Accounts Dept*

Of *COMPUTA SOFTWARE LTD, High St, Kingston-on-Thames*

Telephone *01-632 9632 Ext 275*

Good messages always convey: who, of whom, where located, telephone nos, including STD code and extension.

☑ Telephoned   ☐ Wants to see you
☑ Wants you to phone   ☐ Came to see you
☐ Will phone later   ☐ Will come back later
☐ Returned your call

Most message pads include a tick checklist of back-up information for recipient, of which this specimen shows a sample.

Message *Apparently, our payment for their integrated accounts package ACCOUNTAZED is overdue for settlement. Sum due is £895.00. We stand to lose settlement discount unless we pay within 7 days. Ms Jones can authorise discount if you contact her directly and confirm payment on way.*

The effective message is: clearly written, unambiguous, provides essential detail and indicates follow-up action needed.

Taken by *Jean Roberts*

For follow-up briefing if needed.

Produced by Waterlow Business Forms (A Division of Oyez Stationery Ltd.)
Oyez House, 16 Third Avenue, Denbigh West Industrial Estate, Bletchley, Milton Keynes MK1 1TE.

FORM OA1
2/87

The above specimen preprinted message pad contains spaces for entering key information – names, times, telephone numbers etc. Also, to save time, boxes are included for ticking against appropriate options.

■ **TOP ASSISTANT TIP:**
Always keep such a message pad handy on your desk top, by the phone with adjacent pen or pencil!

USING THE TELEPHONE EFFECTIVELY IN ORGANISATIONS

Nowhere has the impact of IT been more dramatic over the past ten years than in the field of telecommunications. The introduction of fibre-optics technology now enables thousands of telephone conversations to be carried simultaneously along pencil-thin lines. The development of ISDN – Integrated Services Digital Network – has made it possible for international companies like Plessey to design and instal ISDNs in companies which route telephone-calls, computerised digital information, closed circuit TV pictures, fax, telex and videotex messages *all along a single 'plumbed-in' network of wires*! This integrated system links internal users together and routes incoming and outgoing messages both locally and around the world via telephone line and radio signal.

Telephone services have benefited tremendously from the IT developments of the 1980s. In the UK, telephone exchanges are being progressively

upgraded to a computerised digital system which provides users with eight major services:

▶ call waiting warning signal;
▶ abbreviated call coding (often used numbers are given a two-digit number);
▶ up to 27 numbers' repeat last call;
▶ charge advice (details of the cost of a call);
▶ call diversion (routing a call to another handset);
▶ 3-way link-ups;
▶ call-barring (e.g. not allowing a given handset to make long-distance calls).

Programmable PABX systems

Today the telephone switchboards (PABXs – Private Automatic Branch Exchanges) in the reception areas of most organisations are highly sophisticated, thanks to silicon-chip electronics. Office administration managers are now able to control telephone costs by supplying each department or organisational cost-centre with weekly and monthly breakdowns of the costs of their telephone and fax calls.

Similarly, each internal telephone extension may be programmed, for example, to allow its user to dial straight out, bypassing the switchboard; or the same extension may be programmed to go through the switchboard which logs and costs each call. In the same way, an extension may be programmed to dial straight out to the locality, but barred from direct-dialling long-distance calls.

Computerised automatic branch exchange (CABX)

The following table outlines some of the major features of a large computerised automatic branch exchange (CABX), in this case the Ferranti Omni GTE System:

Other major features included in CABX systems are

Amplifying speech
To enable an incoming call to be heard across a room

Night service
Enables incoming calls to be answered by late staying staff after switchboard staff have left

Major typical features of a large CABX system

This table is based upon the Ferranti GTE OMNI System and is kindly made available by Ferranti GTE Ltd)

Some of OMNI's system features

Administration message recording – to provide usage reports

Dictation access – providing a link to dictation services

Group hunting – seeking out any one of a working team's extensions available to take an in-coming call by trying each in turn

Intercom groups – linking users via intercom speakers

Music on hold – playing a soothing tune over the phone while a caller is waiting to be connected

Paging and code calling access – the ability to activate pagers used by roving staff

Standby power – facility to keep system going in event of power failure

Call barring – ability to restrict the range of connections availability on any extension

Some attendant features

Automatic recall re-dial – system keeps trying to connect to a busy number

Break in – facility to break into an active conversation in case of urgency

Call waiting – provision to alert extension user of another call awaiting attention

Camp on busy – ability to wait, having dialled a number until it becomes available and then to ring dialler's extension having effected the connection

Conference – linking of several extension users so all can converse with each other over the phone – system can also include outside callers

Some extension features

Abbreviated dialling – often used numbers are given a short 1/2 digit code to save time

Boss–secretary – direct interconnection

Call forwarding follow me – instruction for incoming calls to be routed from a customary extension to others near to a roving staff member

Call hold – facility to keep line open to caller while specific staff member located

Direct inward dialling – facility to enable incoming calls to be routed directly to selected extension by adding its number to normal organisation's number

Direct outward dialling – facility to access PSTN directly

Do not disturb – cuts phone off while meeting etc taking place; avoids irritating interruptions

Extension to extension calling – for direct in-house phone calls

Call parking

The ability to divert an incoming call to another extension

'No answer' transfer

Facility to re-route a call to another, specified extension

Note: Many of the above features of computerised switchboards are available to the general public with the introduction of BT's System X digital exchanges.

Telephones and desktop terminals

Many executives and their support staff nowadays work very closely with their desktop networked computer terminal. The applications software they employ usually includes an integrated personal organiser package combining WP, spreadsheet, electronic diary, graphics and a *communications package*. This feature connects the user's terminal, telephone extension with the organisation's link to the national telephone system. As a result, calls can be 'dialled' using the keyboard and abbreviated calling features and amplifiers employed instead of handsets. And already on the market is the video phone, where both parties see one another on their VDU screens as they talk!

Becoming IT confident!

As this overview indicates, information technology is transforming the ways in which telephones are used in organisations. New features are being introduced to telephone systems all the time. And so it is very important that you take pains to become IT confident where telephones are concerned, since there is nothing more embarrassing than cutting a caller off by mistake, or being unable to transfer them etc. So, *always make sure you can 'drive' the telephone system where you work competently and confidently!*

Using a telephone with a direct outside line

If you work in a small company you may very well find that the telephone you use is directly connected to your local public telephone exchange. If this is the case, then you need to familiarise yourself with your local telephone directory, which contains information on:

▶ Services available from the operator – e.g. alarm calls and call costing.
▶ Local, national and international call prefix and area codes.
▶ Local useful numbers directory.
▶ Credit charged calls, reversed call charges.
▶ Person-to-person calls.
▶ Telemessages, fax services.
▶ Directory enquiries, sales services.

You should also keep constantly in mind the cost of calls. National telephone companies like BT and Mercury publish cost tariffs in which charges are rated according to the distance of the call. They also produce and update schedules detailing peak and off-peak times when the cost of calls is dearer or cheaper. Calls are always cheaper during the week, for example, after 12.00 pm.

Also, keep firmly in mind that directly dialled calls – Subscriber Trunk Dialling (STD) long-distance in the UK, and International Direct Dialling (IDD) overseas – are *always cheaper than making calls through the operator.*

It is therefore good practice to keep a list of often-used numbers with area codes/prefixes by your telephone for handy reference. Believe it or not, millions of pounds are wasted each year by people dialling wrong numbers – numbers they thought they had correct in their heads. So, whenever in doubt, check it out!

Using an internal telephone extension

If you work in a medium to large organisation, it is most likely that you will use a telephone extension to make and take calls. In this case, it is vital from day one that you obtain a copy of the operating manual or instructions for your particular system, especially if it embodies computerised features.

The following checklist provides you with a guide to some of the commonly occurring features of extensions connected to typical CABXs:

1 Dialling out

Extension users normally access the switchboard console operator by dialling 0 and acquire an outside line by dialling 9. On many systems it is possible also to dial an extension number on the organisation's private line circuit by dialling 7 followed by the number.

2 Handling calls coming in to the extension

Remember that an important part of your role at work may be to act as a preliminary filter of calls and to handle them accordingly. Here the computerised systems offer many useful features which may be activated (if the system operates MF4 handsets) by pressing the R button and then dialling various codes:

▶ Putting an incoming call on HOLD. This enables a secretary, for example, to talk without the caller hearing – for instance, to check with the manager whether he is 'in'.
▶ *Transferring* incoming calls to another extension, for example, when it becomes apparent that another department or staff member is needed.
▶ *Parking* an incoming call; sometimes it is necessary to keep a call in suspension while checking a matter with another extension user etc.
▶ *Shuttling* between an incoming call and an

extension; this feature enables an extension user to move back and forth between two lines without either hearing the other and the user talking.

▶ *Conferencing* is a feature which permits a number of internal extensions and external lines to be linked by the extension users dialling up a code. The secretary may be expected to 'line up' such a conference for her manager.

Note: codes are available to retrieve calls put on 'park', 'hold' or 'transfer'.

In the context of taking calls, it is important to remember that most managers have the system programmed so that their secretaries' extensions intercept all incoming calls to the manager for prior screening.

Making calls

Outside calls may be made either by dialling 9 followed by the prefix and number needed or via the console operator after dialling 0. The following internal features are also available to the extension user:

▶ *Automatic ring back* allows the system to ring the user's number when contact has been made with a number which was not immediately obtainable. The user does not have to hang on to the extension receiver while waiting. This feature also comes into play if an internal extension number is busy when dialled.

▶ *Ring back when in* is a feature where the system notes an extension number is not being answered and then retries the user's call after it picks up the fact that the desired extension has just been used.

▶ *Ring back for an exchange line* contacts the extension user (the bell rings) when an exchange line becomes available if all were busy when the user wished to dial out.

▶ *Piggybacking* is a jargon term used to describe a feature which enables the extension user to contact other extension users on a different but connected CABX system – say of a sister company or subsidiary.

Other useful features

Most systems enable mobile support staff and

managers to have incoming or extension calls forwarded from their home extensions to other assigned extensions. For example, if you plan to spend some time in the reprographics unit, you may arrange for incoming calls to be rerouted there.

▶ *Call forward* diverts calls to another extension and prevents the home extension being used.

▶ *Follow me* allows calls to be routed to further extensions as the user moves around the organisation's buildings.

▶ *Alarm call* allows any user to arrange for a call to be made to a given handset in order to act as a reminder for, say, an important meeting. Secretaries who know they become engrossed in their work use this feature to help them remember their managers' priority appointments or overseas calls to be made, etc.

▶ *Night service* allows an extension user to make and take calls after the operator has gone home.

▶ *Call waiting and intrusion* are features where the handset user is made aware of other callers queuing to talk to him/her (call waiting) and of a need for a priority user to access the line being used or to access the caller directly in an emergency (intrusion).

▶ *Do not disturb* allows the user of any given extension to put a bar on receiving any calls until further notice – vital if sensitive and important interviews and meetings are not to be interrupted, or if a priority task is under way.

While the telephone system in use where you are located may not embody all the features outlined above, it is nevertheless important for you to be aware of them, not least when you are making calls to other organisations.

■ **TOP ASSISTANT TIP**

Nine times out of ten, you make a telephone call which requires the call-taker at the other end to undertake some action on your behalf. Always keep in mind, therefore, that such a person is much more likely to act on your request promptly and conscientiously *if he or she is well disposed towards you* because you made a special effort to get on good terms and establish a friendly relationship.

Golden rules: call making and taking:

The following 'Golden Rules' will help you to become a successful telephone user:

As a call taker

1 Always keep a message pad and pencil handy by the telephone. Delays in finding something to write on cost time and are inefficient. Scraps of paper are easily lost or not recognised as message sheets.

2 Always confirm to the caller your name, job title or your department. Do not hide behind anonymity.

3 Make sure early in the call that you obtain the caller's name, job title, telephone number and organisation. Such information is essential if you need to contact him later, or need to pass on a message.

4 Before you pass a caller on to your boss or a senior colleague, be sure to ask politely the nature of his business. Your senior staff may not always wish to speak to callers and they must know what the call is about before the caller may be told that they are 'in' or 'available'.

5 Take care to note the essential items of the caller's message. Do not be afraid to ask for repeats or spellings when you are unsure. Ask the caller to proceed more slowly if you are taking down a complex message.

6 At the end of the message, repeat its main points as feedback to the caller to ensure that you have neither misunderstood nor omitted anything important.

7 Check that you have the points in 3 above before the caller rings off.

8 Be courteous at all times. It is easy to sound brusque or curt on the telephone. Tell the caller that you will pass on his message or take the necessary action.

9 After the call, convert your brief notes into a fair copy on a fresh message pad if the caller's message is intended for an absent third party and check that everything has been clearly stated.

10 Always pass on messages and take any follow-up action immediately. it is only too easy to forget when something else crops up.

As a call maker

1 Decide what your main aims are *before* you make the call.

2 Make a checklist of your main points *before* you start your call.

3 Have any relevant documents to hand which you may need to refer to. This will save time and you will appear efficient.

4 Have pad and pencil ready to take any notes.

5 Make sure if possible whom you wish to speak to before you start. Otherwise you may repeat your message to several people unnecessarily.

6 *Always* obtain the name of your call-taker – you may need to follow up your call or to check progress.

7 Never guess at telephone numbers – always check. Millions of wrong numbers are dialled each year at great cost.

8 When connected, announce yourself, your company and say to whom you wish to speak. It helps to know people's extension numbers as this saves an operator's time, if you cannot dial through yourself.

9 When delivering your message, speak clearly and do not gabble – the call taker may be writing your message down.

10 Give spellings of names, addresses etc. Also repeat invoice or telephone numbers.

11 Make sure the call taker has understood the essential parts of your mesage. Get him to repeat it to you, if need be.

12 Avoid distractions and interruptions while making the call. You may miss something vital.

13 Remember to thank the call taker for his help. Courtesy costs nothing and is essential at all times.

14 Carry out any follow-up actions before you forget – it is easy to be distracted by the next job or visitor.

15 Remember that using the telephone is expensive. Use the cheaper times; call back rather than be kept waiting.

Checklist for an effective telephone message pad

You may be fortunate and have access where you work to a well-designed telephone message pad.

If not, then use the checklist set out below to design one of your own for desktop publishing and copying.

BOLD TITLE – so you can spot it quickly on a crowded desk.

URGENT and/or CONFIDENTIAL indicators

Spaces in which to write:

MESSAGE FOR
TIME TAKEN
DATE

MESSAGE FROM (with enough space for caller's name and job title)

OF (with enough space for full postal address including postcode)

TELEPHONE NUMBER
FAX NUMBER (increasingly supplied with phone numbers)

MESSAGE (ensure sufficient space supplied)

TAKEN BY (for name of message-taker)

Optional 'tick list' boxes and messages:

☐ Wants to speak urgently

☐ Wants you to return call

☐ Will call back later

☐ Wants to see you

    etc.

Telephone support toolkit

▶ A list of names numbers, addresses and details of contacts, ideally kept in the form of a computer database so that the required information may be called up and displayed on a monitor.

▶ A list of national IDD prefixes for long-distance calls, ideally in the form of a computer database.

▶ Loaded abbreviated numbers for frequently used calls.

▶ Pre-printed message pad and pens.

▶ Up-to-date directory of internal extension numbers.

▶ Access to national/international telephone directories and local/national *Yellow Pages*.

▶ A list of local number prefixes.

▶ Access to LAN/WAN communications module.

▶ CABX operating terminal.

ORAL COMMUNICATION AND RECEPTION ACTIVITIES

Whether they realise it or not, everyone working in an office becomes involved in reception activities from time to time. For example, an assistant may be the only person 'holding the office fort' over the lunch break, or a flu virus may have laid the office low so that for the few still getting in to work it's all hands to the pump. Or again, both departmental manager and secretary may be tied up in a meeting, so that someone else has to pick up the job of answering the phone and greeting visitors.

As you can see, there are many occasions when office staff have to assume reception activities with little or no warning. This being the case, it is important to be aware of the skills involved and to have a clear understanding of the expectations built into the receptionist role by customers and colleagues alike.

Customer Care Rules – OK!

Of recent years many organisations in both private and public sectors have come to realise how crucial to their survival and prosperity is the customer. Whether as a purchaser or as a member of the local community, customers are the lifeblood of virtually all organisations. No customers – no sales or services – no jobs!

As a result of concerted efforts by senior management teams, many companies and public service agencies have today developed policies of *customer care*. In other words, the needs of the customers are kept continually in mind. Even within the organisation, this idea is maintained. For example, personnel who use the facilities of a reprographics unit are its customers, a firm's employees are the customers of those staff who produce the weekly and monthly payrolls. And so, whether dealing with an external or internal customer, each and every member of staff is trained and motivated to produce work of the highest quality for the particular customers they serve each day.

The customer and reception

Staff who work full-time in the reception foyers of large organisations have it instilled into them that *they provide the first and lasting impression a visitor receives of the organisation*. By the same token, theirs will be the first voice on the telephone heard by someone ringing in. As a result, they take particular pains to:

▶ look well turned out in their dress and appearance;

▶ maintain at all times a polite and friendly manner which is not, however, over-familiar;

▶ keep their reception resources – directories, internal telephone lists, visitors' book, office room occupation charts etc – up to date and tidy;

▶ look after the general appearance of the reception area and furniture, removing old newspapers and notices, ensuring that furniture is clean and comfortable and that flowers and plants are regularly watered;

▶ ensure that coffee and/or tea-making equipment and cups etc are in good repair, 'squeaky clean' and wholesome at all times;

▶ keep a check on the equipment they use – telephones, switchboards, PCs, fax machines etc – so that communication does not break down.

In this way, the customer or visitor arriving at the reception area gains a good first impression of the organisation, that, in effect:

▶ his custom or business is important and valued;

▶ the organisation cares about the image it is communicating to the outside world;

▶ positive actions are taken to put the visitor at ease, to connect him or her with their host within the organisation as promptly as possible;

▶ waiting time is made as comfortable as possible by offering the hospitality of a hot (or cold) drink and appropriate newspaper or magazines to read, or telephone to use if need be.

The following checklist provides you with an overview of the features and facilities of a reception area – whether in a front-of-house foyer or part of a department.

Important features of an effective reception area

Reception point Should be a focus, easily seen and recognised but without the appearance of a barrier.

Telephone system Must be capable of connection with all internal extensions and have the capacity to handle the volume of incoming calls so that callers are not kept waiting.

Furniture Above all, reception furniture must be smart and clean; armchairs, an occasional table, magazine rack and facilities to hang overcoats and hold umbrellas are essential.

Lighting Should be warm and pleasant and strong enough, near visitors' chairs, to read by.

Décor Interior designers favour calm pastel shades like greens, ivories and oatmeals, rather than aggressive reds, harsh yellows or cold blues.

Living plants The texture and shape of living plants and flowers are most important in enlivening impersonal office fixtures and fittings.

Magazines and newspapers Should always be current. Out-of-date reading material creates a 'don't care' image; some firms like to include copies of their house magazines.

Refreshments It is now common practice to be able to offer fresh coffee, tea or soft drink.

Access to an outside line Some reception areas include notices offering access to an outside phone line as a courtesy.

Sources of information Local/national/international telephone and fax directories, internal telephone and fax directories, key personnel home telephone numbers etc.

(see checklist below)

Sources of information and support in reception

The well-organised receptionist will ensure that helpful sources of information and support are to hand for use in the reception area. These include:

▶ A regularly updated version of the organisation's internal telephone directory of extension numbers and a schedule of company personnel names, designations and locations.
▶ A set of local/national telephone/telex/fax directories.
▶ Appropriate handbooks and Yearbooks, such as: *Kelly's Directory of Streets, The Municipal Year Book, British Rail Timetables* etc.
▶ A schedule of key telephone numbers including those for use in emergency, the manager's home telephone number, the company doctor/nurse, the duty security officer, etc.
▶ Details of the organisation's instructions and arrangements for emergency evacuation and assembly points.
▶ A first aid kit and manual.
▶ Duplicate maps of the organisation's premises and grounds (to help guide visitors) and maps/plans of the locality.
▶ Telephone/spoken word message pad and notebook to take messages and to log callers and visitors.
▶ A visible system to log office staff as 'in' or 'out'.

Logging in and out

As a result of bitter experience, many companies today are extremely careful about their security. In the past too many agents of competing firms have managed to gain entry to complexes and engage in industrial espionage simply by getting past reception, and, for example, donning a white smock in a toilet and carrying a clip-board about from workshop to laboratory!

Nowadays, therefore, all visitors are most likely to be obliged to sign in on a visitors' book at reception and be logged in and out by the receptionist. They may also have to prove their identity (say at an arms factory) and be given a visitor's badge to wear. Almost certainly they will be escorted wherever they go if the organisation is at all sensitive about its security.

Fig. 7.1 *Example of a visitor's book*

DATE	ARRIVAL	NAME	ORGANISATION	TO SEE	LEAVING TIME
22/6/9-	11-00	JACK BROWN	Apex office Systems	JEAN WATTS	11-45

Sometimes completed by receptionist

In addition, organisations which are situated along busy main streets in cities usually have a 'panic button' device for summoning commissionaires or security staff if, say, someone who is drunk and disorderly wanders in off the street.

The daily appointments register

Large organisations, such as national head offices in multi-storey office blocks, employ a system whereby departmental secretaries send details of appointments a day or week ahead to the receptionist who then produces a complete list for each day of visitors who are expected, including times of arrival, their names and organisations, who they have come to see, and the room locations. Such a schedule supports security and public relations, since, on arrival, the visitor may be welcomed by name and impressed by the fact that he or she is expected.

Fig. 7.2 Example of an appointments schedule

Date Day Time (From To)	Wednesday 12 September 11-30 – 12-00 pm.		
Name Alice Hurst	**Organisation** Yellow Pages	**To See:** John Wright, Advertising manager	**Dept.** Room No. 209 Floor 16

Communication qualities needed for reception

Whether you are engaged in full-time reception work, or become involved as the result of working in an office, the following guidelines will help you establish your own code of communication practice when undertaking reception activities.

Always remember that, no matter how busy or preoccupied you may be, your visitor or caller will gain perhaps a lasting impression of your organisation by the way *you* behave and respond!

Communication skills for effective reception

A friendly face and greeting

Visitors tend to be somewhat stressed on visiting an organisation – they may be expected to bring off an important deal – and so a friendly and outgoing greeting is always welcome:

> 'Good morning, madam, welcome to Educational Publishing! How may I help you?'

Establishing credentials

It is always important to establish the visitor's credentials (who exactly is he or she?) and to check out whom he or she wishes to see. This is often achieved most diplomatically by asking the visitor to sign in to the visitors' book. By so doing, the visitor's identity and company will quickly become apparent without the need to ask directly.

Note: But never be too shy to ask politely:

> 'Would you mind confirming your name and organisation, please.'

If the visit is made in good faith, no resentment will be caused.

Contacting the visitor's host

Entrepreneurial sales representatives have been known to slip past reception by claiming arranged appointments which are a fiction! It therefore pays to contact the visitor's host along these lines:

> 'Would you like to take a seat Mr Phillips, I'll tell Miss Pearson that you are here . . . (rings Miss Pearson) I have a Mr Phillips in Reception, here to see you at 11.15 . . .'

Such an approach cannot be faulted by the visitor, and gives Miss Pearson the opportunity either to confirm the appointment or to refute it. If confirmed, then the receptionist can say:

> 'Miss Pearson's secretary will be along directly to take you to her office.'

If, however, the appointment is a 'try-on', then the receptionist may be instructed (by Miss Pearson over the phone) either to deny access:

> 'I'm afraid that Miss Pearson is tied up in a meeting all day. Would you care to telephone her secretary for an appointment?'

Or, if the visitor's business is felt to be important,

> 'Miss Pearson is tied up today, but her secretary will be along directly to make a firm appointment for you.'

In such ways, access to busy executives is controlled without situations becoming fraught or politeness being strained – perhaps in the hearing of other visitors.

Dealing with delays

Sometimes a visitor's contact may be delayed by a telephone call or meeting with a superior. In such situations the effective receptionist obtains first an informed estimate of the likely length of the delay:

> 'Mr Jackson sends his apologies. He's temporarily detained with the MD, but will be here in no more than ten minutes . . .'

and then makes the visitor feel comfortable:

> 'In the meantime, can I get you a coffee or tea? . . . You'll find today's newspapers in the rack to your left.'

Having made the visitor comfortable, the receptionist should keep an eye on the clock to ensure that ten minutes does not become twenty without telephoning to the contact's office to find out the reason for any further delay. This call also acts as a prompt and reminder to the staff involved.

Checking the visitors' book

Before the visitor is collected and badges fixed to lapels, the receptionist should check out the Visitors' Book unobtrusively and, where appropriate cross-check the entry to that of the Appointments Register for the day.

Dealing with difficult visitors

Sooner or later, the receptionist will need to cope with a difficult visitor or telephone caller. Working on reception is like being at the front line – people tend to aim their irritations and frustrations at the receptionist simply because he or she is available and represents the organisation.

Communication techniques in difficult situations include the following approaches:

> **Never, ever allow an irate person to cause *you* to lose your temper**

A wise saying goes: 'Once you've lost your temper, you've lost!'

Calm your visitor/caller by offering direct help:

> 'I can see why you're upset, and I'll take down your details so as to pass them on directly.'

The act of showing sympathy and offering positive action usually serves to calm people bit by bit.

Make a checklist of the major aspects of the problem and who in the organisation is the best person to deal with the matter.

Contact this person (ideally out of the hearing of the irate visitor) and brief him or her on the problem. Always seek to get him or her to reception to escort the visitor to a private room – nobody likes to hear raised voices in the reception area.

And keep in mind: while it is tempting to seek to resolve such problems alone and unaided, it is wiser to seek the help of a senior colleague with authority to make quick decisions and to trouble-shoot the incident without delay.

Another kind of difficult visitor or caller is the one who claims a personal friendship with a senior member of staff, and who uses this as a lever to try to get to see him or her without an appointment.

As you never can tell, it pays to contact the manager's PA or secretary and to relay the details:

> 'Mrs Carstairs has arrived in reception. I understand she is a friend of the Marketing Director and would like to see him directly . . .'

Such an approach is diplomatic. It does not immediately deny access, but should alert a PA or secretary directly. From this point on, the ball is in the court of the office of the manager concerned, from whom the receptionist can take the cue.

Logging the visitor out

Just as important as checking a visitor in is the process of logging him or her out. Some visitors' books include columns in which to note times of arrival and departure. This is of particular importance in the context of emergency evacuation of premises, when it is vital to know precisely who is in the building. For this reason also, many receptionists are given the job of logging staff in and out of the building.

Needless to say, identity badges are reclaimed at reception to prevent any future security lapses.

Reception and telephone messages

Full-time receptionists soon learn not to volunteer to pass on messages other than the genuinely urgent. The receptionist who gladly accepts the 'I'll take 'em all' message-relaying role will soon be snowed under! A better technique – and one that saves the firm money is:

> 'I'm afraid Mrs Keen is out of the office today. May I suggest you call again tomorrow?'

Thus the onus – and the cost of the follow-up call – is on the initiator, and the receptionist can attend fully to the next incoming call.

TAKING PART IN INTERVIEWS

Perhaps the most demanding aspect of oral communication is taking part in an interview, especially if it is part of the job application process. Interviews occur for a number of different reasons in organisations, since the face-to-face exchange of information is felt to be the best way of:

▶ gaining an insight into someone's personality as part of the recruitment process;

▶ getting to the heart of an interpersonal problem;

▶ uncovering information which people are reluctant to write down;

▶ arriving at a clear understanding about what constitutes acceptable conduct, or required observation of company regulations in a disciplining situation;

▶ negotiating and agreeing targets for the year ahead;

▶ establishing whether a member of staff is ready for promotion.

In other words, the interview is used by managers as a part of the following processes:

RECRUITMENT ▪ TROUBLE-SHOOTING ▪ COUNSELLING ▪ DISCIPLINING ▪ PERFORMANCE MEASURING ▪ JOB APPRAISAL ▪ PROMOTING ▪ FACT-FINDING ▪ NEGOTIATING

Some interviews – notably for recruitment or promotion – are conducted by panels of interviewers such as the line manager involved, the personnel manager and a senior member of the organisation. Others, however, take place on a one-to-one basis, since the interviewee is much more likely to 'open up' if the interview is considered by both parties to be confidential and private.

Some organisations consider the panel approach too stressful for interviewees in the job selection process and organise instead several one-to-one interviews after which the interviewers get together to compare notes and arrive at a decision.

The interview as a transaction

Whatever the reason for an interview being held, it is best regarded by both interviewer and interviewee alike as a transaction, as a process in which both parties seek to obtain outcomes which they have thought about and identified in advance.

For example, in the job selection interview, the employers will be seeking to find out whether each candidate has the knowledge, experience, interpersonal skills, motivation and development potential to carry out the job on offer and to grow with the firm. Similarly, the candidate will need to be assured about the organisation's financial position (i.e. that redundancy is unlikely in the foreseeable future if the post is accepted), that the key features of the post offer job satisfaction, that pay, holidays, pension scheme and general conditions of service are attractive and so on.

As a result of this transaction approach, the interviewer(s) and interviewee have key questions to ask and respond to. And so this section examines oral communication techniques in the context of asking and answering questions, and pays particular attention to the job selection interview.

The job selection interview

As the chart on page 192 illustrates, the job selection interview is part of an extended and involved process. Not unnaturally, employers take pains to ensure that they appoint only high quality staff. Round pegs in square holes can cause much turmoil and hiring is generally easier than firing.

Information available to the interviewer or panel will come from:

▶ your application form;

▶ your curriculum vitae
(a summary of your education, career to date, qualifications, attainments and interests);

▶ your covering letter of application;

▶ confidential references (if taken up with your permission prior to the interview).

As you can see, the interviewers have quite a lot of information to assist them. Fortunately you will have supplied most of it. But it does pay *to keep photocopies of all documents sent to an employer in connection with a job application*. If you are making a series of applications, you may not otherwise recall what precise information you gave to whom.

What influences the interviewing panel?

Before examining the techniques of being an interviewee, it pays to know what will influence the interviewers and guide them to a choice of candidate. The following checklist indicates the key influencers which you should take pains to display to your best ability:

Techniques of communication in interviews

Overcoming nerves

Feeling nervous both before and during an interview is perfectly natural. But to communicate such nervousness – by NVC signals like sitting in a hunched-up position, twisting a ring or speaking in breathless, jerky phrases – tends to make interviewers feel embarrassed for being the guilty parties who made you nervous in the first place! You must therefore take pains to control any nervousness or shyness. Good advice before you enter the interview room is to take in some deep breaths with your diaphragm. This will quieten the nervous stomach muscles which make your speech short-winded. Concentrate also on the fact that your interviewers are probably as nervous as you are and want you to perform well. But most of all, concentrate on what you know to be your strong points in connection with the post. Think positively like the American Football coach eyeballing his team before a big match:

> 'I know you can do it, you know *you* can do it, so let's get out there and *do* it!'

Giving off the right NVC signals

Try to think during the interview about the signals your body language is giving off. If the interviewers have put you at your ease, don't allow yourself to slump or sprawl in your chair. Avoid your gestures becoming over-excited or over-dramatic. Always make sure that you are communicating a professional sense of the occasion – neither too familiar nor too overawed.

When being asked a question by an interviewer, look in his or her direction and show that you are taking in the major points. But avoid your eye contact becoming a fixed stare!

Remember to smile at appropriate moments and to respond similarly to an interviewer's efforts to be light-hearted. No one likes to feel that their interviewing approach has the effect of overwhelming or intimidating a candidate.

Watching for NVC signals

The alert interviewee watches closely at all times – even when speaking – for NVC signals among the interviewers. For example, nodding heads and friendly expressions indicate that what the interviewee is saying is going down well and should be reinforced or emphasised. Frowns, pursed lips or negative murmurs indicate just the opposite. Similarly an interviewer may signal a desire to break in, in which case the thinking interviewee pauses graciously to take on a follow-up question. Yet again, signs of impatience like tapping the table with a pencil may signal that the interviewee has spoken for too long and should stop so as to allow the next question. As you can see, monitoring the interviewers' NVC signals can pay handsome dividends!

Listening and thinking before speaking

Although the interview process can throw candidates off guard, it is important to make oneself concentrate on the question being posed, so as to think quickly about:

▶ What is this question really getting at?
▶ How can I relate it to my experience and knowledge?
▶ Wow! This question's hit me between the eyes! How can I edge around it and get back on to safer ground?
▶ Are there any underlying traps or follow-ups to this question?

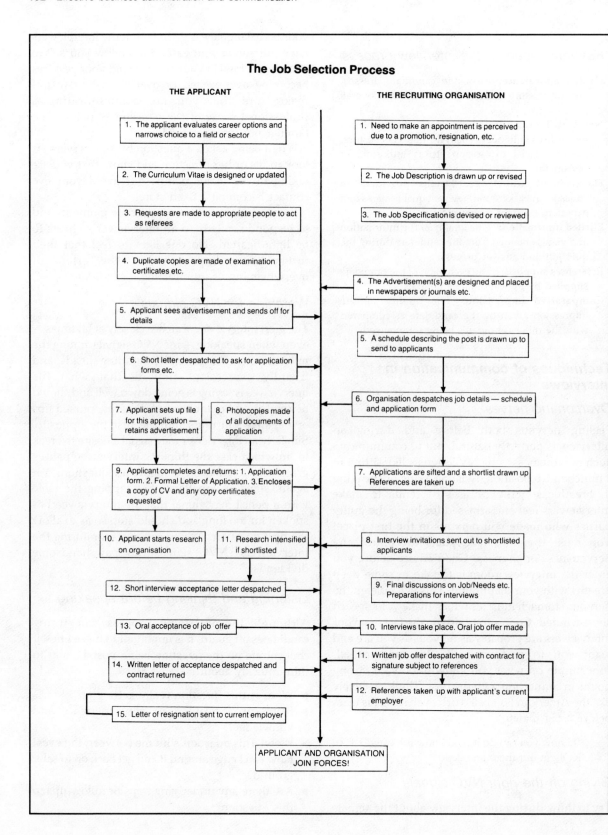

The Job Selection Process

THE APPLICANT

THE RECRUITING ORGANISATION

1. The applicant evaluates career options and narrows choice to a field or sector

2. The Curriculum Vitae is designed or updated

3. Requests are made to appropriate people to act as referees

4. Duplicate copies are made of examination certificates etc.

5. Applicant sees advertisement and sends off for details

6. Short letter despatched to ask for application forms etc.

7. Applicant sets up file for this application — retains advertisement

8. Photocopies made of all documents of application

9. Applicant completes and returns: 1. Application form. 2. Formal Letter of Application. 3. Encloses a copy of CV and any copy certificates requested

10. Applicant starts research on organisation

11. Research intensified if shortlisted

12. Short interview acceptance letter despatched

13. Oral acceptance of job offer

14. Written letter of acceptance despatched and contract returned

15. Letter of resignation sent to current employer

1. Need to make an appointment is perceived due to a promotion, resignation, etc.

2. The Job Description is drawn up or revised

3. The Job Specification is devised or reviewed

4. The Advertisement(s) are designed and placed in newspapers or journals etc.

5. A schedule describing the post is drawn up to send to applicants

6. Organisation despatches job details — schedule and application form

7. Applications are sifted and a shortlist drawn up References are taken up

8. Interview invitations sent out to shortlisted applicants

9. Final discussions on Job/Needs etc. Preparations for interviews

10. Interviews take place. Oral job offer made

11. Written job offer despatched with contract for signature subject to references

12. References taken up with applicant's current employer

APPLICANT AND ORGANISATION JOIN FORCES!

Speech mannerisms while speaking

Take pains to monitor what you are saying as you say it. Avoid repeating meaningless phrases such as:

> You know; If you see what I mean; kind of; etc.

By the same token avoid umming and erring as you speak. Try always to speak in completed sentences and remember that it is better to make a short silent pause as you collect your thoughts before making your next point.

Pacing what you say

It is not easy to know when you have provided a sufficient response to a given question. Nerves can make a candidate gabble on in a torrent of words which only serve to irritate the panel. On the other hand, short or monosyllabic answers can prove equally frustrating to a panel trying to provide opportunities for candidates to show what they know.

So keep an eye on your questioner. Pause regularly so as to provide an opportunity for any follow-up questions and, as a rule of thumb, make your answers shorter rather than longer.

Monitoring the quality of what you say

In the interview situation it pays to be honest when invited to give views on a topic, but also to provide a plausible reason for your viewpoint and to show that you are aware of conflicting views:

> 'I should personally prefer to work in an area of self-contained offices rather than in a large, open-plan office. I think that people generally work better where there is more privacy and smaller work groups. But I do appreciate that open-plan offices are more flexible in their design and less expensive to install.'

Also, try to avoid making sweeping generalisations that you do not justify with a good reasoned example:

> There's simply no comparison between a desktop PC and an electronic memory typewriter!

Much better is this response to the question 'Would you prefer to work with a desktop PC or an electronic typewriter with built-in memory?'

> 'It would very much depend on the kind of work I was doing. A desktop PC is much more versatile, providing as it does different software applications like WP spreadsheets and graphics. However, if I were solely concerned with text processing, then a good quality electronic typewriter might well prove faster and simpler to operate. And, depending on the printer connected to the PC, might well provide a better letter quality end product.'

Such an answer displays the ability to speak fluently and to weigh up pros and cons 'off the cuff'. It also displays a reassuring knowledge about the equipment under discussion.

Asking your own questions

Almost certainly towards the end of the interview the panel's chairman will say something like:

> 'Well you've been very patient with all our questions, is there anything you'd like to ask us?'

At all events avoid the response:

> 'No, not really, you seem to have covered everything pretty well . . .'

Even if this is true, such a response sounds lame and ineffectual. A better approach is along these lines:

> 'Well as a matter of fact, I did jot down one or two points to check out. (Taking card with questions on from pocket or handbag) If I may refer to my checklist . . . First, would you mind going over the salary conditions? Is there an annual salary review with this post?'

Effective candidates always take a prepared checklist with them on topics such as:

▶ What are the opportunities of promotion from the advertised post?
▶ If successful in my application, would I be eligible for further training and development?
▶ Can you give me an indication of the kind of equipment I would work with?
▶ Are there any opportunities with the post of study release to the College of Technology?

Such questions display an interest in personal development and provide an opportunity of finding out how committed the organisation really is to developing its personnel. But note: it is not advisable to make a dash in asking your own questions to those about salary and holidays!

Rather, show first an interest in questions about your developing in the job and where it leads etc.

The making and accepting of the job offer

In the private sector, the panel chairman is likely to end the interview with words like these:

> 'Thank you Mr/Mrs/Miss . . . for coming in for this interview. I hope you didn't find it too daunting. We'll be in touch in a day or two.'

A suitable response from the candidate would be:

> 'Thank you for inviting me. I shall look forward to hearing from you in due course.'

Private sector organisations rarely offer jobs on the spot. They usually take up references first and write to the successful candidate *after the interview day* to make a job offer subject to satisfactory references being taken up. Some public sector organisations call the candidate back into the interview room and make a job offer there and then. In such cases, the offer is expected to be accepted by the candidate. It is customary for those who decide that the post is not for them to communicate their withdrawal while the interviews are taking place.

Offers and acceptances of appointments need always to be confirmed in writing by both sides.

ACTIVITIES AND ASSIGNMENTS Oral and non-verbal communication skills

■ **THE QUICK CHECK-IT-OUT QUIZ**

1 In what way should regional accents and dialects be regarded in terms of oral communication?
2 Draw up your checklist of do's and don'ts for effective spoken word communication.
3 What is the importance of delivery and intonation when using the spoken word?
4 Make a list of irritating speech mannerisms to avoid in oral communication.
5 What are the key influencers of the spoken word?
6 Explain briefly the main features of non-verbal communication.
7 How does a knowledge of NVC assist the communicator in face-to-face situations?
8 What is meant by the term paralinguistics?
9 Draw up a checklist of good practice for a message taker.
10 Outline briefly the components of an effective message pad.
11 What is a PABX telephone system? How does it work?
12 What impact has IT had in recent years on telecommunications?
13 List some of the main features of a computerised automatic branch exchange.
14 What major areas of information would you expect to find in a BT telephone directory?
15 What principal services are obtainable from an internal telephone extension linked to a CABX system?
16 List the major resources and facilities available to a receptionist and visitors in an efficient reception area.
17 Explain the purposes of a Visitors' Book and a Daily Appointments Schedule.
18 As a receptionist, how would you cope in general terms with a difficult visitor?
19 In what situations in organisations are interviews particularly employed?
20 What tips could you give a candidate about communicating successfully in a job selection interview?

Case study activities

The following three case studies provide activities which develop NVQ competences in:

• *Receiving and responding to a variety of given information.*

- Adopting behaviour and language suitable for a particular work context, including register and style.
- Modifying speech and responses according to interactions with others.
- Relating and interacting effectively with individuals and groups.
- Working effectively as a member of a team.
- Relaying information in writing which is presented in a format that is clear, easily assimilated and appropriate for the use intended.

Case study 1

'TELL THEM I'M ON MY WAY!'

A reception case study

Shirley Stephens, an office assistant at Britalite Lamps Limited, works in the company's purchasing office. At present she is alone in the office during the lunch-break. Mr Hawkins, purchasing officer, has just left the office.

The telephone rings and Shirley takes the call:

'Hello? Who? Oh, Mr Simpson, production manager. You wanted Mr Hawkins? Well, he isn't here. He's out at the moment. Where? Oh, well, he didn't say, exactly, but I'm sure he won't be long. I see. You want him to ring you the moment he gets back. Oh, my name's Shirley. What? Oh, Stephens. yes, I'll tell him it's important. Right.'

At this point Tony Gupta, from the accounts department walks into the office:

'Excuse me.'

'Yes?'

'I've come down from accounts. Miss Carter wants your expenses sheet for last month. Supposed to have been sent up last week.'

'Oh. Well that's Jim Riley's fault. He's at lunch at the moment.'

'Well, can't *you* give it to me? I've rung down for it twice already!'

'Well, I would, but Jim's got his own particular filing system. He's very touchy about who tampers with it. *He* knows where everything is, but I wouldn't know where to start looking! Oh, all right, I suppose I can try.'

As Shirley starts to rummage through Jim Riley's papers, a clerk from the mail room arrives:

'Got a memo here for Mrs Catchpole. Marked urgent!'

'Oh well, put it down over there somewhere will

you. I'm tied up at the moment trying to find a wretched expenses sheet. Now where was I? . . . It's no good! We'll have to send it up to you this afternoon.'

'*Please* try to let me have it today. I can't get on till I've got it.'

Tony Gupta leaves and the telephone rings:

'Hello? Personnel? Oh. *Who* did you say? Carol Wainwright. Oh, Carol, I'm afraid not. Because she left about a week ago. Quite suddenly. How do you mean? Well it's not my job to tell you when people leave. If only people would give us a chance to get on here, without constant interruptions . . . Yes, I'll tell Mr Johnson. Oh! Now I know why you don't know! Mr Johnson's been off sick for the past fortnight. Bunion's been troubling him again . . . Well, Jean Parker does some of his work for him. Look, couldn't you give her a ring after lunch? Oh, all right, I suppose I could tell her to send you the details.'

Shirley rings off as Janet Goodson arrives from the company doctor's office:

'Hello, Shirley. How's things?'

'Don't ask! I've been rushed off my feet!'

'Well, I've just come from Dr Tanner. He's just had a call from the hospital. They've had a cancellation and could start the therapy treatment for your back. The appointment's for 2.30. You've just about got time if you hurry.'

'That's great news! Thanks! Tell them I'm on my way!'

With that, Shirley grabbed her coat and hurried off down the corridor, glancing anxiously at her watch.

■ *DISCUSSION TOPICS*

Discuss the following topics in small groups or in a general class session.

1 Read through the case study carefully. What shortcomings can you identify in the running of the purchasing office at Britalite Lamps?

2 How well did Shirley handle the callers and telephone-calls during the lunch-break?

3 What suggestions could you make for improving the way in which the purchasing office is organised and run?

■ *WRITTEN ACTIVITIES*

1 Rewrite the dialogue of the case study in the way that you think Shirley's conversations should have been conducted.

2 First check the section on message taking on page 184 and then write out the messages which you think Shirley should have written to the members of staff.

■ *ORAL ACTIVITY*

The following assignment should be role-played in pairs. The dialogue may be tape-recorded by individual pairs of students and the various interviews played back for discussion by the class.

One student should play the part of Mr Hawkins and the other the part of Shirley Stephens. Mr Hawkins has called Shirley into his office to take her to task over the way she handled matters during the lunch-break. Shirley does not feel she is entirely to blame.

Case study 2

'MORNIN' DARLIN'!'

A case study on handling an extrovert visitor

VISITOR: Mornin' Darlin'! Scott's the name and selling copiers' me game! Give Colesy a buzz and say I'm here would you please.

RECEPTIONIST: Good morning. I'm sorry I didn't quite catch your name . . . Are you Mr Scott or Scott Something . . . And is it Mr John Coles our Accounts Manager or Susan Coles our Assistant Office Administration Manager?

VIS: Yeah, that's right! No, don't mind me, only teasin'! It's the lovely Miss Susan I'm here to see. And the name's Scott Johnson – two teas, no sugar, get it?

REC: Oh I see. Well if you'd just sign in the Visitors' Book, I'll tell Miss Coles you're here. (*Rings Susan Coles extension*) . . . Oh, I see, I thought you were expecting to . . . No, no, I'll tell him.

Miss Coles says she's not expecting to see you today and is very tied up.

VIS: Ah, that'll be with tidying up the details of your new leasing contract with Copyco I 'spect. She did mention it. That'll be the mid-range model over there I think, just arrived has it? They usually send that one for testin'.

REC: Yes, it arrived only an hour ago and it's already in everybody's way. Look, I'm sorry but I've got other things to do than gossip with you all day!

VIS: You're quite right – let's do it after hours. Fancy a disco tonight? Followed by an Italian at Franco's? Tell you what, while you're makin' your mind up, just give Barry Jones a tinkle in Marketin'. He said he wanted to see me when I was next passin'. No, better than that, I'll slip up and surprise 'im mesself. Bit of a lad ol' Barry. (*Scott takes the stairs two at a time.*)

REC: I say! Wait a minute you're not supposed to . . . And you haven't filled out the Visitors' Book . . .

VIS: No, no, don't worry, I know where he lives!

■ **DISCUSSION POINTS**

1 Using the case study as a basis for discussion, examine how a crafty extrovert like Scott Johnson can best be handled by an effective receptionist.

2 In your opinion, where did the receptionist begin to go wrong and lose control of the situation?

3 What specific mistakes of the receptionist's did you spot?

4 What techniques did Scott use to gain access to the building and a sales prospect?

5 In the circumstances, what immediate action should the receptionist take?

Group activity

In small groups of three or four, discuss first how you think the receptionist should have handled Scott Johnson, and then rewrite the Scenario, starting your version from:
REC: Good morning . . . (after Scott has announced himself.)

Case study 3

'I HAPPEN TO BE A PERSONAL FRIEND OF THE MANAGING DIRECTOR!'

A case study on dealing with a difficult visitor

RECEPTIONIST: Good morning. Welcome to Eurocarriers, how can I help you?

VISITOR: Look, I'm in a hurry! Just ring up to Jack Cousins your Sales Director and tell him his old pal Fergus is down here waiting for him and he's late!

REC: I'm sorry, I'll need to have your full name and the company you represent – it's our standard procedure.

VIS: Look young lady, I haven't the time to bandy words with you. I happen to be a personal friend of the managing director! And if you don't stir yourself, I'll make sure he gets to hear of this PDQ!

REC: I'm sorry, sir. But I'll contact Mr Cousins' PA and ask her to come down to have a word with you.

(*Receptionist telephones PA's extension*) Hello, Fiona? There's a gentleman in reception called Fergus who is apparently a personal friend of Mr Cousins. I gather they are both late for an engagement off the premises, and he is insisting on seeing Mr Cousins immediately. Could you please come down to have a word with the gentleman? . . . No, no, you won't find a Mr Fergus in your appointments diary – that's his first name . . . Well, could you ask Mr Cousins to vouch for him personally? . . . He's tied up . . . But what about his meeting with the gentleman I have here . . .?

VIS: Oh, really, this is quite intolerable! Let me speak to her! (*Grabbing the phone.*) Now just you look here Fiona Whoeveryouare, I imagine Jack's forgotten our lunch date, and the client I am introducing him to, so if you value your job you just get hold of Mr Cousins and remind him of our date. Got it?

■ **DISCUSSION POINTS**

1 Consider the case study in terms of the problems which can ensue when handling an aggressive and difficult caller. How well did the receptionist cope with the situation? How do you rate her tone and general approach?

2 To what extent was the visitor responsible for the developing situation? How might he have handled matters better?

3 How well did Mr Cousins' PA, Fiona, react to the situation? Are there any aspects of her response which you would have handled differently?

4 What might either the receptionist or PA do directly to seek to retrieve the situation? Or did they act quite responsibly and therefore need to do nothing?

What would *you* do as either the receptionist or Fiona from the point where the scenario ends?

Group activity

In small groups of two or three, first decide what should be done in order to retrieve the situation outlined in the above scenario. Then write or tape your version of the rest of the scenario to its close. Compare your version with those produced by your co-worker groups and agree together on which approach is most likely to resolve matters.

Case study 4

WHAT MADE YOU APPLY FOR THIS POST?

A job selection interview case study

```
          WESTERN ENGINEERING LIMITED

            Required as soon as possible

              General Office Assistant

               to work in the Administration
                        Department

        We seek a bright and lively assistant with competent
        filing, bookkeeping and administrative skills; keyboarding
        and WP ability advantageous.

        Apply in writing to:
        The Personnel Manager, Western Engineering Limited,
        Box 23, MIDDLETON, Midshire MD3 4RG
```

Miss Jacqueline Singleton has been called for an interview for the post of office assistant in the office administration department of Western Engineering Limited:

JK: Good morning. Miss Singleton isn't it?

JS: Yes. Good morning.

JK: My name is John King, personnel manager, and this is Mrs Pauline Hope, office administration manager. Oh yes, do make yourself comfortable. I hope you had a good journey . . .

JS: Not too bad, thank you.

JK: Fine. Well now, you have applied for the post of general office assistant in our office administration department. As the details mentioned, the post has arisen because of the increase in the work of the department. You would report immediately to Mr Harrison, the senior clerk, and you would undertake a range of duties, including filing, some bookkeeping, petty cash recording, invoice processing and so on.

JS: Oh, I see.

JK: Now I see you are currently following a business education course at Westleigh College of Technology. What exactly does it involve?

JS: Oh, well, we do communication, word processing, office studies, computerised accounting, office organisation – that sort of thing. Oh, and there's an activities afternoon on a Wednesday. I'm doing car maintenance because I want to get a car when I'm seventeen.

JK: I see, and which of those subjects do you like best?

JS: I like word processing, and some of the communication. We do discussions, and case studies. The accounting's a bit boring sometimes . . .

JK: And what is a case study?

JS: It's a sort of problem, I 'spose. You sort of have a topic with a problem in it which you have to sort out.

JK: Do you think case studies help you to learn?

JS: Sometimes. But sometimes our group just argues and we don't always manage to agree!

JK: Yes, well some problems occur just like that here it seems, sometimes! And what examinations will you be taking?

JS: I think it's called the National Business Institute's Stage II Diploma.

JK: Oh yes, of course. Are you going to pass do you think?

JS: Hope so!

JK: Well I'm sure you'll do your best. Now, Mrs Hope has some questions to ask you.

PH: Hello, Jacqueline. As you know, I'm the office administration manager and you would be working in my department. Now, when you're not busy studying, what sort of leisure activities do you enjoy?

JS: Well, I like badminton, and dancing . . .

PH: What sort of dancing?

JS: Disco mostly.

PH: Do you belong to any clubs at the college or a youth club?

JS: No. I go around with a group of friends. I'm going steady with someone.

PH: I see. Now tell me, what made you apply for this post?

JS: Oh. Um. Well, I suppose I need a job! My dad says Western Engineering's got a good reputation. He used to work here.

PH: Did he, that's most interesting. But what about yourself? What attracts you to office work?

JS: Well, I like working with people . . . and word processing. I've always liked paperwork, I used to help me dad when he was a pools collector.

PH: Fine, and how about filing. With which systems are you familiar?

JS: Uuuuum. Mm. Well, the usual ones, in filing cabinets and folders and electronic filing. It's really great how quickly you can get to a file on a PC!

JK: Right, thank you Jacqueline. Now, is there anything you'd like to ask about the post?

JS: . . .Not really. You seem to have covered most of the points . . .

JK: Right. Well, thank you very much for coming. I'll be writing to you in a day or so. Please see my secretary about your travelling expenses. Goodbye, and thank you again.

■ **DISCUSSION TOPICS**

In small groups, examine this case study. Would *you* have given Jacqueline the job? Did she interview well? What would you have said or done in her place? Would she get the job?

Group activity

In groups of five or six, role-play three interviews of about ten minutes each with three class members playing the candidates, one John King, Personnel Manager, and one Mrs Hope, the Office Administration Manager. In advance of the interviews each candidate should compose a letter of application and before commencing, both as candidates and interviewers, make notes of the questions you intend to ask. Also, the interviewers should agree on a 'who does what' structure for the interviews.

Activities to develop competence and confidence:

The following activities develop NVQ competences in:

- *Adopting behaviour and language suitable for a particular work context.*
- *Receiving and relaying both oral and written messages.*
- *Receiving and making telephone calls.*
- *Receiving and assisting visitors.*
- *Composing business documents (forms).*
- *Working with others in a group.*
- *Presenting a positive image of the organisation.*
- *Providing information and advice to customers and clients.*
- *Using information sources.*
- *Applying design and creativity.*

Accent and pronunciation

1 Check the clarity of your vowels, diphthongs and consonants by tape-recording the following sentences by yourself:

Blue Skies Tours mean fine, warm days!

Mining underground often requires working in confined spaces.

Tempered steel displays both strength and elasticity.

Strict adherence to company regulations is essential.

Advertising is quickly becoming an integral part of people's lives.

Picking grapes is a popular choice for a working holiday.

Baking bricks is a back-breaking business!

Play back your recording and check that:

- the open vowels are really open;
- -ed, -ing endings are not clipped;
- 'h's have not been omitted;
- 's' and 'z' sounds are clear;
- syllables have not been slurred;
- consonants are clearly sounded.

Intonation and emphasis

2 Study the following extracts from three different work situations. Consider how you would use intonation, emphasis, pauses and voice-levels to make them as effective as possible when spoken. Re-write them using the key signs employed in the example on page 173. Then record them on to tape and submit your version for evaluation by your group:

'I wanted to speak to you about a personal matter as you know I have been with the company now for eighteen months as far as I know my work has always been satisfactory and I feel that I have been a conscientious employee I should therefore like to ask you for an increase in my salary.

'I have called you in to discuss a most serious matter with you during the past three weeks I have received a number of complaints from customers upset by your apparent rudeness while serving them I propose to outline the circumstances of each complaint from the customer's point of view and then to ask you for your own account of what allegedly took place.'

'Charlie we're in trouble Johnson's have just phoned a large order in but they must have it by tomorrow morning I told them I couldn't promise anything until I'd spoken to you is there any chance of your fitting in another production run I'd certainly appreciate it if you could use your influence.'

Non-verbal communication

3 If you have access to a camera or video TV equipment, make a series of slides or a short film to show a range of NVC signals. You may also wish to add an explanatory commentary.

4 Select a particular mood or feeling and mime it using NVC signals for the rest of the group – who must guess the mood.

5 From magazines and newspapers, collect a series of photographs which display certain NVC signals; remove any written clues and then mount the photographs on a placard. The rest of the group should then hold a competition to decide who can correctly define the signals in the pictures. The results should be scored against a prepared solution checklist.

6 During the course of a single day, make a note of any particularly interesting NVC signals you see and what you think they indicated. Swap experiences in a general group discussion.

■ *DISCUSSION TOPICS*

1 Studying other people's NVC behaviour amounts to taking unfair advantage of them.

2 Can people pretend and transmit false NVC signals, or do such signals tend to provide a true indication of someone's mood or attitude?

3 A sharper awareness of NVC improves a person's ability to communicate effectively.

4 NVC signals are mostly the result of the observer's imagination!

Written assignment

Compose a descriptive paragraph which indicates clearly to the reader the NVC signals of someone who is either worried, excited or impatient.

Message taking and relaying

Carry out the following activities in pairs:

1 Devise a message of not more than 100 words on the subject of one of the following:

a You are a van driver for Ace Refrigeration Limited. You have broken down in a country lane and have walked a mile to the nearest phone. You need to get a substitute articulated lorry to your location quickly, or 12 tons of frozen desserts are likely to melt as the temperature is in the 80s!

b You work for a company of training specialists. One of your top trainers, Peter Short is due this afternoon to give a presentation and hold a workshop on the subject of 'After Sales Service for Motorite Garages Limited' at their Bristol headquarters. Unfortunately Peter has rung in to say his wife (who is expecting a baby imminently) is poorly and he doesn't want to leave her.

You could offer another speaker on 'How To Increase Your Sales', or, 'Developing A Flexible Work Force', or you could arrange an alternative meeting
. . .

By arrangement, deliver your message over the telephone to either your Transport Manager, or Mr/Ms Leslie Gardner, Motorite's Training Manager. If possible, record the telephone conversations and play them back for constructive comments from your class.

Before commencing, consider carefully the role you have been given. Think about the needs of the organisation you represent and how you would react in real life. Make notes of the main points you wish to get across.

Telephone scenarios for role-play development

The following telephone situations may be used as the basis for role-playing simulation exercises or developed for group discussion and analysis purposes.
It is helpful to tape-record simulations for your class to assess later.

1 An irate customer succeeds in being connected to the General Manager of Home and Leisure Department Stores Ltd. He proceeds to complain in no uncertain terms about a defective television set he purchased from his local branch and the company's failure to rectify matters.
2 A prospective applicant rings in response to the current advertisement for the post of trainee sales representative in the Sales Department. The personnel manager's secretary takes the call. Her principal is at a meeting.
3 You receive an urgent telephone call, as assistant to the Personnel Director, from the Works Manager wishing to inform your boss that important negotiations with trade union negotiators have just broken down. The officers of the union are about to recommend an immediate strike with official backing if their demands for a new bonus incentive scheme are not met. The Personnel Director is attending a conference.
4 The personnel assistant of the County Treasurer receives a telephone call from one of the Treasurer's personal friends who insists on speaking to him. He is at an important meeting and has left instructions that he does not wish to be disturbed. The friend maintains that he wishes to speak to him upon a personal and confidential matter and will not, apparently, be put off.
5 As assistant to the Chief Buyer of Smartahomes Building Contractors Ltd, you receive a call from a sales representative wishing to speak to the Chief Buyer about a new line. The Chief Buyer tells you to handle the call.

With a little help . . .

With a little help from your teacher or lecturer, in pairs develop one of the above telephone scenarios into a role-play enacting the situation outlined. Tape-record your dialogue for playback and assessment by your group.

Reception practice and simulation activities

1 Design a Visitors' Book for recording the particulars of callers to an organisation which you think will prove simple and easy to use, yet which obtains all the necessary information from the caller.
   Compare your design with those produced by others in your group.
2 Design a form for recording incoming orally communicated messages. Try to produce a design which follows the general sequence of the message-taking process and which is quick and easy to absorb while ensuring a place for each important component of the message.
   When you have completed your design, check it against several existing designs which are either available in local stationers or have been produced by local firms.
3 Likewise, design a schedule (or computer database record) which will record the appropriate details of staff logging out of premises for business reasons etc and then returning later.
4 First identify the appropriate source of information (e.g. telephone directory) and then obtain and set down correctly the following:

a The customer enquiry telephone number of your local British Rail network.

b The telephone number of your nearest RAC breakdown service.

c The time of the last train on a Friday (in June or November) which will take a client from your nearest local station to London.

d The fax number of the Royal Society of Arts Examination Board, Coventry.

e The postcode of the street in which your main post office is located.

f The name, telephone number and address of your nearest airport.

g The direct dialling (IDD) telephone codes for:
Hungary–Budapest   Austria–Linz   Australia–Perth

Interview activities

1 In pairs, carry out the following interview on one another in succession:

Role A: Yourself as you are.

Role B: A market researcher engaged in finding out what leisure and spare-time interests local students engage in, where and at what weekly costs.
Before commencing, both students should spend about ten minutes working out what specific questions to ask and noting them down clearly.
If possible, tape-record both interviews for subsequent appraisal of the interviewer's and interviewee's oral communication skills.

2 *Location:* High Street Hi-Fi Ltd, Middleton Branch.

Roles: A: An irate customer bringing back a faulty personal cassette player which emits a scratchy background hiss when tapes are played.
B: Sales Assistant, who on examining the player finds a small dent at one corner and therefore suspects that it has been dropped or otherwise damaged.

Scenario: In pairs, play out the 'customer with a complaint' scene. Tape-record it for later class discussion.

3 Assume that you are short-listed for one of the following positions:
accounts clerk; clerical assistant; trainee motor-car or motor-cycle salesperson; sales assistant; receptionist

A panel of three students should devise:

a a display advertisement for the chosen post

b an application form for the post

c details of the post – pay, conditions of service, etc.

A series of candidates should:

a compose a letter of application for the post

b complete the application form

c devise a checklist of questions to ask

After both teams have completed their preparations, the interviews should be role-played and ideally recorded on video-tape or cassette for later evaluation. The panel should award the job to the best applicant and give their reasons for preferring one application to another. Two groups of students should act as observers, one to evaluate the performance of the panel, the other the performance of the candidates. These teams should also give a report on their assessments.

At the end of the assignment, a general discussion should take place to determine what facts have emerged from the simulation, and what has been learned from it.

4 *Location:* Supervisor's Office

Roles: A: Supervisor
B: Office Assistant

Scenario: For the past six weeks the office assistant has intermittently been arriving between ten and twenty minutes late for work in the mornings. Co-workers have become annoyed that nothing seems to be being done about it, and the supervisor decides a disciplinary interview is needed. The assistant has been late for work, partly because of late nights nursing a bedridden parent, and partly because his/her moped has broken down; he/she is saving up to have it repaired, but in the meantime is having to catch the 7.50 bus which is unreliable and sometimes gets delayed by the bypass roadworks.

In pairs, play out the scenario outlined above in 5–10 minutes, and tape-record it for subsequent assessment.

Both role players should first research into company grievance and disciplinary procedures to check out how a first disciplinary hearing is conducted.

5 In groups of three or four, design the following forms and interview support documents, for use in the job selection process of first-time appointments to office support posts:

a a job application form;

b a form to help interviewers note down their assessments of candidates during the interviews.

Work experience attachment assignments

1 Arrange to interview the appropriate manager in order to find out what aspects of accent, pronunciation and 'voice personality' are looked for when recruiting telephone switchboard operators and/or receptionists. Report back to your group on what you discover.

2 Carry out an informal survey of managers, supervisors and secretaries/PAs to find out what aspects of NVC they take note of or tend to use in face-to-face situations. If yours is a retailing organisation, also ask sales assistants about NVC in the context of serving customers. Report back to your group on the kinds of NVC signals which staff consider important to pick up or transmit.

3 Find out what forms/pads your organisation uses to take down and relay messages. Ask for specimens to keep for your base room and revision notes. Check whether there are any guidelines or procedures in force about message-taking. Ask support staff for tips and guidelines which they themselves have adopted. Make an oral report to your group on your findings.

4 Ask your attachment supervisor if you can be shown how the organisation's telephone system works, and seek to shadow a telephonist/receptionist for a morning. Make a note of the IT-related services the system offers staff and incoming callers. See if there are any internally published guidance notes on how to use the system and ask if you may keep a copy. Report back suitably on your findings to your class.

5 Survey the organisation's reception facilities – both general and departmental. Find out what resources and facilities are in use and interview staff so as to find out what demands are made of them and how they respond. Write a short report on your findings for your attachment supervisor. With his or her permission, share your findings with your class.

6 Arrange to interview the organisation's full-time receptionists and some of the departmental secretaries. Find out how they deal with difficult and demanding visitors and telephone callers. Make a checklist of the tips and guidelines you pick up to share with your class.

7 With authorisation, collect specimen blank or completed forms which the organisation uses in connection with:

   a reception activities;
   b telephone calls;
   c interviewing.

Seek to obtain permission to display some or all in your base room. Alternatively, convert the most interesting into OHP transparencies and explain to your class how they work in a presentation of about 5–10 minutes.

8 Interview a selection of managers by arrangement with a view to finding out what they consider to be the techniques of interviewing which they find most helpful. Note them down and collate them into suitably anonymous notes, then give your group an oral report on your findings.

9 Arrange to interview informally a cross-section of the organisation's employees with a view to finding out how they were interviewed for the posts they now hold and what tips they can pass on to someone like yourself on how to be an effective interviewee.

   Write a short article (of between 350 and 500 words) for your school or college newspaper based on your findings. Make sure your article is cleared first with your work attachment supervisor and teacher before publication.

10 Find out whether your organisation's training unit has any material on oral communication skill development. If so, ask if you may be given a copy to share with your class.

Part 8

Persuasive communication

OVERVIEW

Communicating factual information through invoices and statements, factsheets, reports, spreadsheets and memoranda etc is essential to the effective running of business and public sector organisations. But so, too, is the use of persuasion – in meetings, discussions, selling, presentations, advertising, public relations and so on. But, while few would argue the importance of exchanging factual information, for some there is a sense of uncertainty about using persuasive skills at work.

This Part examines the use of persuasive communication in organisations. It examines the ways in which persuasive skills are employed legitimately and shows how to recognise 'below the belt' applications.

In particular, Part 8 surveys the skills of speaking and writing persuasively in a work context, composing posters and notices for internal use, designing display advertisements, writing letters to the Press, selling products or services, persuasion in public relations and image-making.

NVQ references

This Part covers the following BTEC First Diploma In Business and Finance and 'ABC/NWPSS' competences:

BTEC First Diploma

Work Role:

Competences: 5 Presenting a positive image of the organisation, 6 Providing information and advice to customers.

Business Support Systems 1:

Competences: 5, 6 Supplying information for a specific purpose and drafting routine business communications.

Business Support Systems 2:

Competences: 2 Creating and maintaining professional relationships with customers and clients; 3 and 4 Responding to customers' needs for information on products and services and informing them about available products and services.

ABC/NWPSS

Level 2:
Unit 2 Communicating information.

Unit 10 Creating and maintaining business relationships.
Unit 11 Providing information to customers and clients.
Level 3:
Unit 5 Preparing and producing documents.

PERSUASION IN SPEAKING

It's the way that you say it!

The use of persuasion in the spoken word relies not just upon selecting the most appropriate words for a given situation, but also very much upon the ways in which we stress and emphasise the words and the ways in which we slacken or quicken the pace of what we say.

In communicating persuasively through the medium of the spoken word, it pays to keep constantly in mind the following:

How a message is spoken by means of rises and falls in the voice, emphasis of key words and phrases, pauses and rhythms etc, influences listeners just as much as the meaning of the words themselves.

Listeners will take their cue from the way the words are spoken. We are all accustomed to responding in particular ways according to the intonation and style of a speaker.

For instance, the quiz master of a TV game show is constantly seeking to keep up the sense of excitement and tension by talking quickly and excitedly and by laying heavy stress on key syllables, while the news presenter reading a nationwide bulletin on TV will slow down his pace and lower his voice a little to show respect when announcing the death of a famous person, or an accident causing extensive loss of life.

In an entirely different context, the salesperson uses pitch, emphasis and pace to persuade a potential purchaser of the merits of a product. The way in which words are uttered matters just as much as the words themselves.

The following checklist supplies a useful set of guidelines for using skills of intonation, pitch and rhythm in spoken word persuasive communication:

THE SPOKEN WORD: CHOOSING THE RIGHT WORDS

Success in getting the message across to a particular listener or audience in a given context also depends very much on choosing the right words. Speakers of English in this regard are very fortunate since the English language is one of the richest in the world for its synonyms or words which have similar meaning. And so there are plenty of alternative nouns, verbs, adjectives and adverbs to choose from – each expressing a different shade of meaning. Consider for example, the following words which can be used for 'home' or place where someone lives:

Come back to my *place*.
A luxurious *residence*.
At the above *address*.
The accused is *domiciled* in Kent.
No fixed *abode*.
I want to go *home*.

Intonation and the persuasive spoken word

Study the following features of intonation to build your persuasive skills:

Pace and rhythm

Seek to vary the pace of what you say by slowing down and emphasising key words and phrases. But avoid a heavy, regular, 'plodding' way of speaking.

Quicken your pace immediately before key words and phrases:

> '*And undoubtedly the main factor is* <u>our failure to win new business</u>.'

Stress and emphasis

Lay additional stress and emphasis on those words and phrases you want your listener(s) to pick up as particularly important:

> 'It's main features include: *a five-speed* gearbox, *sixteen-valve* engine with *petrol injection* for an extra turn of speed. On the dash you've got extras like a *fuel use recorder* and *seat-belt reminder light.*'

But avoid the temptation to overdo it. Listeners quickly tire of over-emphasis.

Pauses and rests

By pausing before imparting key information, a speaker is able to capture attention and increase an impact:

> 'And, Ladies and Gentlemen, (opening the sealed envelope), the winner is . . . Julia Roberts for her performance in 'Sandstorm'!'

Rises and falls

In speaking, we tend to show that we have reached the end of a sentence or sense group by letting our voices fall:

> 'The referee is glancing at his watch, yes, he's reaching for his whistle – it's all over.'

In the above example, the commentator raises his voice on 'watch' and 'whistle' to indicate there's more to come, then lets it fall on 'over'.

We follow such spoken-word punctuation more than we realise and it helps listeners to pick up meaning and structure.

In each instance, the word for 'home' conveys a different meaning; the Latinate words 'domicile' and 'abode' convey a sense of the impersonal, and 'residence' a sense of the grand, while 'place' and 'home' are much more informal and communicate a much warmer meaning. Instinctively (or as good communicators, more consciously) we choose words from sets like those above to suit a given situation, whether it be among friends or in a formal courtroom setting.

Characteristics of persuasive vocabulary

Subjective not objective: The term subjective means communicating personal feelings and emotions; objective is the opposite – conveying factual data impersonally.

Single/double syllable words not multi-syllabled ones: Words which affect our hearts rather than minds tend to be shorter rather than longer.

Anglo-Saxon/Norse not Latinate root words: Persuasive words tend to stem from Anglo-Saxon/Norse rather than from Latin or Greek. (Check your dictionary for word origins!)

Shorter sentences and sense patterns not longer ones; Persuasive writers tend to keep their sentences short and make extensive use of the full-stop. (They use exclamation marks sparingly.)

Direct, simple, straightforward words not complex, abstruse, involved ones: Successful persuasive writing uses vocabulary which is quick and easy to take in.

Nouns and verbs not adverbs and adjectives: Good, persuasive writers use well-chosen nouns and verbs instead of stringing adverbs and adjectives together in front of them in threes and fours:

The *backpackers toiled* up the hill.

UNSOLICITED SALES LETTERS (USLs)

Many companies choose to promote their goods or services through the medium of the bulk mailshot. Potential customers can be targeted, say, high earners with the earning power to afford a garden swimming pool, or specialist groups like ramblers or anglers who may be expected to purchase products related to their hobbies. Also, selected estates within a suburb or locality may be circularised after a promising result from market research. Moreover, the Post Office offers discounts on bulk mailshots. Unsolicited sales letters posted on a cold canvassing basis – to consumers who have had no prior contact with a company – customarily produce about a 2 to 5 per cent positive response. And so the cost of the total mailshot has to be absorbed into the gross profit of resulting sales – and still leave a worthwhile profit for the company concerned. However, sending thousands of USLs and subsequently paying for the postage and packaging of ordered goods can still prove a lot less expensive than maintaining networks of retail stores or regional sales forces.

Some companies enclose high quality colour brochures or catalogues with their USLs to support the written persuasive word with photographic support and examples.

■ *GROUP ACTIVITY: PERSUASIVE COMMUNICATION – UNSOLICITED SALES LETTER: KLEENAHOME LIMITED*

In groups of three or four, study carefully the unsolicited sales letter from Kleenahome Limited to Mrs White on page 209. Discuss the techniques of persuasive written communication which you detect in the letter. Make a checklist of:

a the approaches employed to persuade Mrs White of the benefits she would obtain by purchasing the products described;

b specific words and phrases which you think have been deliberately used to communicate persuasively. Make notes for each explaining why you think they are/are not effective as used.

Discuss the claims made in the letter and what Kleenahome would need to be able to demonstrate in order for the letter to comply with legal requirements (*Note:* part of your group's activity may be to find out what these legal requirements are. Check with your teacher before starting the activity.)

Compare your notes and discussion points with those of other groups in your class.

KLEENAHOME LIMITED

Kleenahome House
24-28 Broad Street
Fulham
London SW8 1ER

Tel: 071-654 3210

Fax: 071-234 5678

. . . .
Registered Office
Registered No. 745932
Registered in England

18 June 199-

Mrs A White
96 Acacia Avenue
Westonbury
Wessex
WB2 4AK

YES! I CHOOSE KLEENAHOME!

Dear Mrs White

KLEENAHOME PRODUCTS CARE AS THEY CLEAN!

At last you can keep your kitchen and bathroom sparkling bright
and clean without the worry of scratching your plastic, wood or
enamel surfaces with harsh, scouring detergents!

Kleenahome's hardworking research team have developed an exciting
range of new products to meet your demanding standards of hygiene
and cleanliness.

Wipova - our top kitchen cleaner - not only removes dried-in
stains and all the tiny debris of your kitchen's day, it protects
you and your family with its unique formula X24, a powerful
round-the-clock germicide. And Wipova really cares for your
tiled, stainless-steel and plastic surfaces and utensils. It
contains no gritty particles that cut and scratch, leaving
dangerous areas where germs can breed. You can rely on Wipova!

Sparkel, our new all-round bathroom protection agent will bring
all your bathroom fittings back to life! Sparkel has been
specially designed to keep your bathroom 'squeaky clean' and free
from harmful bacteria while caring for all the family! Sparkel
is kind to the tenderest skin and contains our special anti-
irritant ingredient Soothex. You can bring new life into your
bathroom now, Mrs White - thanks to Sparkel!

And Kleenahome has lots more to offer! A full range of brushes
and sweepers, stain and spot removers and carpet cleaning
equipment. Your local sales consultant, Caryl Fraser, will be
contacting you within the next day or so to tell you how
Kleenahome can give you the security of knowing that your home
is clean and safe - for all those you care for most!

And there's more! Simply remove the YES coupon from the top of
this letter, give it to Caryl when she calls, and you will
receive A FULL 20% DISCOUNT OFF ALL YOUR FIRST KLEENAHOME
PRODUCTS!

With best wishes

Sincerely

Jason A Goodheart

Jason A Goodheart
Sales Director

Directors: J.Benson(Managing), J.A.Goodheart, S.B.Fellowes(USA)

The success of this kind of sales promotion and advertising has brought about a sharp increase in the extent of unsolicited mail arriving weekly through consumers' letter-boxes. So much so that the Americanism 'junk mail' is widely used nowadays to describe it. And, not unnaturally, the majority of such mail tends to be 'redirected' straight into the waste-paper bin! So the advertising writer of USLs needs to be an expert in:

▶ immediately catching the eye and creating interest;
▶ sustaining the reader's interest from opening to closing sentences;
▶ convincing the remotely located potential customer to take prompt actions resulting in the advertised goods or services being ordered.

This is a tall order! But over the years a number of persuasive techniques have been developed and elaborated upon:

Opening gambits

THROW THIS AWAY UNREAD IF YOU DON'T NEED £100 PIN MONEY EACH WEEK!

THIS'LL TAKE 30 SECONDS TO READ AND COULD SAVE YOU £1,000 THIS WINTER!

YOU *CAN* LEARN TO MASTER YOUR SHYNESS AND MAKE FRIENDS QUICKLY!

Opening gambits in USLs tend to appeal directly to a common human need or desire – to earn more money in one's spare time, to avoid sudden expenses like burst pipes in winter or to overcome a personal difficulty. Industrial psychologists have identified a number of basic human needs which we all seek to satisfy from time to time:

▶ The need for security.
▶ The need to be socially accepted and popular.
▶ The need to appear successful.
▶ The need to be 'one step ahead of the Joneses'.
▶ The need to stay healthy and delay the onset and physical signs of aging.
▶ The need for fun and excitement.

Effective USLs tend to tap in to one or more of these common needs at the very outset.

Unique selling benefits

Having captured the reader's interest, the USL then proceeds – briefly and appealingly – to describe the product's unique selling benefits. In the specialist world of selling, this term means those particular features which make the product (or service) a better buy for the consumer than any competing one. It is up to the marketing and sales departments to decide what the unique selling benefits are. This could include:

▶ an updated version of the product incorporating new technology ahead of the competition;
▶ superior design and therefore reliability;
▶ higher quality of components and manufacturing care;
▶ better ease of use;
▶ a lower cost than that of competing products;
▶ exclusivity – the user won't find all his or her friends and neighbours having the same dress, tie or jewellery etc.

Such benefits must be communicated in appropriately persuasive language in order to stir the reader's desire to buy. The hard-hitting reasons for purchase must be clothed in attractive words and phrases!

Closing the sale

Like most business letters, the USL needs to convey a closing action statement which will impel the now interested reader to begin the process which will end with a sale being made. In order to achieve this, many USLs make an attractive offer – of a discount from the normal selling price, of a free gift with the purchase, of an additional quantity of the product, or of an extended period of warranty etc. Almost certainly this offer will depend upon a coupon or reply slip (which brings about the sale) being received by a given date:

SEND US YOUR COMPLETED ORDER SLIP WITHIN SEVEN DAYS, AND WE'LL DESPATCH YOUR *FREE GIFT* AND ORDER BY RETURN!

Finally, USLs tend to be signed by business executives with reassuring job titles. And some add a chatty PS in his or her simulated handwriting to add to the sense of having been composed and sent to the customer personally.

SALES LETTERS

Similar in some ways to the unsolicited sales letter – but with some significant differences – is the sales letter. This type of letter is sent by the sales departments of companies to two types of customer:

▶ existing account customers;
▶ prospective new customers.

Selling to existing customers

Sales letters circularised to existing account customers tend to adopt a friendly but not over-familiar tone and act in many ways as newsletters to update the customer network about:

▶ new products or services;
▶ special offers or discounts;
▶ seasonal promotions, such as a media campaign which will advertise garden products just before the Easter Weekend;
▶ competitions which customers may enter based on levels of purchase of products;
  etc.

Some sales letters – especially those in technical markets such as the sale of printing equipment to printing retailers – tend to be more formal/objective and to concentrate on selling the good points of what may be complex equipment specifications. Sales letters from a music cassette and CD wholesaler to retail outlets, however, may be much more informal in the style they use to relay information about, say, rock and jazz musicians' new issues.

What typifies letters to existing customers is the fact that a bond already exists between seller and buyer. This bond has to be created in sales letters to potential customers.

Selling to potential customers

The specimen unsolicited sales letter to Mrs White, a housewife and consumer, (on page 209) adopts an approach which seeks to project Kleenahome as a caring efficient company with a very capable product research team. It also communicates the message that it offers a total cleaning and sanitising service for households and that, as a result, housewives using Kleenahome products can feel totally secure. In this way, Kleenahome creates an image of itself and its products aimed at making the prospective customer want to buy and use what it makes.

Sales letters to potential customers running businesses also seek to win over the customer's confidence in this way. A well-worn but still valid acronym (shorthand way of remembering a phrase by using its initial letters) which applies to the use of persuasive communication in sales letters is:

Awareness
Interest
Desire
Action

AIDA makes the point that, in order to make a sale, the customer's awareness of the existence of the product or service has to be kindled. Then the customer's interest has to be stimulated (perhaps by the emphasis of the benefits that stem from owning the product or acquiring it for resale). As a result, a desire to acquire the product is aroused and the customer takes direct action to effect the purchase.

However constructed and presented, virtually all sales letters to business customers are communicating some or all of the AIDA sales process through the use of persuasive communication.

Hard or soft sell

In the world of advertising the term hard sell is used to describe a sales approach which stressed 'hard'

EXAMPLE OF AN ATTENTION-GETTING ACCOUNT CUSTOMER SALES LETTER

VIKING DIGITAL

YOUR FAVOURITE OFFICE PRODUCTS FOR LESS--OVERNIGHT

Mr D W Evans
Chichester College of Technology
Westgate Fields
Chichester
W Sussex
PO19 1SB

Customer No. 50821   15/04/91

Dear Mr Evans

THIS HALF IS OURS: THIS HALF IS YOURS:

We haven't heard from you since
your first order for office
supplies a few months ago.

That bothers me.   ORDER ATTACHED

Losing a good customer is like
losing a good friend. I can't
let either drift away in silence.

If we're at fault, I'd like to
know, and make it right. Whatever the reason, I do care.

The other side of this "Half"
letter is yours. I'd consider
it a personal favour if you'd
use it.

Yours sincerely

VIKING DIRECT

W Best

William Best
Managing Director

WB:KP

TOLWELL ROAD, LEICESTER LE4 1BR. TELEPHONE;(0800) 424444. FAX NO> (0800)622211
Registered in England No. 2472621

Reproduced by kind permission of Viking Direct

reasons for buying a product – its low price, its superior design, its ease of use etc. A 'soft' sell on the other hand, sells the product by identifying it with moods and feelings we like to have such as 'a fun day', 'inner confidence', 'getting ahead' etc.

Unsolicited sales letters to consumers tend to adopt a hard sell approach in order to get a total stranger to start the purchasing process. While sales letters to potential business customers may at times employ a hard selling approach, on the whole they tend to be more restrained and less 'pushy', since their writers are aware of most business proprietor's built-in resistance to aggressive selling tactics.

However, it is always dangerous to generalise, so make up your own mind by taking part in the following activity:

■ GROUP ACTIVITY: SALES LETTER SURVEY

In groups of three or four, collect specimens of the following kinds of sales letter:

▶ Unsolicited sales letters to consumers.
▶ Sales letters to account customers (in a business–to–business context).
▶ Sales letters to potential new customers (also in a business–to–business context).

Organise your group to make best use of contacts among family and friends, work experience attachment contacts, specimens collected from mailshots etc.

Compare and contrast the use of persuasive communication of different specimens in your collection. List any similarities you can find and note down what you see as differences of approach aimed at different types of customer. Make a display in your base room of the most interesting specimens with explanatory comments for each.

POSTERS, NOTICES AND BULLETINS

Today most organisations attach much importance to their internal communications. So much so, that some firms and local authorities appoint Communication Managers and Information Officers whose responsibilities include the following:

▶ Producing regular newsheets, house magazines and bulletins to inform and update staff, and to maintain morale and a sense of company identity.
▶ Vetting posters, notices, advertisements, and memoranda etc which are displayed on departmental noticeboards.
▶ Acting as information broadcasters within the organisation by ensuring that important developments, acquisitions, achievements etc are well publicised – both inside and outside the organisation.

Such managers are often located within the public relations departments of large organisations. In smaller ones, the job may be given to a personnel/training manager.

Accurate and up-to-date information about an organisation's affairs which is well presented and distributed is essential if grapevine rumours and gossip-spread hearsay are to be avoided. For example, rumours about lay-offs and redundancies may spread like wildfire in a factory in times of recession and so senior management may need to post notices, quashing such rumours which have authority and which are believable. On the other hand, a cash-and-carry food wholesaler may display posters seeking staff to work voluntary overtime when business is booming.

The reasons for designing and displaying posters and notices in organisations are endless, yet each one needs to conform to a common set of design, presentation and content guidelines if it is to be noticed, taken in and acted upon. The following checklist illustrates the major features which go together to make up effective posters and notices:

Checklist of the features of effective posters and notices

1 Size

The size of a poster depends upon the distance from it of the people for whom it is intended. Roadside and railway hoardings, for example, may be as much as six metres high and ten metres long, so as to be visible from motorways and intercity rail routes. Corridor posters, however, may be A3 or A2 in size, but should be easily legible from, say, 1–3 metres distance. Notices tend to be produced on a smaller scale – on A4-sized paper generally, and so operate on a smaller scale and viewing distance of up to a metre.

The most common reason for an ineffective poster or notice is that its message is displayed in such small print that it makes no visual impact and is impossible to read, given its distance from potential readers who may be on the move.

When designing a poster, *always make sure* its message is eye-catching and legible from the point at which its readers tend to be located.

2 Use of colour

Choosing appropriate colours for the card or paper of a poster or notice, as also for the inks of its printed message requires careful thought. For example:

▶ bright reds and yellows tend to 'shout' at passers-by, but
▶ pastel greens, blues, oatmeals and mauves provide a much calmer and quieter effect, and
▶ colours like gold and silver convey a sense of wealth and luxury, while
▶ browns, oranges and beiges give off a sense of mildness and gentle warmth – like a beechwood in autumn.

In a similar way, the various coloured inks which communicate the printed message will definitely have quite different impacts, especially when used in combination with a particular paper colour. For instance, a black print on a bright yellow backing has been scientifically proved to have the strongest visual impact and legibility over the furthest distance. This is why buses and articulated lorries often carry advertisements or logos and trade-names in these wasp-like colours. A royal blue ink on white paper is also highly visible but is more friendly and less aggressive.

The choice of colours and the numbers of inks used on posters are also affected by considerations of cost. For example, a poster or brochure may need to be passed several times through certain types of printing machine so as to pick up different coloured inks on successive runs. Such a process increases costs dramatically. And where sophisticated machines can do the job in 'one pass', the customer has to pay a contribution in each bill towards the purchase and running costs of such an advanced machine.

Whenever designing a poster, you should give careful thought to the type of message it is displaying and the sort of people it seeks to attract, so as to select an appropriate – and therefore effective – combination of colours.

3 Choice of fonts/typefaces

Until recent years, the choice within organisations of the print style in which to present the text of the poster was limited to:

▶ the availability of an efficient signwriter in-house (professional or amateur);
▶ the styles of particular sets of stencils on hand;
▶ the availability of silk-screen printing facilities (a process which allows inks to pass through a silk mesh, where stencilled outlines leave gaps forming alphabet letters, and so pass on to coloured poster paper).

Today, however, IT and desktop publishing, allied to image scanning and enlarging cameras, have created an impressive technology able to produce sophisticated posters in-house within medium to large-size companies. Such posters often contain two or more fonts set in various printer's point sizes – thanks to the wizardry of DTP software and laser printers! To assist smaller firms, local printing and copying bureaux have sprung up in towns to supply on-demand poster printing services.

The result of using DTP-based technology in poster and notice production is that we have become much more affected than we realise by print styles and lettering. So much so, in fact, that we tend to look down our noses at free-hand drawn posters produced with felt-tipped pens etc!

Within the choice available to you, give careful thought to the size and type of fonts you use to convey your message, whether formal and official, 'flash' and cheeky or friendly and reassuring. People *are affected* by the typefaces you employ!

4 Constructing the poster's message

It cannot be over-emphasised that effective poster messages are short and to the point. Just as some posters fail by being too small, so others 'die' on walls and noticeboards by being too wordy!

EXAMPLE OF AN ORGANISATION'S ANNUAL CHRISTMAS DANCE POSTER

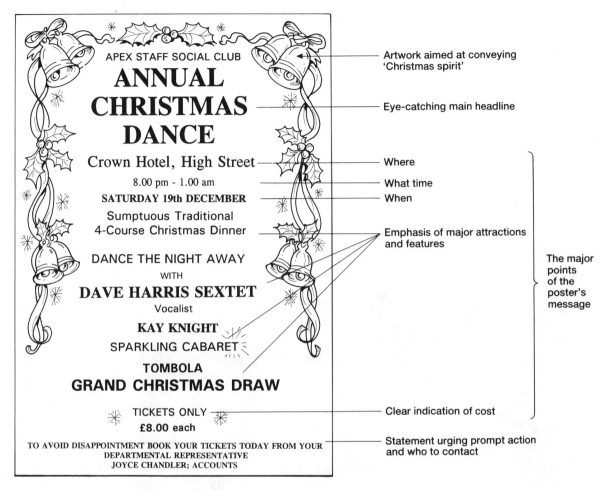

APEX STAFF SOCIAL CLUB

ANNUAL CHRISTMAS DANCE

Crown Hotel, High Street

8.00 pm - 1.00 am

SATURDAY 19th DECEMBER

Sumptuous Traditional
4-Course Christmas Dinner

DANCE THE NIGHT AWAY
WITH

DAVE HARRIS SEXTET

Vocalist

KAY KNIGHT

SPARKLING CABARET

TOMBOLA

GRAND CHRISTMAS DRAW

TICKETS ONLY
£8.00 each

TO AVOID DISAPPOINTMENT BOOK YOUR TICKETS TODAY FROM YOUR
DEPARTMENTAL REPRESENTATIVE
JOYCE CHANDLER; ACCOUNTS

— Artwork aimed at conveying 'Christmas spirit'

— Eye-catching main headline

— Where

— What time

— When

— Emphasis of major attractions and features

— Clear indication of cost

— Statement urging prompt action and who to contact

The major points of the poster's message

Notice the use of white space to highlight the brief message of the poster, which has been edited down to its essentials

Effective poster messages combine:

▶ an eye-catching and interest-arousing headline like:

FREE BEER TONIGHT!

or

Eat as much as you like at unbeatable prices!

▶ brief, clear details of the major features of the poster – what's it about? who is it for? when is it? where is it, what does it cost? etc

▶ a simple to follow action statement such as:

Tickets Available 9.00 am–8.00 pm from College Reception

or:

BE SURE OF YOUR COURSE PLACE BY BOOKING IT NOW WITH YOUR SUPERVISOR!

Always edit out as much as possible from the wording of your poster/notice content. Be ruthless! If your message is too wordy and its sense-groups of words and phrases too long, it just will not get read!

5 Using clip-art in poster and notice design

As well as being able to produce fonts of many different designs and sizes, DTP software and laser printers also enable poster designers to 'import' – that is to introduce into the poster's design – any individual piece of artwork which is included in the software supporting the DTP equipment. Clip-art

– so called because you can clip it to size and 'paste' it electronically on to the poster or brochure being designed – is made up of all sorts of drawings, borders, signs and symbols etc to give a poster visual appeal without the need to produce the artwork from scratch.

Before the advent of DTP, clip-art was produced in large books and arranged in subjects like: sport, education, sales, cars, boats etc.

Clip-art provides visual appeal in posters but should not dominate the poster by being out of proportion and should relate quickly and easily to the poster or notice's message.

Examples of clip-art

DISPLAY ADVERTISEMENTS

Display advertisements, so called because their layout 'displays' both artwork and text, rather than setting it out in prose paragraphs or newspaper columns, follow most of the guidelines we have just examined for posters and notices.

This type of advertisement appears mostly in national and local newspapers, specialist trade journals and the thousands of different hobby/leisure interest magazines sold regularly in newsagents. A display advertisement may be designed to meet all kinds of different aims, including:

▶ to advertise a job vacancy;
▶ to promote a product or service;
▶ to inform a local community of a change in, say, refuse collection arrangements;
▶ to inform the nation generally of an important event such as the taking of a national census;
▶ to publicise charity community events such as sponsored half marathons;
  and so on.

A common factor of many display advertisements is to invite the reader to weigh up two sets of information. For example, the specimen display advertisement on page 218 trades off the skills and knowledge Finer Foods expect in the successful applicant against what it has to offer in terms of the job package detailed. A display advertisement for a county show would also seek to balance out the attractions of the event with the admission and car-parking charges, in the hope that readers would consider the advertisement's offer as a good buy, and so go to the show.

It is therefore useful in designing such advertisements to draw up prior checklists of 'what you are prepared to give' in return for 'what you want to obtain'.

Notice also that the wording of display advertisements (which may cost hundreds of pounds to publish) is short, sharp and to the point. Often, the designer only has space to whet the reader's appetite – 'excellent opportunities for development' may take ten minutes to detail at the job interview. Similarly, 'qualified to NVQ Level 2 in relevant subjects' is a shorthand way for Finer Foods to suggest that it is prepared to be flexible in considering candiates' actual subject passes.

The language of display advertisements varies according to their purpose and targeted readers. Some, say, to advertise a car boot sale may be very 'chatty' and colloquial:

> THE JUNK IN YOUR LOFT COULD PROVE SOMEONE ELSE'S COLLECTOR'S FIND OF THE YEAR!
>
> – AND EARN YOU A PACKET!

While a display job advertisement in a 'heavy' Sunday newspaper for a senior manager's post may be deliberately restrained and formal, using technical language familiar only to those people already working in a specialised field, such as investment and the money market:

> **The successful applicant is likely to have gained extensive experience in the financial services sector and be able to demonstrate a convincing track-record in offshore investment.**

Such a contrast serves to emphasise the point that the choice of words and use of language which go to create a persuasive effect depend entirely on the aim of the advertisement and the kind of reader it seeks to attract. A financial expert seeking a senior post is quite prepared to read through what is often a good deal of continuous prose in advertisements on the appointments pages of quality Sunday papers as a means of gaining a significant increase in his or her earnings and job satisfaction. On the other hand, people thinking of taking part in a car boot sale may decide to try it out on impulse, and therefore need their attention 'grabbed' by eye-catching headlines and punchy, persuasive slogans.

Features of effective advertisement design

▶ Appealing artwork
▶ Use of heavier, emboldened print for major headings
▶ Use of white space
▶ Centring and justifying
▶ Short and sweet entries
▶ Easy to follow language

FINER FOODS LTD ❶

Cash and Carry Wholesale Specialists require an

OFFICE ASSISTANT ❷

as soon as possible to work in their Newtown Food Centre

The successful applicant will be

familiar with current office procedures

IT-confident (ability to use a spreadsheet an advantage) ❸

a self-starter with good communication and customer relations skills qualified to NVQ Level 2 in relevant subjects

Finer Foods Limited offer excellent opportunities for development, with prospects of advancement to office management. Salary according to age and experience. 21 days paid leave p.a., plus public holidays. Special staff discount purchasing scheme. Luncheon vouchers provided. ❹

Further details and forms of application available from:
Mrs Joyce Palmer, Personnel Manager, Finer Foods Limited, Western Business Park, Middleton, Newshire. MT3 4AJ ❺

FFL

1 Attractive design of trading name and logo aimed at communicating a high-quality but friendly company.
2 Title of advertised post emphasised and made to catch the eye by surrounding white spaces.
3 Four key requirements of the post are displayed both centred and well spaced to catch the eye. 'Bullets' have been used to draw the reader's eye to these major features.
4 The major benefits of the post are expressed briefly and clearly. Note the emphasis (by being mentioned first) of the post's development potential, and that Finer Food's selling points for the post move from major to minor.
5 Full details of how to proceed to apply are given, including the name and job title of the recruitment officer and full postal address.

■ **GROUP ACTIVITY**

In groups of three or four study carefully the use of English in the above advertisement. Decide whether it would or would not persuade you to apply. Make a checklist of those parts you think effective (and say why) and also list those parts which you think fail to attract (and say why) and provide your alternative versions.

■ **TOP ASSISTANT TIP**

Whenever asked to produce a draft for any kind of poster, notice or display advertisement, always make time to think about the following aspects, and to jot down your ideas before starting your first draft:

What is the context of my design? Is it serious, important, for a fun event, to be seen as a formal message or as a lighthearted prompt etc? Should my persuasive style therefore be serious or jokey, formal or familiar?

Who is my design aimed at? People in a serious frame of mind, people whose attention needs to be jolted, people who are only likely to give my advertisement fleeting attention, or people who will read it intently because it meets a keen interest etc? How are they likely to respond to the nature of my message?

What techniques of layout and presentation will best convey my message? What font styles, use of white space, centering and other layout features, size of print, choice of colours, type of paper, inclusion of clip-art or one-off artwork etc?

ACTIVITIES AND ASSIGNMENTS *Persuasive communication*

■ *THE QUICK CHECK-IT-OUT QUIZ*

1 Explain briefly the importance of the following in oral communication:
   stress and emphasis
   pace and rhythm
   pauses and rests

2 Explain how the choice of particular words can affect the way in which an idea is conveyed. For example: home/residence/domicile.

3 What features of style would you expect to find in persuasive writing?

4 Explain the difference between words which are:
   Subjective or Objective
   Old English or Latinate in origin
   Concrete or Abstract

5 What does the following stand for? AIDA

6 Describe the main features of a typical unsolicited sales letter.

7 What are the characteristics of a well-designed poster?

8 How does the choice of colour influence persuasive communication on posters and brochures etc?

9 In what ways does the choice of type fonts affect persuasive communication?

10 Explain the use of clip-art in persuasive communication.

11 What techniques of persuasive communication would you expect to find in a display advertisement?

12 For what reasons do organisations submit press releases to newspaper publishers?

■ *DISCUSSION TOPICS*

1 In what circumstances may the techniques of persuasive communication be justifiably used in organisations?

2 In what situations do you think it would be unfair/immoral/underhand to employ persuasive communication techniques in business?

3 Do you think that consumers are really always aware of 'being got at' through techniques of persuasive communication, so that they are really totally ineffective anyway?

4 In your experience, do you think that the controls on advertising are sufficient, or do they need tightening up?

5 'I only ever buy something because it's exactly what I want, and only after very carefully shopping around!' How accurately does this describe you? What prompts people to make impulse purchases?

Case study activities

The following case study provides activities which develop NVQ competences in:

- *analysing and evaluating the values, opinions and beliefs of others;*
- *receiving and responding to a variety of given information;*
- *selecting and composing appropriate methods of visual communication;*
- *producing creative design ideas;*

- *working effectively as a member of a team;*
- *providing a positive image of an organisation;*
- *composing and relaying information in writing which is presented in a format which is clear, easily assimilated and appropriate for the use intended.*

Case study

'IT'S OUR IMAGE – THAT'S THE PROBLEM!'

'It's our image – that's the problem!' sighed Sharon Lee, Entertainment Secretary of the Student Association of Thurleigh College at the monthly meeting of the Committee. 'We just don't seem to be able to attract people to come to our events. Look at the sandwiches and bridge rolls Lena gave away after last month's Halloween Party!'

'Yeah, I 'eard about that,' replied Darren Wilkes. 'Couldn't get to it mesself – United was playing at home in the League Cup.'

'There! That makes my point!' exclaimed Sharon. 'If we can't even get the Secretary to come to our do's, what is the point? We might as well disband the whole outfit!'

'Hey, steady on, Sharon,' broke in Wayne Franklin, the Association's Chairman, 'Darren does his bit. He's been a stalwart . . .'

'Yeah, sorry, Darren, I'm just brassed off with the flak I'm taking over the poor attendances lately.'

'Look, I've been listening to you doom-mongers for the past ten minutes bemoaning our fate! It's no good just rabbiting on about it. It's time we put a really good campaign into action to promote the Association,' interrupted Sonal Patel, Honorary Treasurer. 'And next month's Annual General Meeting would be a good place to start! But before that why don't we try to find out what our members want in terms of social facilities and events and then advertise them properly! Oh, sorry Sharon I didn't mean to imply . . .'

'No, please Sonal, don't apologise. I think you're absolutely right. Look, why don't you and I exchange Committee roles for a while? You're obviously the one to run with this . . .'

'Yes, why not, Sonal?' prompted Wayne. 'You're the one doing the BTEC Business Diploma. Let's defer the rest of the agenda and concentrate on this – if everyone agrees . . .?'

After a further hour's discussion, the Committee asked Sonal to head an *ad hoc* working party to revamp the Association's social events image and programme of activities. In the pipeline over the coming three months were:

The Christmas Party – a light-hearted affair in the Main Hall 8.00 pm–12.00 am on Friday 17 December, with Christmas Buffet, Bar, Disco and Cabaret.

The UNICEF Charity Pram Race – an annual event to be held on 20 January 199— at 1.00 pm around a railed-off College Campus circuit. Teams of two in fancy dress compete from among both student and staff bodies. The 'baby' in the pram of each team collects coins thrown by spectators in a plastic bucket, with a prize for the fastest pair and another for the collector of most money.

The Annual General Meeting of the Student Association
Not very well attended in the past. To be held this year on 12 December 199— at 12.30 pm in the Main Assembly Hall. If students were persuaded to attend, the meeting could help in

providing decisions and views to shape Association policies and plans.

Before the Committee Meeting ended, Wayne Franklin drew its members' attention to the vacancy for a Committee Member to fill the role of Staff-Student Liaison Officer. This Committee post had proved very important in the past, since its occupant sat on a number of College Committees including:

The Academic Board

The Student Services Committee (which runs the Student Common Room, Careers and Counselling Services)

The Library Committee

In addition, the Staff–Student Liaison Officer chairs the Student Association Committee which meets fortnightly with the Principal and Vice Principal to discuss matters of interest and raise issues of concern.

'Lastly, Sonal,' said Wayne, 'if it's not asking too much, do you think your Working Party could come up with a display advertisement to be displayed on College notice boards to recruit a Staff–Student Liaison Officer? We really could do with someone who's not afraid of sticking up for the Association, and who's not going to be overawed by sitting on committees with College staff.'

'I'll see what I can do,' answered Sonal. 'I'll talk to Ranjit. He's very good with DTP.'

Case study activities

■ DISCUSSION TOPICS

1 Does a Student Association in a College or School have an image? If so, what sort of action plan could its Committee undertake to improve it?

2 Should the Committee have accepted Sharon's suggestion that Sonal take over her role, or should she have been persuaded by the Committee to see out her responsibilities for the rest of her term of office?

■ GROUP ACTIVITIES

In groups of three or four carry out the following tasks:

The Christmas Party

1.1 Design an A3 poster to advertise the Christmas Party. Use coloured inks, crayons or paint to simulate its eventual printed appearance.

1.2 Compose a 30-second audio advertisement for the Christmas Party to be broadcast over the Refectory's public address system at break and lunch times.

1.3 Create the design for the Christmas Party tickets, which will include a lucky draw number.

1.4 Draw up a list of suggestions for the décor of the Main Assembly Hall based upon a theme related to Christmas.

The UNICEF Charity Pram Race

2.1 Design a display advertisement about 20 cm wide and 15 cm deep to advertise the Pram Race. Its aim is to get as many local inhabitants as possible to support the Race during their lunch hour, and to give generously to the UNICEF Charity which the Association has dedicated this year to children in need in Africa. The advertisement will appear two days before the Race in the weekly *Thurleigh Gazette*.

2.2 Devise a suitable advertising/promotional campaign to be mounted within Thurleigh College with the aim of getting as many participants for the Pram Race as possible – from both staff and students – and to obtain as big a turn-out as possible.

Your campaign includes the distribution of an A5 advertising leaflet with an entry form on its reverse side for would-be participants. Design and produce a suitable leaflet.

NB Effective designers will take the trouble to find out what UNICEF's logo looks like and will include it in their designs!

The Annual General Meeting

3.1 Design a suitable notice to draw students' attention to the forthcoming AGM and to persuade them to attend – especially as the provision of future social events will be an important agenda item.

3.2 Draft that part of the Entertainment Secretary's Annual Report which makes reference to the poor attendance at past events and which outlines what actions the Committee intends to take to improve support.

Remember that the main aim is to persuade the Association's members that it is in everyone's interests to support any new initiatives, and that a fresh start is needed.

The Vacancy for a Staff–Student Liaison Officer

4.1 Design a display advertisement for posting on College noticeboards inviting student applications for the post of Staff–Student Liaison Officer. Interested students should write a short letter to the Chairman setting out the reasons why they think they are right for the post.

4.2 As an invidivual, compose the letter to Wayne Franklin referred to in 4.1 above.

Activities to develop competence and confidence

Passages for discussion

Read and examine carefully each of the following passages in order to assess what makes them effective (or ineffective) as persuasive communication. Consider the structure of their main points, their overall style and tone, the use of vocabulary and their general register or degree of formality/informality etc:

1 KRYSTAL BRINGS THE WHITE BACK INTO WASHING!

2 *All* the family loves Crackaflake cereals – they make breakfast fun, while doing everyone a power of good!

3 The new line of Sheerline Eleganza tights are most attractively displayed in a space-saving, free-standing merchandiser. The easy, self-serve design of the merchandiser makes it so simple for your customers to select their own size and preferred colour. All you need to do is ring up the sale! Moreover, our sales representative will call regularly to ensure that you are never out of stock. With Sheerline Eleganza, we've taken the legwork out of your tights sales problems!

4 Good evening all! That's right missus, you can wake up now, the star turn's begun! Here, that's enough of that cackling up in the balcony – I *am* a star turn you know. What! Now listen. You're lucky to have me. Oh, yes, the manager was saying to me

just now, we've got a rough lot out there tonight! Yes, missus, not the usual sort we like to get in here, you know – he said it's the weather – most of 'em only come in to eat their fish and chips in the dry!

5   Harry, I know you've done your share of cleaning out the stockroom, but Nick's off sick today, and the boss is bringing one of the directors round tomorrow on a tour of inspection. I'd appreciate it if you would give it a careful check over, because if I leave it to you, I know it'll be tidied properly.

6   I quite realise that the improvements to the staff canteen were promised to be carried out during the current financial year. At the time, management gave the undertaking in good faith. As you all know, however, this has proved a most disappointing year for sales, and orders are well down on last year. As a result, there simply isn't the money available at present to carry out the necessary repairs. But I am sure that everyone here accepts the need for the firm to control its outgoings most carefully if we are to survive the current recession . . .

7   *Your company needs you!*
So . . . *always* wear your safety-helmet! We just cannot afford to lose your expertise and experience. Besides, we rather think it suits you!

8   Ladies and gentlemen, it gives me great pleasure to have the honour to address you this evening on such an important occasion, when I know that you will collectively be recalling the illustrious history of our celebrated and august Society, founded as you will all doubtless recall in the year 1892 by a few far-sighted and public-spirited educationalists, prompted by their abhorrence of the profound lack of educational opportunity which existed in the then . . .

9   Listen, Carol, I know Mr Hendricks is not the easiest manager to work for – but he'll provide the work experience you need to get on here. Yes, I agree that he can be abrupt and overbearing at times, and, yes, say things which can be hurtful and upsetting. But I'm absolutely sure that's just his way. He never *means* to be rude or domineering. And another thing, the Apex Contract has given all of us a lot of extra work in order to meet the deadline. And with the managing director overseas, Mr Hendricks has been under a good deal of additional stress. Now you just dry your eyes and go and freshen up in the Ladies. I'll have a word with Mr Hendricks. Don't worry, he won't know we've spoken. And remember – he has a high regard for your secretarial qualities. You just stick up for yourself! Give as good as you get, and you'll have him eating out of your hand!

10   SPARKLE washing-up liquid will bring a bright lustre to all your china and cutlery. It shifts even cold and burned-in grease, and costs no more than ordinary washing-up liquids. Change to Sparkle and you'll see a world of difference!

11   Sun-Searcher Holidays *guarantee* your holiday satisfaction! All our hotels are vetted by our specialist tour inspectors. Only the most sun-favoured resorts win a place in our Sun-Searcher Holiday Plans, and once you have chosen your own sun-kissed holiday haven – your problems are over! Our highly-trained teams of couriers are constantly – yet discreetly – on hand to help you get the most from your precious holiday time, with suggestions for day-tours or evening visits, and they can handle your holiday problems – from safety-pins to baby-sitters!
    If blue skies, warm sand and clear seas are your holiday dream, ring Freefone 0800-800-900 and Sun-Searchers will make your dream come true!

Persuasive communication: an integrated assignment

1 Your work experience attachment organisation's Staff Association has decided to enter two teams of three men and three women for next year's London Marathon. In order to minimise any possible injuries or attacks caused by a lack of fitness in participants, the Marathon's organisers require certificates of ability to run 26 miles after structured training. The Staff Association's aim is to raise £5,000 towards a scanner for your local hospital through community sponsoring of the two teams.

Your attachment supervisor is the PR representative of the Association's Committee and has asked you to help the project:

1.1 Draft a three-minute oral presentation for a Staff Association Meeting which will brief members on the background and history of the London Marathon, explain what is involved in taking part and seek volunteers to join a Training Group which will meet regularly for eight months to train for the Marathon.

First carry out your research and then produce your notes for giving an oral presentation plus any AVA support material. Then give a simulated presentation to your class.

1.2 Design a suitable poster to recruit volunteers to join the Training Group.

1.3 Then, (assuming that training is under way) compose a short article for your company newsletter which provides information about the progress of the 10 staff in training (four reserves are also training), and which details how much so far has been collected for the scanner etc.

1.4 Assume that the Marathon has taken place. Your two teams did well: the men finished in the 1500–1700 rankings, and the women in the 1200–1300 positions. £6,942.24 was raised for the scanner. The Association's chairperson, Julia Rigby presented a cheque for this amount to Sir Jack Tanner, Senior Consultant Neurologist at St Mary's General Hospital. Over 12,000 local residents sponsored the charity run.

Compose a letter for publication in your local weekly newspaper thanking everyone you think appropriate for the contributions they made to the London Marathon Charity event.

2 Your company, Wellbeloved, Selby & Partners, Advertising Agents, has decided to purchase an upgraded computer for its Graphics Department, in order to improve the quality of its general design and artwork. As a result, you now have a Valiant PC Turbo computer – only three months old, but just out of warranty – which you wish to sell. The Valiant has the following specifications:

▶ 40 Mb of memory on hard-disk.
▶ 12-in colour monitor with VGA quality resolution.
▶ Mouse and graphics tablet.
▶ Adaptor boards installed for desktop publishing, graphics and importation of scanned material.
▶ Printer ports suited to advanced laser printers.

The Valiant would be ideal for a small firm which designs and prints advertisements, brochures and leaflets etc for local businesses. Your Graphics Department manager has suggested an asking price of £1,290, with some surplus disk storage units and a keyboard cleaning kit thrown in.

First make sure you are familiar with the specialist terms in the above specification, then design a suitable display advertisement of approximately 17 × 12 cm for insertion in *Graphics News*, a monthly magazine for commercial computer users in the design and media field. Your firm is based at Tower House, 122 Chester Road, Warrington, Lancs. WA12 6EG.

Activities to develop competence and confidence

1 A senior partner of Johnson, Haines and Beckett, solicitors, 4 East Parade, Middleton, Newshire, MT4 6BG, telephone, Middleton 876584/6 requires an office assistant to support his PA. Hours are: Mon–Fri 9.00 am–5.30 pm, one hour lunch break; three weeks paid holidays, usual fringe benefits, and starting salary around £6,500 pa. Might suit a school/college leaver.

   Design a suitable display advertisement for the post to appear in the local weekly newspaper.

2 Family Foods PLC, a nationwide supermarket chain is about to open a new store in Westerton, Midshire, at 109/113 High Street. The firm is anxious to ensure that as many local residents as possible are aware of the superb shopping facilities and range of food products. You have been asked to design a leaflet to be posted through residents' letterboxes which will advise local people of the time, date, hours of opening, range of goods, shopping advantages, etc. Using graphic, visual and written persuasive communication techniques, design a suitable leaflet.

3 At a cost of £1.3 million, the Newtown Borough Council has almost finished building a brand new Community Youth Centre at 5 Parkside Road, Newtown, Wealdshire NT2 WS4.

   The Centre will be managed by Chris Barnes, an experienced Youth Leader (telephone Newtown 567342) and the premises will include facilities for discos, aerobics, circuit-training, drama, badminton, billiards and snooker, a snack bar and meeting rooms, etc.

   The council is keen to see the centre fully used and, as an assistant to the council's information officer, Mrs Patricia Simpson, you have been asked to design a brochure to send to schools, colleges and clubs in the area to persuade teenagers to join in the Centre's activities. *Note:* the Centre aims to cater for young people between the ages of 13 and 19.

   Either singly, or in groups, design a suitable brochure.

4 Liaise with your school or college's student committee and arrange to design, print and distribute posters or notices for a forthcoming social or sports event.

5 Design a suitable poster for display in a training office, workshop or laboratory to remind student users of the need to take care and avoid causing or being involved in accidents.

6 Design a poster to be displayed in your school or college aimed at preventing litter and to encourage staff and students to be more conscious of the need to care for their environment.

7 Consider carefully the current course you are following, and the type of students it aims to help. In groups, design a promotional 'kit' which could be sent to any potential student enquiring about joining the course next year.

8 Either individually, or in groups, design a sales brochure aimed at promoting the sale of *one* of the following:

   a hair shampoo; a toilet soap; an after-shave lotion; a toothpaste; a perfume; a talcum powder; a men's hair lotion/spray.

9 Assume the role set described below and compose an appropriate short speech (of

not more than two minutes) which you think will meet your brief. After rehearsal, deliver your speech to your group:

You are the trade union representative for your Department (the Office Administration Dept. of Sentinel Insurance PLC). Your union is the National Office Workers Association (NOWA). Trade union members include clerical assistants, word processing operators, filing assistants, data processing operators and secretaries etc. At this time NOWA has a pay claim being considered by management of 11.5 per cent (Two months ago, inflation was running at 12.5 per cent). Because of inflation, lending and mortgage rates are very high and everyone is feeling the pinch. Today you received a confidential letter from NOWA head office to tell you that the negotiating team have reluctantly agreed to submit a pay offer of 8.5 per cent to the membership which carries their recommendation for acceptance. This proposed settlement was made in the light of Sentinel's concern about possible redundancies due to the recession. Your General Secretary wants you to put the case for acceptance to your members.

10 You work for Horridges, a national departmental store group with a reputation for high quality merchandise sold at competitive prices. You work in the Gift Department and Christmas is in just six weeks' time. Your manager has been given the job of selling a large quantity of pocket-sized colour television sets which run on both mains and batteries. The TV screen is some 6 centimetres square. Picture definition and colour faithfulness are remarkable in such a small set. The amplification is also very acceptable given that the sets should be ideally placed about 40–50 centimetres from the viewer's head. The sets, made by Syundai Electronics of South Korea, can transmit all UK TV signals and are easily adaptable for use abroad on holiday or business. Encased in a discreet, matt-black casing with simple push-button controls, the Syundai Microtel Television Set costs £129.99, inclusive of VAT.

Your manager would like you to compose a commercial to promote the Microtel – in keeping with Horridge's image – which will be broadcast at intervals in the Gift Department in the run-up to Christmas, to support a special sales counter and promotion. Devise a suitable commercial of not more than 45 seconds duration. Practise delivering it on an audio cassette, and then play it back to your group for comment. You may add any realistic details about the Microtel that you wish.

Part 9

Visual, graphic and number communication

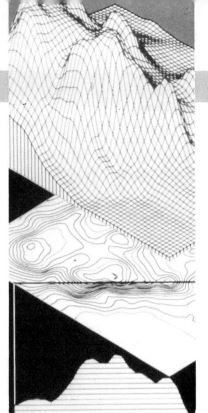

OVERVIEW

This Part shows you how to communicate successfully through the media of diagrams, charts, tables and graphs. It also provides an overview of the use of photographs, cartoons, icons and symbols in business communication. In addition, this Part examines the use of colour and patterns in visual communication and surveys the impact upon the reader of contrasting type fonts and sizes used in desktop publishing. Lastly, it provides helpful guidelines on designing and using visual aids as part of an oral presentation.

NVQ references

This Part covers the following BTEC First Diploma in Business and Finance and 'ABC/NWPSS' competences:

BTEC First Diploma

Business Support Systems 1:
  Competences: 5 and 6 Supplying information for a specific purpose and drafting routine business communications, 7 Producing alpha-numerical information in typewritten form.

Business Support Systems 2:
  Competences: 3 Responding to customers'/clients' requests for information on products, services, 8 Processing information in spreadsheets.

ABC/NWPSS

Level 2:
  Unit 2   Communication information
  Unit 3   Data processing
  Unit 11 Providing information to customers/clients
  Unit 13 Information processing

Level 3:
  Unit 2   Researching and retrieving information
  Unit 5   Preparing and producing documents

THE IMPACT OF VISUAL COMMUNICATION IN THE 1990s

Inevitably, the widespread use of television, video cassette, film and photograph has had a massive impact on how people absorb and respond to information. Many families today, for example, regularly watch more than four hours of television each evening – amounting to over a day per week!

Newsagents such as W H Smith Limited nowadays stock video cassettes of films, pop music, sports and fitness programmes along shelves which used to hold books. And the book publishers themselves have recently introduced 'visual novels' which tell extended stories in picture form, with dialogue set in balloons, rather like Asterix comic books.

All such trends highlight the development of a society in which most people read little but are extremely responsive to visual and graphic communication. All around us today visual symbols are used to transmit messages – sometimes about a matter of life or death – like the one for high-voltage electric current on national grid pylons or electrified railway lines. All over Europe, standardised road signs aid drivers crossing through several countries in the space of a day, while at home, advertisers constantly seek our attention by using graphic communication techniques creatively.

POPULATION TREND OF 16–19 AGE GROUP IN UK 1985–1991

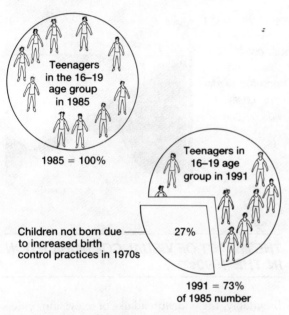

Teenagers in the 16–19 age group in 1985

1985 = 100%

Teenagers in 16–19 age group in 1991

Children not born due to increased birth control practices in 1970s — 27%

1991 = 73% of 1985 number

Fig. 9.1   Use of symbols to depict population trend

SALES OF FOUR MAIN PRODUCTS IN FIRST QUARTER THIS YEAR

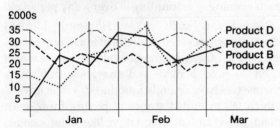

£000s

35
30
25
20
15
10
5

Jan   Feb   Mar

Product D
Product C
Product B
Product A

Fig. 9.2   Use of a graph to show comparison of sales of a range of products
Note: quantities – here between £0 and £35,000 – are usually plotted against the vertical axis of the graph, and time – here January to March – along the horizontal axis of the graph. Also the use of contrasting colours for each product line would have more visual impact than the use of variously broken lines in black only shown above

In the field of computing software design much imagination has gone into the creation of icons (picture symbols) which stand for certain operations. An icon of a printer displayed on a VDU and touched by a cursor or finger will activate a computer's printing instructions; a dustbin likewise erases a file and a filing cabinet calls up a filing operation and so on.

Such visual symbols have the advantage of being internationally understood by video recorder users, car drivers, call-makers using public phone booths or tourists moving through airports. Indeed, a universal 'visual vocabulary' is fast growing, and our 'wordlist' of such signs and symbols is very much larger than we realise!

Computerised graphics

Today organisations use colour coding as a medium of communication, whether to simplify finding a document or reaching a particular location. In hospitals, for example, tracks of green footprints may lead an out-patient to the X-Ray Department, and blue ones to Casualty. And large business head offices often employ colour codes to mark the locations of particular files.

Managers in organisations also use numbers in tables, charts, graphs and charts to communicate information easy to take in and retain. For example, a circular pie chart can convey very strikingly how the numbers of young people in the 16–19 age range have declined in the UK between 1985 and 1991. In a similar way, a coloured line graph plotting the numbers of a set of products sold against months of the year will help a busy retail manager to brief his staff effectively on what is selling best and what overall sales trends are.

In fact, to convince you just 'how much louder visual charts speak than words', examine carefully the charts described above! As you will see, techniques of visual communication are enormously helpful in relating detailed numerical information. By contrast, using words to convey the same facts is an involved and lengthy business.

Indeed, to enable computer users to work quickly and easily, software programmers have devised a range of icons (picture symbols) representing printers, filing cabinets or dustbins etc to stand for print, erase, or file commands all activated by selecting them with a cursor or finger.

By the same token, graphics packages have been designed which contain attractive and sophisticated charts, graphs, maps and diagrams on to which the user can arrange specific number information. By adding colours to such graphic information, a manager can quickly produce striking film slides or overhead transparencies for presentations and briefings.

USING NUMBERS EFFECTIVELY IN VISUAL COMMUNICATION

At almost every turn in our personal or business lives, we receive information in number form which aims to relay particular data to us. Each month for instance, everyone with a current bank account can receive a statement of the account presented as a numerical listing of pounds and pence – one entry for each cheque issued, standing order or direct debit paid out, and another for each payment into the account from whichever source. Credit card companies like Visa and Access produce similar statements of credit taken up due for payment. Again, at regular intervals (usually quarterly), telephone, water, electricity and gas companies do likewise. And annually, local tax bills like the Council Tax are issued to residents along with brochures which illustrate in pie chart and bar chart form how taxpayers' money gathered in the previous year has been spent.

By the same token, managers and support staff in organisations receive, update or dispatch at daily, weekly, monthly or quarterly intervals number-based information in the form of:

▶ an advice note, invoice, statement or credit note;
▶ profit and loss accounts and balance sheets;
▶ reports of weekly/monthly sales in branches, districts and regions;
▶ schedules of stocks held, in transport or in bonded warehouses;
▶ reports on production quantities and wastage rates;
▶ details of daily weekly and monthly takings in shops, stores, filling stations and public houses etc.

Indeed, the variety of forms of number-based information which organisations feel they need to produce or use to monitor activities is seemingly endless. And for this very reason, managers and assistants take often extensive pains to present such numerical data in ways that *summarise and present it in diagram or chart form so as to make it more easily absorbed and understood.*

The following sections examine these techniques one by one and highlight the communication strengths and weaknesses of each medium in turn.

Tables

Simply, tables are columns of figures where each individual entry has a specific connection with every other one. For example, the till roll issued at the check-out of a supermarket basically details each purchase made and adds each to the next so as to form a final total, which the customer pays. If the customer presents a token of, say, 5 p off the next purchase of a tin of baked beans, this may be shown as a deduction from the balance due on the receipt and the total will be amended accordingly:

SIMULATED SIMPLE + AND – TABLES

+ A	By placing	+ K
+ B	such columns	+ L
+ C	next to others,	+ M
– D	comparisons	+ N
+ E	may be made	– O
= F	between, say,	= P
	the sales of	
	one type of product	
	and another	

Note:
Simple tables often show the sum total of additions and subtractions in listings set side by side.

Other types of table employ multiplication and division rules. For example, a purchase order may list quantities of several different items like this:

PLEASE SUPPLY:			
OUR ORDER NO.:	JULY 24	DATE: 27 July 199—	
Qty	Description	Unit price (£)	Total (£)
50	A4 Reams Bond Paper (White)	3.81	190.50
25	A4 Reams Copy Paper (Ditto)	3.21	80.25
10	A4 Reams Copy Paper (Primrose)	3.39	33.90
			304.65

Here the detailed purchase order multiplies the price of a single item – the unit price – by the total of the quantity:

$$50 \times 3.81 = 190.50$$

Another type of table uses division rules to communicate information:

TO GOODS SUPPLIED: 12 August 199—

Qty	Description	Unit Price (£)	Total Gross (£)	Total Net (£)
25	Cases Liebfraumilch Seidler	41.04	1,026.00	
	Less Trade Discount 25%			769.50
10	Cases Schloss Hardt Burgunder	55.20	552.00	
	Less Trade Discount 22.5%			427.80
			Total:	1,197.30
		Add VAT @ 17.5%		209.53
			Total due:	1,406.83

The above table, in the form of a sales invoice for wines sold in cases of 12 bottles shows the retail price of the Liebfraumilch, as £1,026.00 for 25 cases. This price total enjoys a discount of 25 per cent. To arrive at the correct price payable, the sum of £1,026.00 is *divided by 100 to arrive at the cost of 1 per cent and then multiplied by 75 to produce a total equalling 75 per cent*. Thus a table which includes percentages is working in both division and multiplication. This is also evident from the calculation of the VAT due, which is 17.5 per cent of the total, or £209.53 of £1,197.30.

■ TOP ASSISTANT TIP

Before embarking on the design of a table to communicate data, ask yourself whether a graph, pie chart or bar chart would serve your needs better.

Checklist of essential components of an effective table

1 A clear and simple title summarising what the table is communicating, including 'from' – 'to' dates.
2 The source of the table's data, whether from government statistics or head office monthly sales report etc.
3 Clearly labelled headings over columns of figures: JAN, FEB, MAR etc, or North East, Midlands, South etc.
4 A clear indication of the unit of measurement that the numbers stand for – pounds sterling, dollars, metres, grams etc.
5 Clearly labelled totals or subtotals of listings.
6 Where appropriate, details of the author of the table.
7 And, essential, the date on which the table was drawn up.

Always make sure that the figures in the tables you design are large enough to be read easily and clearly and that they are surrounded with sufficient white space. Also, remember that boxes, vertical lines and dots . . . . help the eye travel across paper and are always helpful in making tables more easily understood.

Briefing note on tables

1 Communication advantages

Tables communicate very accurately – to several decimal point places – number information where the four rules of arithmetic: $+$, $-$, $\times$, $\div$ are used to produce totals. Columns of figures may be set side by side to present information of items to be compared. Tables are also extremely useful for storing such information.

2 Communication disadvantages

When the data entries in tables are many, then it becomes *extremely demanding to unravel what they are communicating*. In other words, the reader becomes lost in a maze of figures which communicate poorly in comparison to graphs, pie- or bar-charts.

Consider, for example, the information set out in the following table:

Discount Hardware Limited
Sales analysis for year ended 19—

Sales
value in
£000

Products	Jan	Feb	Mar	Apr	May	Jun	July	Aug	Sept	Oct	Nov	Dec	
Garden furniture	0.5	0.7	1.2	2.4	3.5	4.6	4.2	2.1	0.6	0.4	0.3	0.1	20.6
Paints	0.8	1.6	2.4	3.5	3.4	2.6	1.7	1.8	1.4	2.1	2.3	0.2	23.8
Tools	0.7	0.5	0.7	0.6	0.5	0.4	0.3	0.3	0.4	0.5	0.7	1.0	6.6
Washing machines	2.0	1.5	2.1	1.7	1.9	2.4	0.8	0.7	0.8	0.6	0.5	0.4	15.4
Refrigerators	2.1	1.4	1.5	1.4	1.8	1.7	1.5	1.7	1.6	1.5	1.4	1.2	18.8
Freezers	1.7	0.6	0.7	0.4	0.4	0.3	0.5	0.9	1.0	0.5	0.6	0.8	8.4
Kitchenware	0.7	0.5	0.3	0,4	0.7	0.5	1.2	0.4	0.5	0.4	0.5	0.8	6.9
Wallpaper	1.1	1.6	1.8	2.2	2.1	1.8	0.6	0.4	0.8	1.2	1.4	0.8	15.8
Total:	9.6	8.4	10.7	12.6	14.3	14.3	10.8	8.3	7.1	7.2	7.7	5.3	116.3

. . . the reader becomes lost in a maze of figures which communicate poorly.

The line graph

Though it may, at first sight, appear somewhat daunting, the line graph is, in reality, an extremely simple form of number communication to devise and interpret. Most line graphs used in business take the form of a grid:

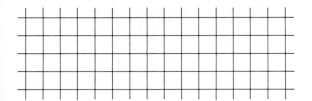

Fig. 9.3 Grid for a line graph

Information is plotted on the grid in a way which tells the reader what happened at a given point. Very often, the graph plots quantities against time. For example, a retail store may sell a certain number of washing machines each month. The manager may wish to keep a careful eye on his sales turnover in washing machines, and may therefore devise a line graph which records the number of machines sold by the end of each month.

In the line graph, then, we have quantity plotted along a vertical axis (from bottom to top), and time plotted along a horizontal axis (from left to right). We can see that in April the manager sold 25 washing machines, and in October, 30.

UNIT SALES OF WASHING MACHINES

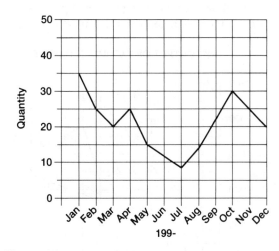

Fig. 9.4 Simple line graph

A more developed form of such a line graph can be used to compare the sale of washing machines in the current year against sales made in previous years.

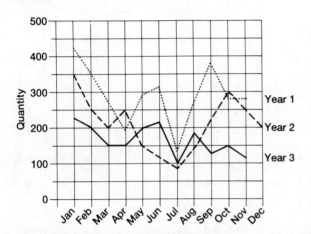

ANNUAL UNIT SALES OF WASHING MACHINES

Fig. 9.5   Line graph to show comparisons

Thus the line graph not only acts as a means of storing information, but also as a means of comparing one set of facts or figures with another in a way which is easily interpreted.

An additional feature of the line graph is that from it, it is possible to predict what is likely to happen in the future.

In the following example the output of the factory fluctuates. It does not move upwards at a smooth rate. But it *does* go on moving steadily upwards over a period of time – here, over the course of the year.

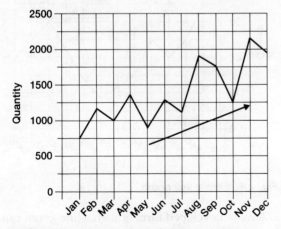

UNIT OUTPUT OF VACUUM CLEANERS

Fig. 9.6   Use of a graph for forward planning

As a result, the line graph's upward trend as plotted makes it reasonable to suppose that the output will continue broadly in the same upward climb in the first few months of the following year. In this way, the graph helps the factory manager to carry out forward planning on the basis of what has been happening in the past.

Such information would be much more difficult to extract from a table of figures, as its visual impact would not be as immediate as the graph's.

■ *PLOTTING RULE*
Always plot the factor which does *not* change (e.g. time) along the horizontal axis, and the factor which *does* change (e.g. quantity) along the vertical axis.

Breaking the vertical axis

Sometimes the items which are to be plotted against, say, quantity and time prove to be very unequal. For instance three items may not exceed a high point of sales amounting to £400.00 in any month, while the fourth may be soaring between £1,200.00 and £1,500.00 in the same months. To manage such differences, it is acceptable to show clearly a break in the grid of the graph by using a drawing symbol – rather like the Spanish tilde sign:

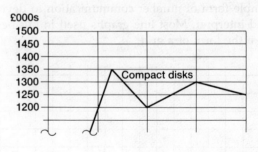

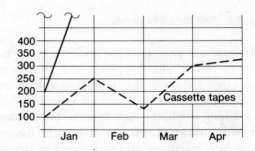

Fig. 9.7   Breaking the vertical axis

~ where the vertical axis line has been broken and restarted at a higher total, as shown in Fig. 9.7.

Selecting an appropriate scale for the vertical axis

It is up to the line graph designer to select the intervals of the scale for the vertical axis, so that the peaks and troughs of plotted performances can be clearly distinguished by the reader, and so that a series of items being displayed *do not jostle together on the 'at the bottom of a deep plate' like tangled spaghetti as shown in Fig. 9.8.*

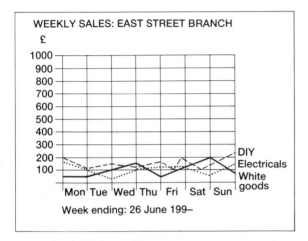

Fig. 9.8 *Graph showing incorrect use of vertical scale*

If too expanded a scale is chosen (as in Fig. 9.9) this also has the effect of flattening out the peaks and troughs which a more compact scale would highlight:

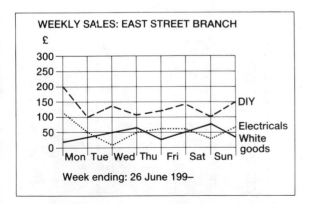

Fig. 9.9 *Graph showing the effect of too expanded a scale*

Avoiding over-crowding the grid

Sometimes – especially if the designer is limited to the use of a black ink on a white paper – the communicating advantages of a line graph vanish amid a woven pattern of dots, dashes and continuous lines. The reason for this is simple: too many items are being displayed too close together (Fig. 9.10).

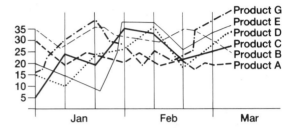

Fig. 9.10 *Graph showing too many items close together*

Briefing note on line graphs

1 Communication advantages

Line graphs make a much stronger and more immediate impact upon the reader's eye – they display 'see-at-a-glance' movements in upward and downward directions. And, importantly, they also indicate trends. In the world of stocks and shares, for example, a line graph illustrating three months' business might show weekly totals rising and falling, but indicate very clearly over the whole three-month period that the value of the shares is steadily rising. Thus line graphs help managers to make informed guesses as to what is likely to happen in the future. Like tables, line graphs also make it possible to compare displayed items – but they do it better!

2 Communication disadvantages

If care is not taken in selecting appropriate scales for the vertical axis, plotted data can become flattened out and crowded together. Also, there is a limit to the number of plotted items which the human eye can readily take in, when shown alongside others. This problem is made worse when the designer is limited to black ink and white paper. Lastly, if vertical scales are selected cunningly, then increases and falls can be made to look much more dramatic than they really are, and so fool the reader!

The bar chart

Another type of visual communication, very similar to the line graph, is the bar chart.

Here, the variable factor is displayed as a vertical column, very much like the column of mercury in a thermometer. The following bar chart shows in visual form the way in which a retail store's turnover for the month of March breaks down according to the range of products sold.

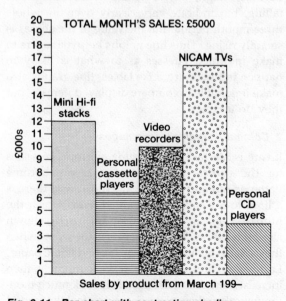

Fig. 9.11 Bar chart with contrasting shading

The bar chart provides a good visual impact for contrasting the respective quantities, sizes or amounts of items which are measured *by a common unit.* Here the unit is pounds expressed on a scale in thousands of pounds.

Note that in order to give a true picture, the columns – mini hi-fi stacks, video recorders, TVs, personal cassette players etc – must all be of the *same width.* And in order to catch the eye, it is helpful to give each bar in the chart an individual colour, or as in Fig. 9.11, contrasting shading.

The bar chart may also be used to compare and contrast items of the same kind measured against, for instance, different periods of time or different sources:

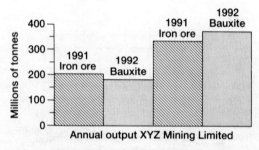

Fig. 9.12 Bar chart showing comparison of output of commodities

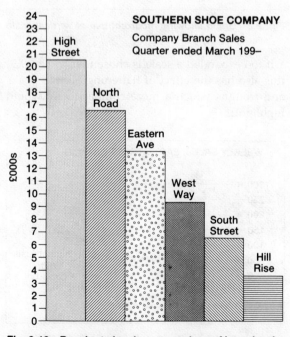

Fig. 9.13 Bar chart showing comparison of branch sales

The pie chart

As its name suggests, the pie chart is made up of a circle or 'pie' of information broken into segments of the circle or 'slices' of a pie! Also, the scale in use is circular, representing 360°, rather than linear:

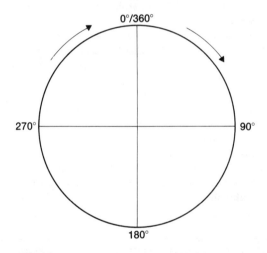

Fig. 9.14 Pie chart

Thus a value of 100 per cent will be equal to 360° on the pie chart.

Four golden rules for devising pie charts

There are four golden rules to remember when the pie chart is considered for illustrating number information visually:

1 The *total value* of the items (100 per cent or 360°) must be known in order to compare items in a pie chart. For example, in comparing the market share of the boot and shoe market controlled by various manufacturers, the total value of *all* boots and shoes sold in the market must be shown – and in pie chart terms will equate to the 360° of the circle. This value may be shown in pounds sterling terms or in numbers of pairs of boots and shoes sold. The market share for each manufacturer may then be indicated by a proportional 'slice of the pie'.

2 Each percentage point of the pie chart will be exactly equal to 3.60°. Thus for example 25 per cent will equal 90° (25×3.60) or a quarter of the pie.

3 It is very difficult for the human eye to gauge exactly the percentage values of similar-size segments of pie. It is therefore essential that the values of each slice of pie are included clearly in percentage terms, which are themselves given the values of the units in which the pie chart is totalled – here pounds sterling.

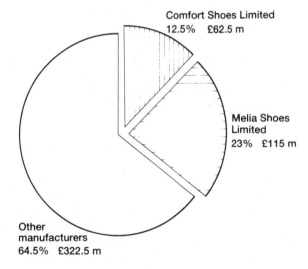

Total market value = £500 m

Fig. 9.15 Exploded pie chart

4 Each segment of the pie needs to be identified clearly – ideally in colour, or else in contrasting black/white shadings – and needs to be given clear values, i.e. what the segment represents in percentage and unit values, and what it stands for in the pie chart. As in all charts, clear titles need to be devised and the year, month, quarter, etc when the comparison was made clearly shown.

The following example shows the share of Comfort Shoes Limited's production made up of ladies boots and shoes:

Comfort Shoes Limited

Product share: ladies' boots and shoes
Period: 12 months ending December 199–

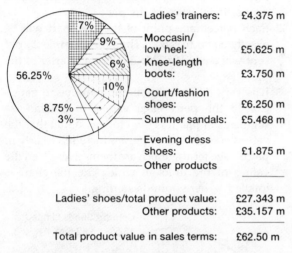

Ladies' trainers:	£4.375 m
Moccasin/low heel:	£5.625 m
Knee-length boots:	£3.750 m
Court/fashion shoes:	£6.250 m
Summer sandals:	£5.468 m
Evening dress shoes:	£1.875 m
Other products	

Ladies' shoes/total product value:	£27.343 m
Other products:	£35.157 m
Total product value in sales terms:	£62.50 m

Fig. 16 Pie chart with shaded segments

Briefing note on pie charts

1 Communication advantages

Pie charts provide an excellent visual means of conveying information about the make-up of various parts which form *a known whole*. They are especially arresting visually when a very small or very large part of a whole is displayed, say, only 7 per cent of all women ever go to prison, or 70 per cent of all UK inhabitants are right-handed. Pie chart design techniques which display the pie in three dimensions or which 'explode' the slice under scrutiny by cutting it out and away from the rest of the pie are particularly striking.

2 Communication disadvantages

The design of pie charts relies on splitting up parts of a circle into fractions or segments which total 360 degrees. But the human eye has great difficulty in distinguishing between slivers of pie which are close in size, and so each slice has to be labelled as equating to, say, 27 per cent or 34 per cent. In this way degrees of the circle have to be converted into percentages to make the pie chart more easily understood. And, like the line graph, if too many

items are grouped closely together, the whole becomes difficult to interpret. As with all visual communication, contrasting colours help to overcome this problem. In a word, pie charts are at their best when communicating information about two to four items which vary noticeably in their sizes.

Checklist of essential components of an effective pie chart

1 The size of the whole pie which is being divided into slices must be known. For example, total of students in college, number of people interviewed etc.
2 Similarly, the subtotals for each slice of pie must be known accurately, e.g. out of 29 students, 14 live less than 3 miles away, and 10 between 3 and 10 miles away from college etc.
3 All the slices to be plotted must be converted into fractions of 360 degrees. 3.6 degrees will equal 1 per cent. Thus 14/29ths (*see above*) equals 48.27 per cent which equals a slice of pie amounting to 173.7 degrees.
4 All slices must be clearly labelled with their respective titles: *Students Living Up To Three Miles Away* and with the appropriate percentage they make up: 48.27 per cent. Sometimes it is necessary to locate such labels outside the pie and link them with line arrows to the appropriate slice.
5 Contrasting shading or colour must be used to distinguish clearly each slice or segment.
6 As always, the chart must have a simple but clear heading, date of composition and source of authorship.

HOW TO WORK OUT PERCENTAGES

One of the most common ways to express a proportion or share of something, is as a percentage:

Fastsnacks have 43% of the sweet market.
'Our target is to increase turnover by 10%'.

'Per cent' means 'part of a hundred'. So a number with a percentage symbol % after it means that it is so many parts of a hundred. For every hundred sweets bought, Fastsnacks made 43 of them. If turnover last year was £100,000, the target for next year is £110,000.

Working out a percentage

Percentages are very easy to calculate. Of course, if there is a percentage key on your calculator there is no problem; if you haven't, follow this method and you should have no difficulty:

Example

What percentage of 350 is 45?

45 as a fraction of 350 is $\dfrac{45}{350}$

so as a percentage would be $\dfrac{45}{350} \times 100$

$$= 12.85\%$$

Fastsnacks turnover for one week is £35,000. Their turnover for the month is £125,000. What percentage of their turnover was earned in that week?

$$\dfrac{£35,000}{£125,000} \times 100 = 28\%$$

Sometimes we may know something as a percentage, but want to work out what it is in real terms. For instance Ajax Pumps' gross profit may be 27% of turnover – but how much profit did they actually make? A retail store increases all its prices by 10%, so what is the new price of that washing machine?

Example

What is 12.5% of 290?
Divide 290 by 100 to find 1%

$$\dfrac{290}{100} = 2.9$$

so 12.5% is 12.5 × 2.9

$$= 36.25$$

The price of a washing machine is £245. The shop selling it wishes to increase the price by 8%. What is the price increase?

1% of £245 is $\dfrac{£245}{100}$

8% of £245 is $\dfrac{£245}{100} \times 8$

$$= £19.60$$

■ **PERCENTAGE ASSIGNMENTS**

1 Calculate what the number 24 is as a percentage of 96
2 Calculate what 150 is as a percentage of 3,000
3 Calculate what 333 is as a percentage of 666
4 Calculate what 14.2 is as a percentage of 58.63
5 What is 60% of £1,345.00?
6 What must a customer pay if he is given a 33.3% discount on £500?
7 What is 110% of £650?

Fractions into percentages

Harridges department store earns its income in the following way:

Ladies' fashions:	4/10
Men's outfitting:	1/6
Electrical goods:	6/20
Food hall:	1/10
Haberdashery:	1/30

These different fractions make it very difficult to compare one department with another. It would be much easier if each amount were given as a percentage.

To convert a fraction to a percentage, just multiply the fraction by 100.

$$\dfrac{4}{10} \times 100 = 40\%$$

$$\dfrac{1}{8} \times 100 = 12.5\%$$

We can now work out as a percentage, what proportion of its income each department of Harridges makes:

Ladies' fashions:	40%
Men's outfitting:	16.67%
Electrical goods:	30%
Food hall:	10%
Haberdashery:	3.33%
	100%

■ **FRACTIONS INTO PERCENTAGES CONVERSION ASSIGNMENTS**

1 Express 5/16 as a percentage
2 Express 13/4 as a percentage
3 Express 23/32 as a percentage
4 Express 3/9 as a percentage

AGE DISTRIBUTION IN THE UK 199–

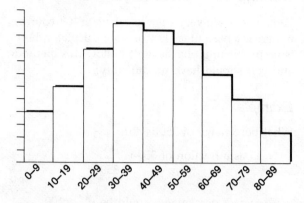

Fig. 9.18   Histogram or distribution chart

Other types of chart

So far we have examined carefully how to produce effective tables, line graphs, bar and pie charts. And these form the most commonly employed charts through which number communication is communicated. Nevertheless, there are a number of additional, specialised charts which you should know about:

Checklist of specialist charts

Flowchart or algorithm

This chart is used extensively in designing computer software and in organising major projects or production lines. It divides an activity into a sequence of logical steps and provides for alternative 'yes' 'no' responses and for feedback of information.

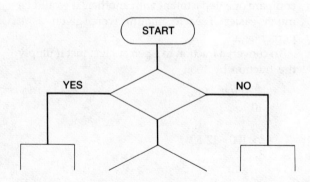

Fig. 9.17   Flowchart or algorithm

Histogram or distribution chart

Such a chart shows clearly the spread of parts which form a known whole. For example how many people in the UK are in a series of age groups between 0 and 100 years. Histograms may take the form of a plotted single line, or a set of side-by-side bars.

Branching tree

The widespread introduction of computerised information has led to branching tree charts being used to classify data and lead a user from the general to the specific by branching off to various pieces of information according to the answers the user gives to linked questions.

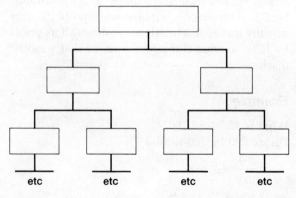

Fig. 9.19   Branching tree

Organisational chart

These charts are used to show the connections between people employed at various levels in organisations or to show links between connected items such as those between central and local government or the divisions of a multinational company etc.

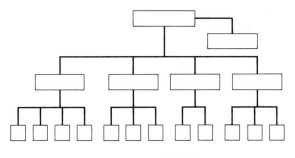

GLOBAL SERVICES LTD

Fig. 9.20 Organisational chart

Diagrammatic chart

Charts which intermix text and number information within drawings which have a visual impact are very widely used to make the words and numbers more interesting and appealing.

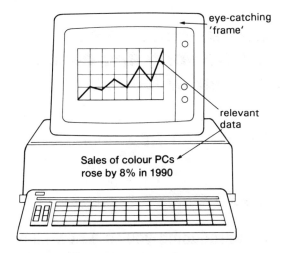

Fig. 9.21 Diagrammatic chart

More exciting documents thanks to laser printers and DTP

The visual impact of printed text has come a long way since the days of manual typewriters, when the entire printed message of a report or sales letter had to be displayed in the same print style, with only capitalising and underlining as the means of emphasising headings or important words and phrases.

Today, thanks to the technology of desktop publishing and laser printing, any trained text processing operator can produce the printed word in an amazing variety of sizes, styles and features.

Indeed, today's managers – whether in sales, marketing, advertising, personnel or accounts – devote much time and effort in devising documents which:

▶ convey a sense of high quality, dedication and professional expertise;
▶ impart a friendly, warm and helpful image;
▶ communicate detailed information crisply, clearly and in easily absorbed sections or paragraphs;
▶ catch the browsing eye with cheeky, punchy or deliberately unusual captions or headlines;
▶ communicate a sense of high seriousness and formality.

As a result of the very wide range of typefaces, fonts and printing features now readily available to organisations in-house, both internal employees and external customers and contacts expect textual and graphic information to be presented in documents in much more exciting and stimulating ways if they are to devote some of their busy time to reading it.

Moreover, as the 20th century moves towards its close, people are tending to watch TV, films and video much more and to read much less. They are therefore much less inclined to wade through pages of text which use the same typeface set in endless prose paragraphs. And, with computers producing more rather than less paper, every printed page arriving on an executive's desk has to compete with a host of others for attention!

■ *TOP ASSISTANT TIP*

As you progress through your career, you will first assist others in producing effective printed information, and then go on to devise and circulate your own.

It therefore makes good sense – from the outset – to become thoroughly familiar with what DTP and laser printing can do to make your printed communications easily read, remembered and therefore acted on!

EXAMPLE OF A SALES LETTER PROMOTING VARIED FONTS AND GRAPHICS BY USING CANON LASER PRINTERS

Canon

Mr D W Evans
Head Management & Busn Studies
Chichester College
Westgate Fields
Chichester
West Sussex
PO19 1SB

Dear Mr Evans,

While the computers in your office might look good, the sad fact is that the documents they produce tend to look boring.

This is no fault of the computers themselves - the problem lies with your printer.

Documents produced on a normal printer look like this half of the letter - the same typeface printed in the same way, on and on and on and on...

Which, when your company wants to present the best image at every opportunity, is disappointing to say the least.

Mr D W Evans
Head Management & Busn Studies
Chichester College
Westgate Fields
Chichester
West Sussex
PO19 1SB

Dear Mr Evans,

Canon would like to add a little song and dance to your office routine.

We'd like to give every document you produce a new image, a new look, a new life.

How?

By introducing you to a new kind of laser printer. A printer that will make you and your company look good on paper.

Fig. 9.22   Sales letter promoting varied fonts and graphics

It can also, of course, end up costing more because you have to pay for impressive presentation documents.

That, or you settle for the drab and boring look.

The funny thing is that all it takes to make your computer system really start working for you is a laser printer from the Canon LBP-8III range.

That's it. Whatever your system, the chances are it can produce great documents.

And who gets the credit? If you don't tell anyone, we won't. Just take a look on the right and start looking good yourself.

Yours sincerely,

Mark Hallam
Mark Hallam
National Distributor
Sales Manager

Imagine it – you could produce any letter, document, or presentation you wanted from your own desk. With amazing graphics, the odd ▲ ✪ ❤ ❑ here and there, with words enlarged, ᵣₑdᵤced, rotated, 𝕯𝕰𝕮𝕺𝕽𝕬𝕿𝕰𝕯, *as*

BIG
as you liked, and all with the quality you might expect from Canon. (You're actually looking at the quality now because this half of *the letter was produced on a Canon LBP–8III.)*

That said, we'd like to offer you the opportunity to use an LBP–8III laser printer yourself – free, for 1 week.

For a week, you can put it through its paces and, if you're not impressed, we'll take it back, no questions asked.

On the other hand, take a look to the left...boring, isn't it?

Yours sincerely,

Mark Hallam
Mark Hallam
National Distributor
Sales Manager

Regd Office, Canon House, Manor Road, Wallington, Surrey SM6 0AJ
Regd No 1264300 England.   A subsidiary of Canon Inc.

EXAMPLES OF CLIP-ART AVAILABLE FROM GRAPHIC BOOKS INTER-NATIONAL LIMITED

Fig. 9.23   Clip-art examples
The selected piece of clip-art is 'imported' into the DTP document being designed on a VDU by a scanner, or a specialised piece of equipment which scans the artwork and then converts it into an electronic file

---

ACTIVITIES AND ASSIGNMENTS *Visual, graphic and number communication*

■ *THE QUICK CHECK-IT-OUT QUIZ*

1 Why are visual and graphic forms of communication widely used in organisations today?

2 What developments in IT technology have improved the quality and variety of visual/graphic communication?

3 In what ways would you expect visual/graphic communication to be used in business and public service organisations?

4 Explain the ways in which a table communicates number information.

5 Explain clearly how to design a line graph.

6 What is the difference between a bar chart and a pie chart?

7 List briefly the advantages and disadvantages of tables, line graphs, bar charts and pie charts for communicating visual and number information.

8 Describe briefly what the following charts are used for:

a a flowchart

b a histogram

c a branching tree

d an organisational chart

e a diagrammatic chart

9 Describe clearly how to calculate a percentage by using a worked example.

10 How do desktop publishing software and laser printers provide varied and appealing printed documents?

11 What is a colour plotter?

12 Explain how clip art is used in desktop publishing.

Case study activities

The following case study activities develop NVQ competences in:

- *applying numerical skills and techniques;*
- *supplying information for a specific purpose;*
- *using a calculator correctly;*
- *processing information in graphics software;*
- *accessing and printing hard copy charts and diagrams.*

Case study

BREAKTIME VENDING LIMITED'S ANNUAL SALES CONFERENCE

You work in the sales department of Breaktime Vending Machines Limited, a national company which sells vending machines for both drinks and snacks to a wide range of industrial, commercial and public sector organisations. Your supervisor has been asked to produce a range of visual aids for the annual sales conference of sales representatives, district and regional managers and senior head office sales staff.

(continued overleaf)

Task 1

The first task you are asked to undertake is to produce a line graph (using a colour graphics package if possible) from the following information:

1.1 Time duration: January–December 199—
1.2 Data: Total sales listed by region
1.3 Regions: Scotland, South West, Midlands, North East, South East, North West, London.
1.4 Sales breakdown:

Sales in £10,000s

	J	F	M	A	M	J	J	A	S	O	N	D
Scotland	24	15	19	31	26	21	16	14	22	30	34	26
S West	8	11	15	17	16	19	23	18	20	16	18	15
Midlands	36	42	51	48	52	60	47	58	43	47	54	41
N East	21	17	23	27	24	31	22	18	15	17	13	12
S East	32	37	41	39	45	39	28	22	29	31	34	26
N West	19	23	16	14	27	34	41	36	43	38	33	29
London	43	56	54	67	59	57	49	51	44	39	46	35

Questions

What does your line graph tell you about:

▶ which is the busiest region?
▶ when Breaktime can expect to be selling most?
▶ in which regions Breaktime's sales strength lies?
▶ what time of year Breaktime could seek to promote new lines when sales are generally low?

Task 2

Your supervisor also wants you to produce a pie chart to communicate as strikingly as possible the following information about the national breakdown of the vending machine market in the same year:

The entire UK vending machine sales in 199— were worth £222.3 million. Breaktime's competitors, Autovend and Vendapax sales were £41.9 million and £82.3 million respectively.

Using this information and that contained in the table for Task 1, design a pie chart to display the share of the UK market in percentage terms as well as total sales for these three major companies; include all other vending machine sales companies under a heading of 'Others'.

Task 3

In order to illustrate comparative sales by region with a strong visual impact, your supervisor has also asked you to use the information given in the table in Task 1 to design a bar chart which shows each region's sales for each month of the year.

Task 4

And in a similar bar chart show each region's sales for the current year (Table 1 above) and for the previous year. Last year's sales were:

Scotland:	2,830,000
S West:	1,770,000
Midlands:	5,910,000
N East:	2,560,000
S East:	3,880,000
N West:	3,270,000
London:	6,120,000

Question

What does your finished bar chart tell you about Breaktime's sales trends over the two years you have analysed?

Task 5

Breaktime is concerned about the age of its national sales force, since it went through a bad patch some years back when a large number of experienced representatives retired within a few months of each other. At that time, the company did not have enough sales representatives in their thirties – keen to develop their careers and already possessing experience – to maintain sales. Your supervisor has therefore asked you to design a bar chart (technically a histogram) to show the age distribution of the current sales force using the following information:

BREAKTIME SALES PERSONNEL

Age Range

	Trainees	Sales Representatives				
	16–20	21–30	31–40	41–50	51–60	61–65
All:	10	8	14	18	21	12
Male:	6	2	6	13	16	10
Female:	4	6	8	5	5	2

Questions

▶ What does your age distribution chart tell you about Breaktime's sales force?

▶ Are they facing any potential problems in the way the ages of their sales staff are distributed?

▶ Can you see any problems facing Breaktime in terms of the comparative numbers of male and female representatives in the distribution age ranges?

Task 6

This is the new organisational sales structure which will be announced at the annual sales conference:

Jean Masterson: Sales Director   Sally Peters her P.A.
Regional Sales Managers:
Scotland: Ray McKendrick
S West: Sheila Vickers

Midlands: Chris Patel
N East: Jack Downey
S East: Jim Butterworth
N West: Joan Fairclough
London: Winston Morris

Each region will also have a Regional Administration Manager. These are new posts yet to be recruited. Also, each Regional Manager has a personal assistant. The regions are broken down into the following districts: Scotland: 4 S West: 3 Midlands: 5 N East: 3 S East: 3 N West: 3 London: 4.

The districts are to be shown, but personnel details will be presented on another chart.

Your task is to design a clear organisational chart with an appealing drawing/diagram representing Breaktime's business activities as a kind of frame for the chart to be set into.

■ CASE STUDY NOTE

Remember that your designs will be used as the basis for a set of overhead transparencies and/or colour film slides, so make an especial effort to produce originals which are clear and lively and which make effective use of colour/shading and layout techniques. If at all possible, use a graphics package and colour plotter/printer.

Activities to develop competence and confidence

1 Having first investigated and made your rough notes, devise an organisational chart which shows clearly how your school, college or study centre is organised.

2 In groups of two, design a chart which will record clearly which students in your group have successfully demonstrated which performance criteria (tasks) for which Units in your NVQ-assessed course of study. The aim of the chart is to maintain a record and also to show readily what each student has completed during each week/month of the course.

3 First research and then design a payslip for the sales representatives of Breaktime Vending Limited which will also detail the repayment of their claimed travelling expenses.

4 Breaktime wishes to transfer its sales transactions from a manual to a computerised system. The products which Breaktime sells on account are:

    1 Beverage Vending Machines:
      (a) 5 × Cold Drink
      (b) 5 × Hot Drink
      (c) 8 × Hot/Cold Drink
    2 Constant Filter Coffee Maker
    3 Sweet and Snack Foods Dispensers

Breaktime also supply the replacement plastic cups, beverage mixing powders (coffee, chocolate, soup etc) as well as stocks of sweet bars and wrapped snacks etc.

In addition, charges are invoiced for regular maintenance services and emergency call-outs.

Task

First carry out your research, and then in groups of two or three, design a computer invoice for Breaktime to issue for sales on account.

■ **RESEARCH TIPS**

Remember that: invoices need unique reference numbers; products generally have product codes and references, as do account customers; dates and clear details of delivery addresses are important; room must be found for extending the price of goods by quantity from a unit price; VAT calculations have to be made and a credit invoice will also be required; and most customers will enjoy a confidential discount which needs to be shown; lastly, many invoices make a reference to previous delivery and advice notes.

Work experience attachment assignments

1 With permission, collect the 'A–Z' sequence of documents your organisation uses to record its account sales transactions, e.g. sales order, stock requisition, advice note, delivery note, invoice, credit note, statement etc.
2 See if you can be given a specimen set of the organisation's petty cash forms and vouchers.
3 Find out how your organisation controls its stock – in, out and balances.
4 With permission, make a checklist of the tasks which are carried out in the organisation using a spreadsheet.
5 With assistance, work through a typical set of documents which are used to monitor the production of the goods your organisation manufactures; e.g. quantities produced, flow of parts, quality control, wastage rates etc.
6 Make arrangements to be shown how the organisation calculates and administers its Value Added Tax responsibilities.
7 Find out what activities and information the organisation records on:

   tables, graphs, pie charts and bar charts, diagrams, slides, transparencies, etc.

   and make a list of the areas you discover.
8 Find out how your organisation presents number and visual information at briefing meetings and presentations for managers.
9 Undertake your research and then design a chart which illustrates the type of activity and document which your organisation produces using desktop publishing equipment. If possible, collect samples in use.
10 Arrange to interview staff who regularly produce number and visual charts and diagrams etc and ask them for their tips on how to design good visual aids.

As usual, and only after obtaining permission, report back on your findings about the above ten activities to your class group.

And also, display in your base room any specimens of good practice you were able to obtain.

Index